Beginning Adobe

G000167666

Beginning
Adobe® AIR™

Beginning
Adobe® AIR™
Building Applications for the Adobe Integrated Runtime

Rich Tretola

Wiley Publishing, Inc.

Beginning Adobe® Air™

Published by
Wiley Publishing, Inc.
10475 Crosspoint Boulevard
Indianapolis, IN 46256
www.wiley.com

To the love of my life, Kim, and my beautiful daughters, Skye and Coral.

About the Author

Rich Tretola is the Rich Applications Technical Lead at Herff Jones, Inc. He is an award-winning Flex developer and was the lead author of *Professional Flex 2* (ISBN 978-0-470-10267-1) from Wrox. He entered the field of Web development in the late 1990s and has been building applications ever since.

Other than Flex, he builds applications using ColdFusion, Flash, and Java (where he is a Sun-certified programmer). Rich is highly regarded within the Flex community as an expert in RIA and is also an Adobe Community Expert. He runs a popular Flex and AIR blog at http://blog.everythingFlex.com, and is the community manager for http://www.InsideRIA.com.

Rich was also selected to be a speaker at the Adobe MAX 2007 conference in Chicago.

About the Technical Editor

Joe Johnston is an Experience Designer at Knoware, an Interactive Design Studio building applications from RIAs to embedded devices. Joe has been using AIR/Flex when it was in the beta stages and uses it daily on all of his projects. He also finds it exciting to build applications to create unique user interaction. You can see more and contact him at http://merhl.com.

Credits

Executive Editor
Chris Webb

Development Editor
William Bridges

Technical Editor
Joe Johnston

Production Editor
Daniel Scribner

Copy Editor
Cate Caffrey

Editorial Manager
Mary Beth Wakefield

Production Manager
Tim Tate

Vice President and Executive Group Publisher
Richard Swadley

Vice President and Executive Publisher
Joseph B. Wikert

Project Coordinator, Cover
Lynsey Stanford

Compositor
Craig Johnson, Happenstance Type-O-Rama

Proofreader
Sossity Smith

Indexer
Melanie Belkin

Acknowledgments

I thank the acquisitions editor, Chris Webb, and the development editor, William Bridges, for their work helping to get the book completed through a constantly changing timeline.

I give special thanks to Danny Joscher, Frank Ferrara, Joey "the Schnoz" Fiorello, and "the Boss," Mr. Fiorello from J&R Discount on Long Island, NY. I spent a great deal of time with these people over many years and learned a lot from each of them. Mr. Fiorello is actually responsible for getting me started in programming by splitting the cost of my first laptop with me. One more thing that needs to be said, especially to Frankie: Let's Go, Islanders!!

Most importantly, I thank my wife and best friend, Kim, and my daughters, Skye and Coral. Anyone who has been through the experience of writing a technical book knows how much time and effort are involved and how important the support of the people closest to you is. I love you all!

Contents

Contents

Contents

Contents

Foreword

By Edward Mansouri

The life cycle of Internet-based applications is taking an exciting turn toward the desktop.

The earliest Internet-based applications used on a large scale by the general public were the ASCII text-based e-mail and web clients of the 1980s, such as the University of Washington's Pine and the University of Minnesota's Gopher.

With the introduction of the first graphical browser, NCSA Mosaic in September 1993, an era of browser-based, graphics-intensive Internet content and applications began and would last more than 13 years.

Over time, remarkable advancements have been made in the browser itself to serve increasingly rich content including audio and video as well as the ability to provide Web developers with client-side run-times with languages such as JavaScript and Microsoft's Active X to further customize the way users interact with Web content. In addition, the presentation capabilities made available to designers continue to accelerate with languages such as Cascading Style Sheets (CSS).

Also, another important technology that has evolved as consistently and reliably as the browser itself is the Shockwave Flash (SWF) file format from Macromedia (acquired by Adobe in 2005).

Flash first appeared on the scene in 1996, largely as a tool in the graphic designer's repertoire for embedding animated and engaging content into a web site.

A few years later, Flash would begin its turn toward appealing not just to designers but also to developers with the advent of ActionScript, a simple yet robust language for scripting the behavior of Flash content.

The ability to ingest data into a Flash "movie" and submit it to remote network locations quickly emerged, as well as the ability to create rich user interfaces derived from remotely assembled data and content.

The Rich Internet Application (RIA) era had arrived.

The promise of a browser-based application that offered some of the same user experiences of the familiar desktop-based application emerged, notably drag-and-drop functionality.

Also, no longer did a web site or web application need to rely on the conventional "stateless" model of the Web in which each page of a web site needed to be unloaded and fully replaced by the next with each click of a hyperlink.

The discovery by JavaScript programmers of the browser's XMLHttpRequest object (and Microsoft's MSMXL object in Internet Explorer) was equally significant and introduced the world to yet another paradigm for Rich Internet Applications with AJAX (Asynchronous JavaScript and XML) — Google Maps, perhaps, is the most famous.

Foreword

Despite these remarkable advancements to the landscape for Internet-based content and applications, the fact remained that all functionality was limited to the restrictive sandbox environment of the web browser.

While AJAX has offered many developers an elegant platform upon which to build Rich Internet Applications, developing an AJAX-based application that will execute with equal reliability across all the major web browsers is a monumental task that requires substantial extra knowledge and coding time.

In 2006, Adobe announced that it was working on a groundbreaking new platform called *Apollo* that would open up incredible capabilities for the Rich Internet Application developer: a cross-operating system runtime that would enable HTML/AJAX-centric developers as well as Flash/Flex-centric developers to build applications that could bring together the best characteristics of a web application with the capabilities of a desktop application.

In March of 2007, Apollo launched as a public alpha and moved quickly to a public beta three months later in June along with a rename of the product to AIR, the Adobe Integrated Runtime.

The ramifications of AIR were immediately recognized as developers blogged and boasted about taking existing HTML/AJAX, Flash, or Flex-based applications and adding desktop components to them as they repackaged them as AIR applications in a matter of hours.

During the remainder of 2007, several special interest communities emerged to evangelize AIR, including Mr. Tretola's own EverythingFlex.com site and my O$_2$Apps.com site, both of which provide a comprehensive array of sample applications, code, and tutorials for AIR developers of all skill levels.

My programming background is in the development of E-Learning software, and my interest in AIR came about from my long-standing goal to bring desktop functionality to the landscape for online students and teachers.

Dating back to 2000, I have attempted to do this with technologies such as WebDAV, Java, and C++. With each attempt, I was unsatisfied with the lack of stability I was able to achieve as well as the inherent complexities involved with the technologies, not to mention the need to tackle much more difficult programming languages.

AIR has provided a way for me to leverage the existing Web development skills I've been building since 1996 (namely, HTML, JavaScript, CSS, ActionScript, Flash, and Flex) to build useful desktop-based functionality that allows my users to do things such as dragging and dropping files from the desktop to an Internet-based online classroom — something virtually impossible in a strictly browser-based application.

It became apparent that it was not only what you could do with AIR that appealed, but the ease with which you could do it.

For the creative designer, you will love how AIR lets you mix HTML and Flash content together. Using techniques such as the Flex Builder HTML Component, you can create custom-shaped HTML interfaces that can offer your clients and users a great first impression and experience.

Furthermore, the reach you'll attain with your AIR applications will likely be far beyond any other alternative.

Over the last two decades, the Adobe company has developed nearly universal recognition of their PDF file format. Furthermore, they have been able to attain Flash Player presence on nearly 99 percent of the world's Internet-connected computers. They have the experience, resources, and, clearly, the desire to bring AIR to similar heights.

Mr. Tretola's book, *Beginning Adobe® AIR™*, is a great resource to get you started building AIR applications and will continue to serve you as you move further into building your first killer Rich Desktop Application.

Mr. Tretola does a masterful job in developing an understanding of the nuts and bolts of AIR applications and provides very equitable coverage of the primary programming paradigms available for AIR developers (Flex, Flash, AJAX, or a combination of the three).

The practical examples and source code made available in this book have provided and will provide me with invaluable inspiration and reference materials as I continue building my own desktop-based E-Learning applications.

Congratulations on your decision to build AIR applications. I hope you will have as much fun with AIR as I have. To become involved with a technology that may well be poised to define how people interact with the Internet over the next few decades is an exciting opportunity, and Mr. Tretola's book will give you a firm basis from which to start.

Introduction

AIR (Adobe Integrated Runtime) was first introduced by Adobe in early 2008 with the goal of offering a cross-platform runtime for the development of desktop applications. Although there are some platform-specific features, the AIR APIs make "write once, deploy anywhere" possible for the development of desktop applications.

What makes AIR unique is that the languages used to produce AIR applications are not new languages. They are languages that have been used in Web development for many years. These languages include HTML with JavaScript (AJAX), MXML (Flex), and ActionScript. By making it very easy for existing AJAX and Flex/Flash developers to write desktop applications, the time to learn it is extremely brief for those with experience in these languages. This should also help the adoption rate of the AIR development platform.

This book follows a step-by-step process, walking you through the features of the AIR development platform. It is designed to get you familiarized quickly with many of the features of AIR. I highly recommend that you continue your learning process by understanding and using the ActionScript and MXML documentation that is provided by Adobe.

Whom This Book Is For

Although there are some simple examples of creating applications using HTML within Dreamweaver CS3 and Flash-based AIR applications using Flash CS3, the primary language in this book will be MXML and ActionScript, and the primary development tool will be Flex Builder 3. If you have been using Flex or ActionScript, the samples shown will be very easy for you to understand. If you have no experience with Flex but do have experience with any other tag-based XML language, you should do just fine.

What This Book Covers

This book covers many of the features of AIR that will allow you to build desktop applications that follow traditional desktop application architecture. It covers multiple methods of data storage, including both local within the file system and embedded database as well as storage on remote servers. It also demonstrates many features that allow your AIR application to interact with both the Mac OS X and Windows operating systems.

How This Book Is Structured

This book has been broken down into four parts plus two Appendixes, each covering specific areas of AIR. These parts are as follows:

❑ **Getting Started** — Part I introduces the Adobe Integrated Runtime and discusses Rich Internet Application development platforms as well as Rich Desktop Applications. Next, we cover the different programming languages and the development tools for creating and packaging AIR applications.

❑ **Adding Data** — Part II focuses on getting data into AIR applications from XML, ColdFusion, JSON, and Web Services.

❑ **AIR APIs** — Part III covers the many AIR-specific APIs that handle interactions with the Operating System including file system access, windowing, SQLite embedded database, and more.

❑ **The AIR Components** — Part IV covers the file system components as well as the HTML component.

Appendix A is a bonus section that takes an existing Flex application and converts it to AIR, adding AIR-specific features along the way.

Appendix B demonstrates some of the possible answers to the exercises that accompany some of the chapters.

What You Need to Use This Book

The samples in this book have been built using both the Mac OS X and WindowsXP operating systems. You can use either for many of the samples; however, there are some that are specific to one or the other. Although you can compile all of the samples within this book with the free AIR SDK, your life will be much easier if you use Flex Builder 3, which can be downloaded as a free trial.

Source Code

As you work through the examples in this book, you may choose either to type in all the code manually, or use the source code files that accompany the book. All the source code used in this book is available for download at www.wrox.com. Once at the site, simply locate the book's title (either by using the Search box or one of the title lists), and click the Download Code link on the book's detail page to obtain all the source code for the book.

Because many books have similar titles, you may find it easiest to search by ISBN; for this book, the ISBN is 978-0-470-22904-0.

Once you download the code, just decompress it with your favorite compression tool. Alternatively, you can go to the main Wrox code download page at www.wrox.com/dynamic/books/download.aspx to see the code available for this book and all other Wrox books.

Errata

We make every effort to ensure that there are no errors in the text or in the code. However, no one is perfect, and mistakes do occur. If you find an error in one of our books (such as a spelling mistake or faulty piece of code), we would be very grateful for your feedback. By sending in errata, you may save another reader hours of frustration, and at the same time, you will be helping us provide even higher quality information.

To find the errata page for this book, go to www.wrox.com and locate the title using the Search box or one of the title lists. Then, on the book details page, click the Book Errata link. On this page, you can view all errata that have been submitted for this book and posted by Wrox editors. A complete book list including links to each book's errata is also available at www.wrox.com/misc-pages/booklist.shtml.

If you don't spot "your" error on the Book Errata page, go to www.wrox.com/contact/techsupport.shtml and complete the form there to send us the error you have found. We'll check the information and, if appropriate, post a message to the book's errata page and fix the problem in subsequent editions of the book.

p2p.wrox.com

For author and peer discussion, join the P2P forums at p2p.wrox.com. The forums are a Web-based system for you to post messages relating to Wrox books and related technologies and to interact with other readers and technology users. The forums offer a subscription feature to e-mail you topics of interest of your choosing when new posts are made to the forums. Wrox authors, editors, other industry experts, and your fellow readers are present on these forums.

At http://p2p.wrox.com you will find several different forums that will help you not only as you read this book, but also as you develop your own applications. To join the forums, just follow these steps:

1. Go to p2p.wrox.com and click the Register link.

2. Read the terms of use and click Agree.

3. Complete the required information to join, as well as any optional information you wish to provide, and click Submit.

4. You will receive an e-mail with information describing how to verify your account and complete the joining process.

You can read messages in the forums without joining P2P, but to post your own messages, you must join.

Once you join, you can post new messages and respond to messages other users post. You can read messages at any time on the Web. If you would like to have new messages from a particular forum e-mailed to you, click the "Subscribe to This Forum" icon by the forum name in the forum listing.

For more information about how to use the Wrox P2P, be sure to read the P2P FAQs for answers to questions about how the forum software works, as well as many common questions specific to P2P and Wrox books. To read the FAQs, click the FAQ link on any P2P page.

Beginning
Adobe® AIR™

Part I
Getting Started

Introducing AIR
(Adobe Integrated Runtime)

AIR (Adobe Integrated Runtime), which was originally code-named Apollo, is a cross-operating system runtime that allows developers to build and deploy rich Internet applications to the desktop using their existing skill sets. AIR applications can be built using HTML, AJAX, Adobe Flash, and Adobe Flex. The version 1.0 release supports both Mac OSX and WindowsXP and Vista. Adobe has also confirmed that a Linux version of the runtime is on its radar.

So, what exactly does this mean to developers? First and foremost, it means that if your current skill set includes HTML/JavaScript (AJAX), Flex, or Flash, you already have everything you need to create a desktop application that will install on a Windows or Mac computer. Therefore, you don't need to know Java, C++, C, or any of the other traditional desktop languages to create and distribute full-fledged desktop applications.

It also means that since Adobe has created these runtimes, Adobe is the one responsible for ensuring that your application performs the same on any of the operating systems that AIR supports. If you are coming from a Flash or Flex background, you already know how nice it is to write an application that performs the same within the Flash player in a traditional web browser. If you are coming from an HTML/JavaScript background, you have undoubtedly suffered through countless frustrations and hacks to get your web page to show up the same in many different browsers. Well, if you have suffered through this experience with HTML and the browser, I have good news for you. You will suffer no longer when your HTML/JavaScript application is deployed as an AIR application, since it will be running within the Adobe Integrated Runtime.

Online versus Desktop Applications

The traditional definition of an *online application* is one that runs within a web browser while connected to the Internet. A *desktop application* has traditionally been one that runs on the local computer whether there is an Internet connection or not. New programming models like AIR have begun to blend these ideas and create hybrid applications in which some of the data are stored locally, while additional data may be loaded into the application when an Internet connection exists. Or the application can synchronize its data or files when an Internet connection exists for use later when an Internet connection no longer exists. Google via its Gears API has also begun to create browser-based applications that can cache data within an embedded database for offline use.

There is no doubt that the convergence of online and desktop applications into occasionally connected applications will continue. With tools such as AIR, it is easier than ever to create applications that can perform well whether an Internet connection exists or not.

The Runtime Environment

The runtime environment is what guarantees the consistent experience across different operating systems and the versions of each. For example, there is an API within an AIR application that handles the creation of a new file or folder. The AIR developer writes the application using this API. The runtime then translates this request into an operating-system-specific call, ensuring that the file or folder is created in the native way that the operating system normally handles the creation of a file or folder.

The runtime itself is distributed both as a stand-alone install package catered to each operating system, or it can be packaged and distributed along with an AIR application. Once the runtime exists on a user's machine, it will handle the responsibility of installing new AIR applications as well as maintaining a version history of itself, which is fully backward-compatible. The backward compatibility will allow developers to build applications that target a specific release of the runtime but also ensure that a future runtime release doesn't break an existing application.

A few of the unique features of the Adobe Integrated Runtime include an integrated web browser based on the Safari WebKit as well as an integrated database based on the SQLite embedded database distribution. These are a just a few of the features unique to AIR that will be discussed later in this book.

The AIR File

The .air file extension is a new file extension from Adobe that's used to signify an application built to run on the Adobe Integrated Runtime. When a developer creates a new AIR application, it is compiled to an AIR package with the .air extension, for example, HelloWorld.air. When a user downloads the HelloWorld.air package, the runtime recognizes this as an installer package and will then install the application to the operating system. The application itself will either be an executable .exe file extension on Windows or an .app file extension on Mac. Once the application is installed, the original HelloWorld.air file is no longer needed and can be deleted, as it is needed for distribution and installation.

The Tools

Adobe has made it possible to create and distribute AIR applications with absolutely no cost at all. It again (as it did with Flex 2) offers a free SDK that can be used to package AIR applications using a command window with the ADT library. The SDK also allows the compilation of the application to a temporary file for testing purposes. The temporary file is created using the ADL library and runs the application without the need of installing it to the operating system.

Flex Builder has also been updated to version 3 and now includes the AIR tools. Flex Builder 3 makes it easy to create, test, debug, and package AIR applications, and although this is not a free tool, in my experience it is worth every penny. This book focuses on building applications with the use of Flex Builder 3.

Adobe has also released extensions for both Dreamweaver CS3 and Flash CS3 to integrate the creation and testing of AIR applications within these tools. These tools are covered in Chapters 4 and 5.

The AIR SDK

The AIR SDK is a free library offered by Adobe, which allows you to test an AIR application using the `adl` command and also compile the application to a distributable AIR package using the `adt` command. There is no GUI (graphical user interface) offered, although it is not very difficult to set up an ant task to call these commands from an editing tool like Eclipse.

ADL

The `adl` command is part of the free AIR SDK and allows for the testing of AIR applications without the need to package and install the AIR application. After navigating to the directory that contains your application through a terminal window, the sample syntax for `adl` would look like this:

```
adl HelloWorld-app.xml
```

For more information on testing and debugging an application with `adl`, refer to Chapter 5.

ADT

The `adt` command is also part of the free AIR SDK and allows for the compiling and packaging of an AIR application to an AIR package for distribution and installation. After navigating to the directory that contains your application through a terminal window, the sample syntax for `adt` would look like this:

```
adt -package -storetype pkcs12 -keystore cert.pfx HelloWorld.air
HelloWorld-app.xml HelloWorld.swf
```

For more information on packaging an application with `adt` and creating a self-signed certificate, refer to Chapter 6.

Flex Builder 3

Flex Builder 3 is an update to the Eclipse-based Flex Builder 2 and is available either as a plug-in to Eclipse or as a stand-alone installation. Flex 3 has many additional features over its predecessor. The biggest feature and the one that we're most interested in for this book is the inclusion of AIR functionality. Flex Builder 3 makes Flex-based AIR applications extremely easy to build using either the source or design views. It also includes a nice interface for testing AIR applications as well as compiling and creating AIR deployment packages. Among the many new features, Flex Builder 3 also includes the ability to compile applications with a specific SDK. Flex Builder 3 has a mid-level price tag, but the ease of use, along with the fact that it simply lets you develop faster, certainly justifies its price.

Dreamweaver CS3

Adobe has created an extension for Dreamweaver CS3 to help ease the creation and testing of HTML/ JavaScript AIR applications. Dreamweaver has been the premier development tool for HTML/JavaScript for many years, and this new extension will make it easy for developers currently using Dreamweaver to deploy AIR applications. For more information on using Dreamweaver CS3 for AIR development, refer to Chapters 4 and 5.

Flash CS3

Flash has been the dominating force in rich Internet content for more than 10 years, and the Flash development tool has been used by millions of Flash developers. Adobe has released an extension, which allows Flash developers to easily test and package their applications for deployment in the Adobe Integrated Runtime. For more information on using Flash CS3 for AIR development, refer to Chapters 4 and 5.

Installing the AIR Runtime

Installing the AIR runtime is as simple as installing any other piece of software. Simply download the runtime from Adobe.com, and the installer will install or update the AIR runtime on your system.

Set up the SDK on Mac

The following assumes that you have the SDK in a folder named *AIRSDK* and that it resides directly under the root of the OSX hard drive. See Figure 1-1.

Open Terminal.app and type **pico .profile**, as pictured in Figure 1-2. Now click Enter, and you should see something like Figure 1-3. Now, append :/AIRSDK/bin/ to the PATH variable (see Figure 1-4) and click Ctrl+o and then Enter to save the updated file. Close the Terminal window.

Open a new Terminal window, type **adl -help**, and then click Enter. You should now see something like Figure 1-5, which shows that the command was found and displays the help information. You can also try running adt -help. See Chapter 5 for information on how to use adl and adt to test and compile AIR applications.

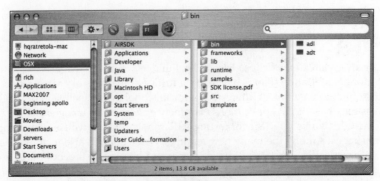

Figure 1-1: The location of the AIR SDK.

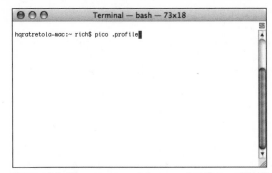

Figure 1-2: The command for opening the profile file for edit.

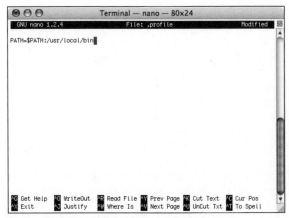

Figure 1-3: The .profile file before editing.

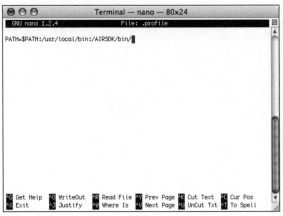

Figure 1-4: The .profile file after the AIR SDK has been added.

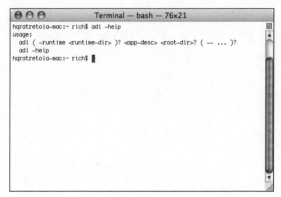

Figure 1-5: The Terminal screen after running
`adl -help`.

Set up the SDK on Windows

The following assumes that you have the SDK in a folder named *AIRSDK* and that it resides directly under the root of the C: drive at C:\AIRSDK. See Figure 1-6.

Open up the Windows control panel and select System. This will open the System Properties dialog box. Now choose the Advanced tab, and you should see what is shown in Figure 1-7.

Clicking on the Environmental Variables button will open the Environmental Variables dialog. Now, scroll through the list of System Variables until you find the `Path` variable. With the `Path` variable selected (as shown in Figure 1-8), click on the Edit button. This will open up an Edit window that will allow you to append the variable for the AIR SDK. Scroll to the right through the current Variable Values and add a semicolon and the C:\AIRSDK\bin so that your Variable Value looks similar to what is shown in Figure 1-9. Click OK and then click OK through the remaining windows to apply the variable.

Figure 1-6: The location of AIRSDK on WindowsXP.

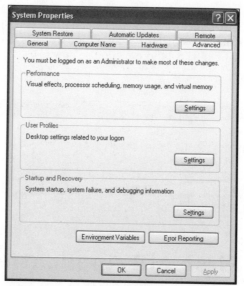

Figure 1-7: The System Properties with Advanced tab selected.

Figure 1-8: The Environmental Variables.

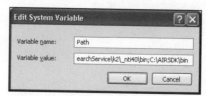

Figure 1-9: The Edit window for the Path variable.

Now, click on the Windows Start menu, and then choose Run and enter **cmd** in the prompt. A command window should open. Type **adl -help** and then click Enter, and you should now see something like Figure 1-10, which shows that the command was found and displays the help information. You can also try running adt -help. See Chapter 5 for information on how to use adl and adt to test and compile AIR applications.

```
C:\WINDOWS\system32\cmd.exe                                    _ □ ×

C:\>adl -help
usage:
  adl ( -runtime <runtime-dir> )? <app-desc> <root-dir>? ( -- ... )?
  adl -help

C:\>
```

Figure 1-10: The results of adl -help.

Create Your First AIR Application

Proceed through the following steps to create your first AIR application.

❑   Open Flex Builder 3 and select File ➪ New ➪ Flex Project from the navigation menu at the top of the screen. See Figure 1-11.

❑   Next, enter **MyFirstAIR** as the Project name, and select "Desktop application" (runs in Adobe AIR) in the "Application type" section. See Figure 1-12.

❑   The next screen allows you to choose an output location; just leave it as it is. See Figure 1-13.

❑   The fourth step allows you to set the source folder, the main application file name, and the application id. It also allows you to add library assets (SWC files, etc.). Leave it as it is and click Finish. See Figure 1-14.

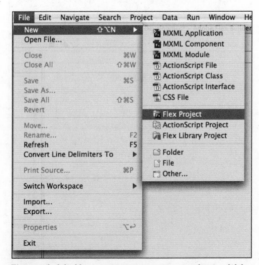

Figure 1-11: How to create a new project within Flex Builder 3.

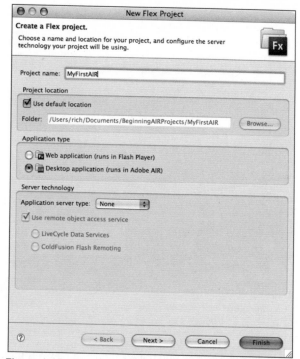

Figure 1-12: Step 2 in the creation of a new AIR project.

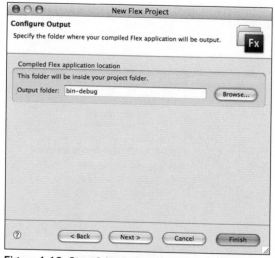

Figure 1-13: Step 3 in the creation of a new AIR project.

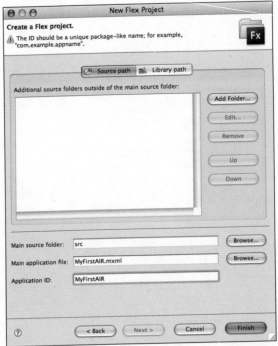

Figure 1-14: Step 4 in the creation of a new AIR project.

You should now have a new AIR project named *MyFirstAIR* and a main file named *MyFirstAIR.mxml*. Figure 1-15 shows the new project within the Flex Builder 3 Navigator view. You can see that a MyFirstAIR-app.xml file also has been created. We discuss this file and its properties in Chapter 6. Figure 1-16 shows the MyFirstAIR.mxml file within the Flex Builder 3 Source view.

Figure 1-15: The newly created
AIR project within the
Flex Builder 3 navigator.

Figure 1-16: The newly created
MyFirstAIR.mxml file.

OK, you're now well on your way to your first AIR application. Now simply add a label component to the MyFirstAIR.mxml file.

```
<mx:Label text="My First AIR application" horizontalCenter="0"
fontWeight="bold" fontSize="20"/>
```

Your completed MyFirstAIR.mxml file should now look like Listing 1-1.

Listing 1-1: The completed MyFirstAIR.mxml file

```
<?xml version="1.0" encoding="utf-8"?>
<mx:WindowedApplication xmlns:mx="http://www.adobe.com/2006/mxml"
layout="absolute">
  <mx:Label text="My First AIR application" horizontalCenter="0"
    fontWeight="bold" fontSize="20"/>
</mx:WindowedApplication>
```

Now run the application by clicking on the green arrow and selecting MyFirstAIR, as pictured in Figure 1-17. This will create a test version of the MyFirstAIR application using ADL. Your results should look like Figure 1-18.

Figure 1-17: Example showing how to run the MyFirstAIR application.

Figure 1-18: The MyFirstAIR application.

Summary

This chapter offered an introduction to AIR and the development tools. It also offered instructions on setting up the AIR SDK on both the OSX and Windows operating systems. Finally, there was a step-by-step demonstration on creating your first Flex-based AIR application.

The next chapter will focus on the definitions of Rich Internet and Rich Desktop applications as well as the many vendors who are trying to gain a piece of this expanding market. Some of the largest names in technology like Microsoft, Sun, and Adobe are offering tools to create Rich Internet and Rich Desktop applications. Each has its own implementation catered to creating these applications, and we will look at each.

Exercise

Create a new AIR application within Flex Builder, switch to Design view, drag a few components onto the workspace, and run the application.

Rich Internet/Desktop Applications

Before discussing Rich Desktop Applications, it's important to understand the history of Rich Internet Applications and the various technologies that are included under the title of RIA. More and more software venders are attempting to get a piece of the RIA space. At the time of this writing, there are developer tools from companies like Adobe, Sun, Microsoft, Mozilla, and OpenLaszlo, as well as freeware like AJAX.

What Is RIA?

A *Rich Internet Application (RIA)* is an application that runs in the traditional browser but utilizes an intermediate layer that can bypass the traditional Page Refresh that has been a standard of most current web applications. The most common tools that can achieve this intermediate layer include JavaScript used in Asynchronous JavaScript and XML (Ajax) applications, as well as Flex or Flash using the Flash Player. Other RIA solutions include OpenLaszlo (which utilizes the Flash Player as well as Ajax), XUL (which is dependent on a Mozilla-compatible browser), and the Microsoft Silverlight.

Adobe Flash

Adobe Flash creates the SWF file type that runs within the Flash Player. Adobe Flash is currently in version 9 within the Adobe Creative Suite 3 software collection. Flash has been around for more than 10 years and was originally known as FutureSplash before being acquired by Macromedia and renamed as *Macromedia Flash*. Flash was a completely new way of building content for the Internet. It allowed for the creation of vector-based animations that could be embedded within a web page. Although Flash was originally used mainly for creating animations and introduction pages for web sites, it quickly developed into a way to create engaging Internet experiences. With the original release of ActionScript 1.0 and the ability to load data easily into Flash 5 applications, developers began to create the first truly Rich Internet Applications. The methods used were somewhat complicated for traditional developers to grasp. With the release of the forms-based Flash applications with Flash MX 2004 and ActionScript 2.0, building RIAs with Flash became much easier; however, it still lacked the feel of traditional software development, since it continued to rely on timeline-based applications. This all changed with the initial release of Flex 1.0.

Adobe Flex

Like Adobe Flash, *Adobe Flex* compiles to SWF and runs within the Flash Player. Flex, which is currently in version 3, was first introduced in 2003 as Macromedia Flex 1.0. When Flex was first introduced, it was billed as a programming language that was more suited to the needs of traditional programmers, since it was 100 percent code-based as opposed to the timeline-based Flash. As with Flash, Flex compiles to the SWF file format. Flex 1.0 utilized the tag-based MXML language, which is an XML-based language, and ActionScript 2.0, which was the standard for Flash at that time as well. Flex 1.5 was an upgrade over Flex 1.0 and continued to use ActionScript 2.0 as the scripting language that accompanied MXML.

Flex 2.0, introduced in July of 2006, was a major shift in the target audience for the product. While Flex 1.0 and 1.5 focused on enterprise-level companies and were priced accordingly, Flex 2.0 introduced the free Flex SDK (Software Development Kit) as well as free versions of the Flex server. This greatly increased the number of developers interested in building applications with Flex. Flex 2.0 also took a leap ahead of Flash by introducing ActionScript 3.0. This was a major change from ActionScript 2.0, since it was now truly an object-oriented scripting language — and one that was very familiar to those who were already creating applications using traditional software development languages like C or Java.

Flex 3, introduced in 2007, continues to offer free versions. It also again made a major shift in target audience by becoming an open-source project. Although at the time of this writing, the Flex 3 open-source project is just getting under way, it's predicted that this will again bring many more developers into the Flex development space.

XUL

XML User Interface Language (XUL) is an XML-based language developed by the Mozilla project. It is a tag-based language that contains many predefined widgets (buttons, radio buttons, etc.) that will be rendered only by a Mozilla-compatible browser such as Firefox. Although it can also be used in the creation of RIAs, XUL has been most widely used in the creation of Mozilla applications and extensions.

OpenLaszlo

Like Flex, *OpenLaszlo* can compile to SWF, and, because it is open source, it is also free for developers to use. OpenLaszlo applications are built using JavaScript, as well as an Extensible Markup Language (XML)-based programming language named *LZX* and compiled to SWF. It is very similar to Flex, and because it was available for free, it garnered a larger amount of attention during the days of Flex 1.5. Because OpenLaszlo compiles to SWF, it enjoys the same write-once-run-anywhere feature that is synonymous with Flex and Flash applications. The one advantage to OpenLaszlo over Flex is that the next version of OpenLaszlo (code-named *legals*) will allow write-once-and-compile to either an SWF or a dynamic HTML (DHTML), or Ajax, application. The major disadvantages of OpenLaszlo are that it has a smaller set of built-in components than Flex, and it has always been at least one full version behind in optimization for the most current Flash Player.

HTML/AJAX

Ajax is a combination of HTML or Extensible HTML (XHTML), Cascading Style Sheets (CSS), and JavaScript to create an application-type feel from a standard web-page request. CSS and JavaScript can be used to trigger updates to the visual aspect of the page, and XMLHttpRequests can be used to fetch data in the background of the page. The combination of these techniques allows a single web page to change its appearance and update its data without any additional page requests from the server. There are many limitations to this type of RIA, including compatibility issues with browser versions and differences in (or lack of) JavaScript support necessary for the RIA to perform as expected.

Windows Presentation Foundation/Silverlight

Windows Presentation Foundation (WPF) consists of an engine and a framework, which will be pre-installed in Windows Vista and introduces XAML as a new tag-based language. *XAML* is very similar to Adobe Flex MXML as it is a tag-based XML language with attributes in which each tag creates an object model class. XAML tags are fully extendable, allowing developers to create custom classes. XAML along with C#, which is the programming language, would correspond to MXML and ActionScript 3 in Adobe Flex.

WPF is used both for traditional desktop applications and for browser-based RIAs using the *Silverlight* name. *Microsoft Silverlight* is a cross-browser, cross-platform plug-in for delivering the next generation of .NET-based media experiences and rich interactive applications for the Web. Silverlight offers a flexible programming model that supports AJAX, VB, C#, Python, and Ruby, and integrates with existing Web applications. Silverlight supports fast, cost-effective delivery of high-quality video to all major browsers running on the Mac OS or Windows.

With Microsoft's backing, WPF/Silverlight and XAML are sure to make a large contribution to Web 2.0 and RIA. Microsoft has stated that it will also introduce WPF/E, which stands for Windows Presentation Server Everywhere. WPF/E will provide support for other browsers and platforms. One major advantage of WPF is that it will support 3D out of the box, which is something that's been lacking in the Flash Player. A disadvantage of WPF is that it doesn't run within the Flash Player, and it will be a long time before Microsoft can expect the same penetration of its runtime as the Flash Player.

JavaFX

JavaFX is a new product from Sun designed to compete in the Rich Internet Application market. JavaFX is based on Java technology and includes a set of runtime environments, widgets, and scripting environments. As of this writing Sun has released two implementations. The first, JavaFX Script, was created to target Java environments, and it allows developers to create rich media and content. JavaFX Script has the ability to make direct calls to Java APIs, thus making it a very powerful language. The second implementation is JavaFX Mobile, which targets mobile devices. The JavaFX product line promises to provide Java developers the tools to create rich applications using traditional Java technologies.

History of RIA

Although the concept of a web application that performs more in line with the traditional desktop application has been around for years, Macromedia first introduced the term RIA in March of 2002. Since this introduction, there have been great advances in the tools and languages used to create RIAs. The growth of Flash and Flex, along with the use of AJAX by companies like Google, has really catapulted RIA to the forefront of web technology. The recent addition of tools from Microsoft and Sun will certainly spread the use of RIA even faster in the coming years.

Benefits of RIA

RIAs offer many benefits over traditional web applications. Following are a few of the many advantages of RIAs:

❑ RIAs offer a richer interface that provides a more engaging user experience without the need for page reloads.

❑ RIAs offer real-time feedback and validation to the user, triggered by user events.

❑ The look and feel of a traditional desktop application can be accomplished with an RIA.

❑ RIAs can include a full multimedia experience, including audio and video.

❑ RIAs have capabilities such as real-time chat and collaboration that are either very difficult or simply impossible with traditional web applications.

Moving to the Desktop

Both Google and Adobe currently have tools in beta that will extend traditional web applications to the desktop. *Google Gears* is a browser plug-in for Firefox that embeds a SQLite database engine within the browser, thus allowing for data synchronization and offline browsing. The first product that Google integrated with Google Gears technology was the Google Reader, which has been a traditional web application. Google Gears has given Google Reader the ability to download the contents of RSS feeds to the embedded database. This allows the user to read the contents of these RSS feeds while offline.

Adobe has made a huge push toward moving web applications to the desktop with the release of the *Adobe Integrated Runtime* (AIR 1.0). AIR has given developers the ability to write desktop applications using traditional web technologies like HTML and JavaScript as well as Rich Technologies like Flash and Flex. AIR also has the ability to detect whether an Internet connection exists, which gives the developer the option of refreshing locally stored data with data from a server.

Microsoft and Sun will undoubtedly add support to make it easier to move applications offline using JavaFX and Silverlight.

Traditional Desktop Applications

Desktop applications have been in the hands of the general public for as long as the personal computer has been around. Many of the technologies used to build these applications have been dependent on the computer's operating system or must be compiled to run on a specific operating system. Java and the Java Virtual Machine have crossed some of these boundaries by providing a runtime to interpret the application byte code to run on multiple operating systems including Linux, Windows, and OSX.

C

Bell Telephone Laboratories developed C in 1972. *C* is a procedural-based programming language that was originally developed for the Unix operating system. It has been used extensively in desktop application development and is the predecessor to C++. C is written as a human-readable language comprised of structures. It must be compiled to byte code and can be compiled to run on multiple platforms. C is a weakly typed language as opposed to C++ and Java, which are strongly typed and will throw more compiler errors due to typing issues.

C++

C++ is a separate language from C but built upon the concepts of C. C++ was originally called *C with Classes* as it was an upgrade to C with the addition of classes. C++ is a strongly typed language and is an Object Oriented (OO) language. OO means that C++ supports polymorphism and inheritance. C++ allows developers to write classes containing methods, properties, and so forth. C++ is ideal for larger applications, as classes allow for code reuse and are more manageable than the less organized C. C++ is also a language that must be run through a compiler.

Java

Java is an Object Oriented language that borrows many of its principles from C and C++ but has stronger OO principles. Java is currently recognized as the most popular computing language in existence today. As previously mentioned, Java compiles to byte code, which, in turn, is interpreted by the *Java Virtual Machine (JVM)*. The JVM is specific to an operating system and is built to provide consistent results independent of the operating system. This is part of Sun's goal of write once, run anywhere.

Summary

Although it remains to be seen who will be the dominant force in RIA (Rich Internet Applications) and RDA (Rich Desktop Applications), Adobe certainly has a nice head start, with Flex being a mature product and AIR on the way. The large profiles of the other companies putting resources toward gaining market share will only accelerate the spread of RIA and RDA.

The next chapter will examine the languages involved in creating AIR applications, including ActionScript 3, MXML, HTML, and JavaScript.

The Programming Languages

AIR applications can be built using several different programming languages including MXML, ActionScript 3, HTML, JavaScript, and CSS. An application can be built with just one of these or a combination of some or all of them. This chapter will offer some background and definition of each of the AIR programming languages.

AIR Flex/Flash Applications

AIR applications built with Flex or Flash may use ActionScript 3 as the base language for the application. The application can be built entirely with ActionScript 3 when working with either of these platforms.

Flash applications are generally built using the visual tools of the Flash development environment to create visual content. These applications are traditionally timeline-based with ActionScript 3 being used to support and extend the functionality of the visual interface.

Flex applications are usually but not always built with a combination of MXML and ActionScript 3. MXML simplifies the visual components and their layout, while ActionScript 3 adds functionality.

MXML

MXML is an XML-based language that was first introduced by Macromedia in 2004. MXML is a declarative tag-based markup language, and since its introduction, it has proven very successful for component layout within Flex user interface design. As an XML language it is very structured and validates against an Adobe DTD.

MXML is mostly used for component layout to design the visual aspects of a Flex or Flex-based AIR application. For example, `<mx:ComboBox>` adds a combo box to the display, `<mx:Button>` adds a button object to the display, and `<mx:DataGrid>` would add a data grid.

MXML can also be used to define other objects that are not visual objects. A few examples of these are <mx:WebService>, which defines a connection to a WSDL file; <mx:NumberValidator>, which is used to validate data; and <mx:Binding>, which can be used to bind data between components. MXML components can also be extended to create custom components and even combined to create composite custom components. This ability makes it very easy to create reusable components that can be shared across applications.

MXML can be written with any text editor or can also be edited using the visual editing tools of Flex Builder 3. MXML components can also be styled either within the properties of the component tag or using an external CSS style sheet.

Although it is possible to create complete applications using only MXML, the real power of this language is shown when combined with ActionScript 3.

MXML ultimately compiles to SWF, which is the file format created to run within the Adobe Flash Player.

Listing 3-1 shows an example of an MXML file that includes a Button and Label component.

Listing 3-1: A sample MXML file

```
<?xml version="1.0" encoding="utf-8"?>
<mx:VBox xmlns:mx="http://www.adobe.com/2006/mxml">

    <mx:Label text="Label"/>
    <mx:Button label="Button"/>

</mx:VBox>
```

ActionScript 3

ActionScript 3 is a robust mature programming language that is object-oriented and offers a very familiar syntax to users of other programming languages like C#, Java, and JavaScript.

ActionScript 3 and JavaScript are very similar, as both are derived from the European Computer Manufacturers Association (ECMA) document ECMA-262, which is the international standard for the JavaScript language. ActionScript 3 is based on the ECMA-262 Edition 4 specification, so this is where the similarities come in between the two languages.

Since ActionScript 3 is object-oriented, it gives developers the ability to extend the ActionScript classes that are part of the Flex Framework to create custom components and objects.

Integrating ActionScript with MXML gives developers all the tools needed to accomplish just about anything with Flex. AIR has taken this even a step further as there are far fewer security restrictions when building AIR applications than is the case with Flex web-based applications.

As with MXML, ActionScript will compile to the SWF file format.

Listing 3-2 shows an example of a custom ActionScript 3 class named `AngleButton`. This class extends the `mx.controls.Button` class and sets the rotation of the component to 45 degrees.

Listing 3-2: The `AngleButton` custom class

```
package
{
  import mx.controls.Button;

    public class AngleButton extends Button
    {
        public function AngleButton()
        {
            super();
            this.rotation = 45;
        }
    }
}
```

Using the Documentation

Adobe has provided documentation for both MXML and ActionScript objects in the form of *ASdocs*, which are very similar to JavaDocs. Understanding how to read and use these documents will allow you to use MXML and ActionScript to their fullest potential. Figures 3-1 through 3-11 show some snippets of the documentation for the MXML Button component. Each image shows a different section of the properties, events, styles, and so forth, of the button.

Figure 3-1, which is the topmost section of the documentation, shows the inheritance of the Button component. Looking at this section, we can easily see the parent objects of a Button as well as what package it is in and what it implements, as well as what it subclasses. Figure 3-2 offers a brief description of the object you are researching. The next item in the documentation of the Button is an example of the syntax used to create the Button. This is shown in Figure 3-3. Figures 3-4 through 3-7 show the additional properties and methods, both public and private. Each can be expanded to show the inherited properties and methods. Figure 3-4 shows an example of the inherited protected properties after the documentation interface was expanded to show them. Each of the inherited items will show an arrow to indicate that it is inherited from a parent somewhere up the inheritance tree. Shown in Figures 3-8 through 3-10 are the events, styles, and effects available for the Button object. Each of these also can be expanded to show inherited items. Finally Figure 3-11 shows the public constants available for the Button object.

Package	mx.controls
Class	public class Button
Inheritance	Button → UIComponent → FlexSprite → Sprite → DisplayObjectContainer → InteractiveObject → DisplayObject → EventDispatcher → Object
Implements	IDataRenderer, IDropInListItemRenderer, IFocusManagerComponent, IListItemRenderer
Subclasses	AccordionHeader, CheckBox, LinkButton, PopUpButton, RadioButton, ScrollThumb, SliderThumb

Figure 3-1: This example shows the inheritance of the Button.

The Button control is a commonly used rectangular button. Button controls look like they can be pressed. They can have a text label, an icon, or both on their face.

Buttons typically use event listeners to perform an action when the user selects the control. When a user clicks the mouse on a Button control, and the Button control is enabled, it dispatches a `click` event and a `buttonDown` event. A button always dispatches events such as the `mouseMove`, `mouseOver`, `mouseOut`, `rollOver`, `rollOut`, `mouseDown`, and `mouseUp` events whether enabled or disabled.

You can customize the look of a Button control and change its functionality from a push button to a toggle button. You can change the button appearance by using a skin for each of the button's states.

Figure 3-2: The definition of the Button.

MXML Syntax ▾Hide MXML Syntax

The `<mx:Button>` tag inherits all the tag attributes of its superclass, and adds the following tag attributes:

```
<mx:Button
    Properties
    autoRepeat="false|true"
    emphasized="false|true"
    label=""
    labelPlacement="right|left|bottom|top"
    selected="false|true"
    selectedField="null"
    stickyHighlighting="false|true"
    toggle="false|true"

    Styles
    borderColor="0xAAB3B3"
    color="0x0B333C"
    cornerRadius="4"
    disabledColor="0xAAB3B3"
    disabledIcon="null"
```

Figure 3-3: Sample syntax of the Button component.

Public Properties

▶ Show Inherited Public Properties

Property	Defined by
autoRepeat : Boolean Specifies whether to dispatch repeated buttonDown events if the user holds down the mouse button.	Button
data : Object The data property lets you pass a value to the component when you use it as an item renderer or item editor.	Button
emphasized : Boolean Draws a thick border around the Button control when the control is in its up state if emphasized is set to true.	Button
label : String Text to appear on the Button control.	Button

Figure 3-4: The Public Properties of a Button.

Protected Properties

▾ Hide Inherited Protected Properties

Property	Defined by
⬆ **resourceManager** : IResourceManager [read-only] A reference to the object which manages all of the application's localized resources.	UIComponent
textField : UITextField The internal UITextField object that renders the label of this Button.	Button
⬆ **unscaledHeight** : Number [read-only] A convenience method for determining the unscaled height of the component.	UIComponent
⬆ **unscaledWidth** : Number [read-only] A convenience method for determining the unscaled width of the component All of a component's drawing and child layout should be done within a bounding rectangle of this width, which is also passed as an argument to updateDisplayList().	UIComponent

Figure 3-5: The Protected Properties of a Button.

Public Methods

▼ Hide Inherited Public Methods

Method	Defined by
Button() Constructor.	Button
⬆ **addChild**(child:DisplayObject):DisplayObject Adds a child DisplayObject instance to this DisplayObjectContainer instance.	DisplayObjectContainer
⬆ **addChildAt**(child:DisplayObject, index:int):DisplayObject Adds a child DisplayObject instance to this DisplayObjectContainer instance.	DisplayObjectContainer
⬆ **addEventListener**(type:String, listener:Function, useCapture:Boolean = false, priority:int = 0, useWeakReference:Boolean = false):void Registers an event listener object with an EventDispatcher object so that the listener receives notification of an event.	EventDispatcher

Figure 3-6: The Public Methods of a Button.

Protected Methods

▶ Show Inherited Protected Methods

Method	Defined by
clickHandler(event:MouseEvent):void The default handler for the MouseEvent.CLICK event.	Button
mouseDownHandler(event:MouseEvent):void The default handler for the MouseEvent.MOUSE_DOWN event.	Button
mouseUpHandler(event:MouseEvent):void The default handler for the MouseEvent.MOUSE_UP event.	Button
rollOutHandler(event:MouseEvent):void The default handler for the MouseEvent.ROLL_OUT event.	Button
rollOverHandler(event:MouseEvent):void The default handler for the MouseEvent.ROLL_OVER event.	Button

Figure 3-7: The Protected Methods of a Button.

Events

▶ Show Inherited Events

Event	Summary	Defined By
buttonDown	Dispatched when the user presses the Button control.	Button
change	Dispatched when the selected property changes for a toggle Button control.	Button
dataChange	Dispatched when the data property changes.	Button

Figure 3-8: The available Events of the Button component.

Styles

▶ Show Inherited Styles

Style	Description	Defined By
borderColor	**Type:** uint **Format:** Color **CSS Inheritance:** no Color of the border. The following controls support this style: Button, CheckBox, ComboBox, MenuBar, NumericStepper, ProgressBar, RadioButton, ScrollBar, Slider, and any components that support the borderStyle style. The default value depends on the component class; if not overriden for the class, the default value is 0xB7BABC.	Button
color	**Type:** uint **Format:** Color **CSS Inheritance:** yes Color of text in the component, including the component label. The default value is 0x0B333C.	Button
cornerRadius	**Type:** Number **Format:** Length **CSS Inheritance:** no Radius of component corners. The following components support this style: Alert, Button, ComboBox, LinkButton, MenuBar, NumericStepper, Panel, ScrollBar, Tab, TitleWindow, and any component that supports a borderStyle property set to "solid". The default value depends on the component class; if not overriden for the class, the default value is 0.	Button

Figure 3-9: The available Styles of the Button component.

Effects

▼ Hide Inherited Effects

Effect	Description	Defined By
⬆ addedEffect	**Triggering Event:** added	
⬆ creationCompleteEffect	**Triggering Event:** creationComplete	
⬆ focusInEffect	**Triggering Event:** focusIn	
⬆ focusOutEffect	**Triggering Event:** focusOut	

Figure 3-10: The available Effects of the Button component.

Public Constants

▼ Hide Inherited Public Constants

Constant	Defined by
⬆ **DEFAULT_MAX_HEIGHT** : Number = 10000 [static] The default value for the maxHeight property.	UIComponent
⬆ **DEFAULT_MAX_WIDTH** : Number = 10000 [static] The default value for the maxWidth property.	UIComponent
⬆ **DEFAULT_MEASURED_HEIGHT** : Number = 22 [static] The default value for the measuredHeight property.	UIComponent

Figure 3-11: The Button component's Public Consants.

Knowing how to use the Flex/ActionScript documentation will make your life a lot easier as you build applications. Although additional references, books, and best practices are always useful for gaining an understanding of how to build applications, the documentation should be what you fall back on, so knowing how to use and understand it is essential.

AIR HTML Applications

AIR applications can also be built using traditional web languages like HTML, JavaScript, CSS, XHTML, and DOM. *HTML* has been the backbone of the Internet for many years and is something that almost anyone who has even opened a text editor to edit a web page is familiar with. Since AIR has given us the ability to create desktop applications using simple HTML, the size of the possible AIR development community is tremendous. HTML-based AIR applications can use JavaScript to extend the application and give it additional functionality. JavaScript also has the ability to communicate with ActionScript. This gives HTML-based AIR applications enhanced with JavaScript the ability to utilize many of the AIR features without the developer needing to know the ActionScript language.

HTML (Hypertext Markup Language)

In late 1991, the first public definition of HTLM was made available in a document by Tim Berners-Lee titled, "HTML Tags." It described 22 HTML tags of which 13 still exist today. This very simple markup language gave the early Internet developers everything they needed to format mostly text-based web pages. HTML has grown over the years from the original to HTML 2.0, which was completed in 1995. In 1996, the World Wide Web Consortium (W3C) became the authority to maintain the HTML standard, and in early 1997, HTML 3.2 was officially published. Not long after that, in late 1997, HTML 4.0 was published, followed by HTML 4.01 in 1999. In 2000, HTML also became an international standard (ISO/IEC 15445:2000). HTML 5 is still an editors' draft and has yet to be officially published. Listing 3-3 shows a basic HTML file that includes a head (<head>) tag with a title (<title>) tag nested within, a body (<body>) tag with a few headings (<h1>, <h2>, <h3>) of different sizes, a paragraph (<p>) tag with a few break tags (<br/>) and a hyperlink tag (<a href>) within. Figure 3-12 shows the results of the HTML code of Listing 3-3.

Listing 3-3: A basic HTML file

```html
<html>
  <head>
    <title>This is a title</title>
  </head>

  <body>
    <h1>Heading</h1>
    <h2>Heading 2 (smaller)</h2>
    <h3>Heading 3 (smaller than 2)</h3>

    <p>This is a paragraph tag
    <br/>
    <br/>
    There are two break tags above, which will leave vertical space
    <br/>
    <a href="http://blog.everythingflex.com">Visit my Web Page</a>
    </p>
  </body>
</html>
```

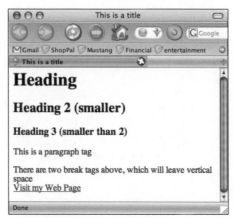

Figure 3-12: A basic HTML file.

JavaScript

JavaScript is a dynamic scripting language that is both weakly typed and prototype-based. JavaScript was originally known as *Mocha* and then later *LiveScript*. It was renamed *JavaScript* as a marketing ploy to capitalize on the popularity of Java. JavaScript was first included in the Netscape 2 browser in 1995 and has been updated since. The most current version of JavaScript is version 1.7. Adobe AIR has support for JavaScript 1.5, which is based on the ECMA-262 standard. The AIR JavaScript engine is built by integrating the WebKit open source browser engine project. JavaScript is executed client side, which means that the user must have JavaScript installed and accessible in order for the code to run correctly. This is sometimes a problem when using JavaScript within web-based applications; however, since the JavaScript engine is part of the AIR runtime, you can be certain that your code will perform as expected when running within an AIR desktop application.

Listing 3-4 shows an example of an HTML file with several JavaScript blocks included. Within the <body> tag the document.write() method is used to write text to the document. The link tag calls the showAlert() function when clicked, which shows a JavaScript alert. The results can be seen in Figure 3-13.

Listing 3-4: A sample HTML file with multiple JavaScript blocks

```html
<HTML>
  <HEAD>
    <SCRIPT LANGUAGE="JAVASCRIPT">
      <!--
      function showAlert(){
        alert ("Javascript Alert")
      }
      -->
    </SCRIPT>
    <TITLE>Page Title</TITLE>
  </HEAD>
  <BODY>
    <SCRIPT LANGUAGE="JAVASCRIPT">
      <!--
      document.write("Written by JavaScript");
      -->
    </SCRIPT>
    <a href onClick="showAlert()">Click Me</a>
  </BODY>
</HTML>
```

Figure 3-13: An HTML file with JavaScript.

CSS (Cascading Style Sheets)

CSS (Cascading Style Sheets) is a language built for styling HTML or XHTML web pages. Colors, fonts, layouts, backgrounds, and so on are commonly defined within a style sheet. CSS helps to separate the styling of an application from the presentation layer. Prior to CSS all styling was done in line with the underlying HTML. CSS not only changed this but actually allowed for the same underlying HTML to be displayed differently by simply swapping out a few of the CSS styles. The CSS principles are also part of the Flex styling package and can be applied to MXML in a very similar manner to HTML. Styles are not only applied to the outermost container tag but also apply to nested tags. CSS styles can be applied to a tag by name or can be applied to a tag within the tag itself.

Listing 3-5 contains two CSS styles; the first applies to all instances of the <h1> tag and will make the text output show as green. The second style, named *bold*, only applies to areas that are specifically set where the class property of the <p> tag is set. Therefore only the "bold" font will output as bold, while the "normal" font will show as regular text. The results of Listing 3-5 can be seen in Figure 3-14.

Listing 3-6 contains two CSS styles; the first will apply a font size of 36 to all instances of a Label component within the file. The second Label will show both large and bold with italics, as the CSS style will apply the 36-point font to the Label, and then the styleName being set to boldI will set the text bold and italic. Finally, the Button component has only the boldI style attached and no CSS defined for the Button by name, so the label will show as bold and italic in the default font size. The results of Listing 3-6 can be seen in Figure 3-15.

Listing 3-5: An example of CSS within an HTML file

```html
<html>
  <head>
    <title>CSS HTML Example</title>
    <style type="text/css">
      h1 {
        color: #008000;
      }
      .bold {
        font-weight: bold;
      }
    </style>
  </head>
  <body>
    <h1>Green Header</h1>
    Normal Font
    <p class="bold">Bold Font</p>
  </body>
</html>
```

Listing 3-6: An example of CSS within an MXML file

```xml
<?xml version="1.0" encoding="utf-8"?>
<mx:WindowedApplication xmlns:mx="http://www.adobe.com/2006/mxml">
  <mx:Style>
    Label {
      font-size:36;
    }
    .boldI {
      font-weight:bold;
      font-style:italic;
    }
  </mx:Style>
```

(continued)

Listing 3-6: An example of CSS within an MXML file *(continued)*

```
<mx:Label text="Large"/>
<mx:Label text="Large and Bold" styleName="boldI"/>
<mx:Button label="Bold and Italic" styleName="boldI"/>
</mx:WindowedApplication>
```

Figure 3-14: An example showing HTML with CSS.

Figure 3-15: An example showing the use of CSS within an MXML file.

XHTML (Extensible Hypertext Markup Language)

XHTML (Extensible Hypertext Markup Language) is a rigid implementation of HTML that is built on XML. Since it is much less forgiving than HTML, which can output correctly even when it does not validate properly, XHTML must be properly formatted. The reason this is important is that XHTML can be validated using automated techniques, while HTML must run through custom parsers. What this means is that an XHTML document can be validated against a custom DTD or namespace. An XHTML file can be set as transitional so that it will still function within older browsers or can be set to use a DTD, which forces strict code validation. In Listing 3-7, you see a file set to validate against a strict DTD (xhtml1-strict.dtd). In Listing 3-8, you see a file that is set to validate against a transitional DTD. In this listing, notice that the background color of the body is set to blue. This property would not be allowed in Listing 3-7, as a strict DTD would not validate the bgcolor property because it has been deprecated and should be replaced by a CSS property.

Listing 3-7: A document using a strict DTD

```
<?xml version="1.0" encoding="UTF-8"?>
<!DOCTYPE html PUBLIC "-//W3C//DTD XHTML 1.0 Strict//EN" "DTD/xhtml1-strict.dtd">
<html xmlns="http://www.w3.org/1999/xhtml" xml:lang="en" lang="en">
  <head>
    <title> Strict XHTML Example </title>
  </head>
  <body>
  Some Text
  </body>
</html>
```

Listing 3-8: A document using a transitional DTD

```
<?xml version="1.0" encoding="UTF-8"?>
<!DOCTYPE html PUBLIC "-//W3C//DTD XHTML 1.0 Transitional//EN"
"DTD/xhtml1-transitional.dtd">
<html xmlns="http://www.w3.org/1999/xhtml" xml:lang="en" lang="en">
  <head>
    <title> Transitional XHTML Example </title>
  </head>
  <body bgcolor="#0000FF">
  Some Text
  </body>
</html>
```

DOM (Document Object Model)

DOM (Document Object Model) is a specification for an API that allows an HTML or XML file to be accessed as an object with a clear navigation through its hierarchy. Each item in the DOM (images, form elements, text, etc.) is accessible by navigating the hierarchy of the DOM tree. This allows for the update of content or structure of HTML and XML documents through the use of JavaScript. Therefore, it is possible to update specific document contents without the need of a full refresh. Using JavaScript, the DOM can be accessed, and specific pieces of the document object can be modified. The DOM can be navigated with the use of dot notation as illustrated in Listing 3-9, which shows the value of the myTextField form field within document's form with the name of myForm being read and shown within an alert window. The results of Listing 3-9 can be seen in Figure 3-16.

Listing 3-9: Access of the DOM through dot notation

```html
<html>
  <head>
  <title>DOM Dot Notation</title>
  <script language="javascript">
  <!--
    function alertIt(){
      alert (document.myForm.myTextField.value);
    }
  -->
  </script>
  </head>
  <body>
    <form name="myForm">
      <input type="text" name="myTextField" value="Hello World"/>
      <input type="button" onClick="alertIt()"/>
    </form>
  </body>
</html>
```

Figure 3-16: Example showing the use
of dot notation when navigating the DOM.

DOM also has the option to access items by id using the `getElementById()` method. Listing 3-10 shows a similar example as Listing 3-9 but this time uses the `getElementById()` method. The results of Listing 3-10 can be seen in Figure 3-17.

Listing 3-10: The use of the getElementById() method

```html
<html>
  <head>
  <title>DOM getElementById()</title>
  <script language="javascript">
  <!--
    function alertIt(){
      alert (document.getElementById('myTextField').value);
    }
  -->
```

```
    </script>
    </head>
  <body>
     <form name="myForm">
       <input type="text" id="myTextField" value="Hello World"/>
       <input type="button" onClick="alertIt()"/>
     </form>
  </body>
</html>
```

Figure 3-17: The use of the
getElementById() **method within**
the DOM.

You can also add items to the DOM using methods like createElement() or createTextNode(), and then adding them to the DOM using the appendChild() method. Listing 3-11 shows the use of these functions. Clicking on the Button object will add some text ("Hello World") to the document. The results of Listing 3-11 can be seen in Figure 3-18.

Listing 3-11: How to add an object to the DOM

```
<html>
  <head>
  <title>DOM appendChild()</title>
  <script language="javascript">
  <!--
    function addText(){
      var divTag = document.createElement("div");
      var someText  = document.createTextNode("Hello World");
      divTag.appendChild(someText);
      document.body.appendChild(divTag);
    }
  -->
  </script>
  </head>
  <body>
    <input type="button" onClick="addText()" value="Add Text"/>
  </body>
</html>
```

The W3C first introduced DOM 1 in 1998 and then updated it to DOM 2 in 2000. DOM 3 was then released in 2004, and this is the most current version.

The HTML control, which is part of AIR, allows for full access of the DOM of the location that is loaded into the control.

Figure 3-18: Example showing elements being added to the DOM.

AJAX (Asynchronous JavaScript and XML)

AJAX (Asynchronous JavaScript and XML) is a development technique using JavaScript and the DOM to manipulate sections of web pages without the need of full-page refresh. Data are retrieved by using the XMLHttpRequest and returned in XML, HTML, JSON, or even plaintext. The data are then parsed, and, through the manipulation of the DOM, portions of the page are refreshed. This not only gives the user the perception of a much more fluid application, but also saves a tremendous amount of bandwidth.

In a traditional client/server model, the AJAX techniques would only work properly when the client's browser has JavaScript enabled. Since Adobe has embedded the WebKit engine, this is not a concern when working with AIR applications, since we as developers can be certain that the application will perform properly.

Summary

This chapter offered a brief definition and sample code for the different languages that can be used to create AIR applications. One, many, or all of these languages can be used in a single application. The next chapter will discuss and demonstrate the tools used to create AIR applications. Flex Builder 3, Dreamweaver CS3, and Flash CS3 are covered.

The AIR Development Tools

Adobe has enabled several of its products to work with AIR. These include Flex Builder 3 for Flex-based AIR projects, Dreamweaver CS3 for HTML/JavaScript-based projects, and Flash CS3 for Flash projects.

Introduction to Flex Builder 3

One of the most significant pieces of the Flex 2 product family was the all-new Flex Builder 2. The original Flex Builder was built on top of Dreamweaver, and, to put it bluntly, the community was not shy about letting Macromedia (now Adobe) know just how bad Flex Builder 1 actually was. Fortunately for the Flex development community, Macromedia acknowledged this, decided to scrap it completely, and started over, using Eclipse as the base for Flex Builder 2. Flex Builder 2 was light years ahead of the original, and most developers now use it as the tool of choice for doing Flex MXML and ActionScript development.

Flex Builder 3 is an upgrade to Flex Builder 2 and has added many new features, including the ability to build and compile AIR applications. The ease of use of Flex Builder 3 makes it the premier tool for building, debugging, testing, and packaging AIR applications.

Most modern systems will not have any problems running Flex Builder 3.

The official requirements from Adobe for Flex Builder are listed below.

Windows

- ❏ Intel Pentium 4 processor
- ❏ 1 GB of RAM recommended
- ❏ Microsoft Windows XP (with Service Pack 2)
- ❏ Microsoft Vista Home Premium or higher
- ❏ 300 MB of available hard-disk space to install

- ❏ Java™ Virtual Machine: Sun JRE 1.4.2 (included), Sun JRE 1.5, IBM JRE 1.5
- ❏ Eclipse 3.2.1 or higher for Plug-in install

Macintosh

- ❏ G4 1.25 GHz PowerPC or Intel-based Mac
- ❏ OS X 10.4.7–10.4.9
- ❏ 1 GB of RAM recommended
- ❏ 300 MB of available hard-disk space to install
- ❏ Java™ Virtual Machine: JRE 1.5 or JRE 1.6 from Apple
- ❏ Eclipse 3.2.1 or higher for Plug-in install

Flex Builder Eclipse Stand-Alone and Plug-in

Flex Builder 3 is available in two different distributions. The *stand-alone version* operates exactly the same as the *plug-in version*, but is a lighter-weight application. The stand-alone version runs on top of a stripped-down version of Eclipse, which makes it a smaller install and a smaller memory footprint. However, for those who have already been using the full version of Eclipse for other development (such as Java, ColdFusion, etc.), Flex Builder comes as a plug-in that installs into Eclipse, just like the many other Eclipse plug-ins.

Flex Builder Perspectives

Flex Builder has multiple perspectives. A *perspective* defines a set of editors and view panels that are useful to the task at hand. For example, Flex Builder will switch to a different perspective if you are debugging an application. Switching to a perspective will alter the views and editors that show within the Eclipse application. Switching perspectives will happen automatically in some situations. The default perspective is the *development perspective,* and it includes a Source mode (Figure 4-1) and a Design mode. The other perspective is the *debugging perspective.*

The Development Perspective Source Mode

The *Source mode* is a basic code editor that will include code hints, code completion, syntax coloring, and real-time error reporting for both MXML and ActionScript code. Figure 4-2 shows the Development perspective with the Outline view of the Source mode enabled. The *Outline view* shows the hierarchy of your MXML code when editing an MXML file, or the properties and methods of your class files when editing an ActionScript class. Either way, you can go directly to a line of code by clicking the entry in the Outline views.

The Development Perspective Design Mode

As shown in Figure 4-3, switching to the *Design mode* makes available two panels on the right-side screen: the *States panel* and the *Components panel.* The *Editor panel* located in the middle of the screen changes to become a visual editor, allowing the drag-and-drop positioning of components, as well as drag and drop of components from the *Components panel.* The *States panel* allows you to create new states that can be designed visually as well. For more information on how to use states, see Chapter 8.

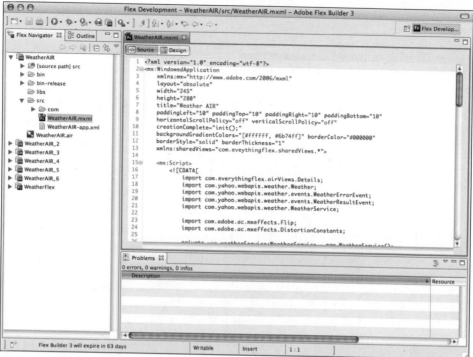

Figure 4-1: The Development perspective in Source mode.

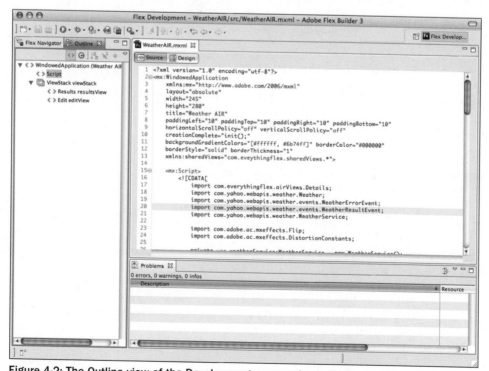

Figure 4-2: The Outline view of the Development perspective in Source mode.

Note that you cannot switch to Design mode when editing an ActionScript file. It is only available for editing MXML files.

Also note that, by default, the Components panel appears in the same pane as the Outline view on the left of the screen, and the States and Properties panels appear on the right.

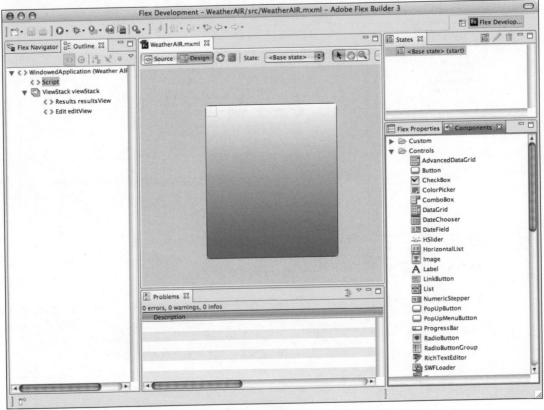

Figure 4-3: The Development perspective in Design mode.

Another part of Design mode, the *Properties view*, has multiple sections, as well as the following Property-view options:

❑ **Standard property-view options** — There are three separate sections within the Standard view of the Properties view.

❑ **Common section** — This allows for editing of the component properties, as shown in Figure 4-4.

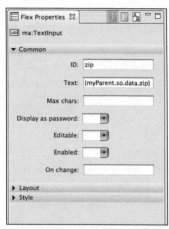

Figure 4-4: The Common section of the Properties view.

❏ **Style section** — As shown in Figure 4-5, this makes use of color selectors, sliders, combo boxes, and buttons to allow for easy editing of the selected component's style properties. The changes are reflected in real time within the Design Editor.

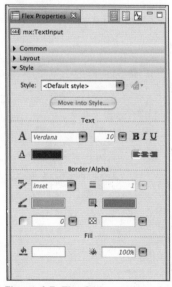

Figure 4-5: The Style section of the Properties view.

❏ **Layout section** — This is the area where you make changes to layout properties, including width and height when working in directional layouts. It also includes x, y, and the layout constraints when working within an absolute layout. Use the checkboxes within the constraint options section to anchor the selected component to one or more corners of the parent container. Figure 4-6 shows the Layout section with a component anchored to the bottom-right corner of the parent container. Any changes made will be reflected in the Design Editor in real time.

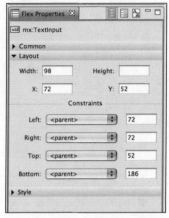

Figure 4-6: The Layout section of the Properties view.

❑ **Category property-view options** — The Category view shown in Figure 4-7 is a tree layout of the available properties. The properties can be edited by updating the text fields next to each property. Some of the text fields will include visual editors to make editing of colors and known property options easier.

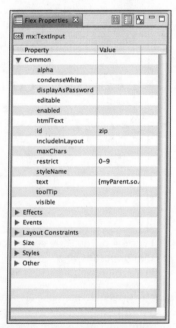

Figure 4-7: The Category view of the Properties view.

❑   **Alphabetical property-view options** — As shown in Figure 4-8, the Alphabetical view includes all of the same properties shown in the Category view, but in a simple alphabetical list, rather than a tree layout. To use the Properties view to make changes to your components, simply click a component within the Design Editor, which will update the Properties panel to show the options available for the selected component.

Figure 4-8: The Alphabetical view of the Properties view.

The Debugging Perspective

Switching to the *debugging perspective* allows you to run the Flex debugger, set breakpoints, watch variables, and step through your code. To switch to the debugging perspective, simply choose Flex Debugging Perspective from the Perspectives menu at the top-right corner of the Editor, as shown in Figure 4-9. The Flex Debugging Perspective will not be available as shown in Figure 4-9 unless it has been opened at least once before. To show it for the first time, you must either click the Open Perspective button in the top right or navigate to Window ➪ Perspective ➪ Flex Debugging.

Debugging Your Application

Flex Builder 3 offers debugging capabilities that allow you to find bugs within your application. A debugger allows you to stop and start the application to find problems, or to examine or substitute values for variables. To debug your application, you must first switch your perspective to the Flex Debugging Perspective using the buttons within the tabs at the top of the Editor window, as shown in Figure 4-9. Once you are in the Flex Debugging Perspective, you can set breakpoints by right-clicking on the line of code you wish to break on, and selecting Toggle Breakpoint from the Context menu, as shown in Figure 4-10. You can also simply double-click on the line of code to toggle on and off a breakpoint.

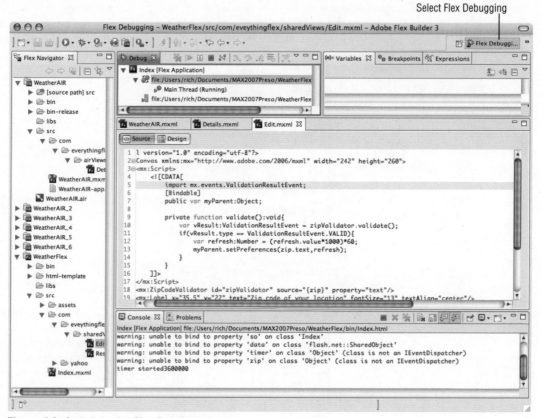

Figure 4-9: Switch to the Flex Debugger.

Note that the Debugging perspective is automatically opened when a breakpoint is encountered, or when a runtime error is thrown.

The Debugging perspective also includes views to read, edit, and watch variables, manage breakpoints, and watch expressions. These include the Console view, the Variables view, the Breakpoints view, and the Expressions view.

Console View

The *Console view* displays any trace statements that are within your source code while your application is running within a debug session. This view will become one of your best friends while debugging your Flex applications. The Console view also displays runtime errors.

Variables View

The *Variables view* of the debugger allows you to easily copy, find, change, and watch your variables while debugging your application. To do so, simply right-click on a variable name, and then use the context menu shown in Figure 4-11 to perform any of the aforementioned functions. Selecting Watch from the Context menu will add the variable to the Expressions view (discussed below).

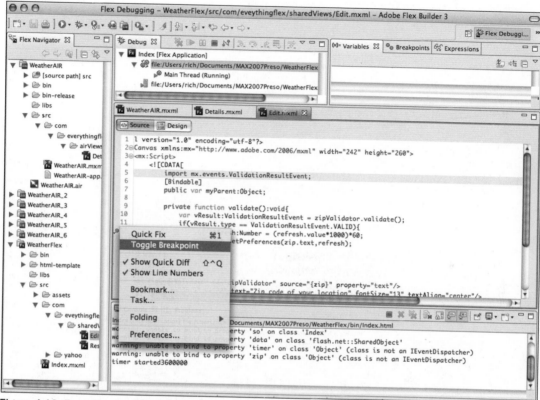

Figure 4-10: Example showing how to add a breakpoint.

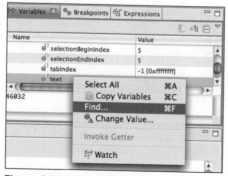

Figure 4-11: The Variables view of the Debugging perspective.

The Variables view contains many icons and symbols that can be a bit confusing. The following table provides definitions for the various symbols.

Symbols	Definition
Red square	Defines a private variable
Green circle	Defines a public variable
Yellow diamond	Defines a protected variable
Blue diamond	Defines an internal variable
Orange box (package)	Defines a variable scoped to a user-defined namespace

The following table provides definitions for the various icons.

Icons	Definition
C icon	Defines a constant variable
D icon	Defines a dynamic variable
S icon	Defines a static variable
Getter Icon	Indicates that the variable has a getter

Breakpoints View

The *Breakpoints view* is an easy place to manage your breakpoints while in a debugging session. As shown in Figure 4-12, you can right-click on a breakpoint and use the context menu to change the status or to remove a breakpoint. You can also use the Breakpoints toolbar for additional functionality, including jumping to the breakpoint within the source code, skipping all breakpoints, and expanding and collapsing the breakpoint tree.

Expressions View

Use the *Expressions view* to add and edit expressions on the variables you are watching. You can also choose to reevaluate the expressions you are watching, because the data may have changed as you proceeded through the debug session. As shown in Figure 4-13, you can right-click on an expression and use the Context menu.

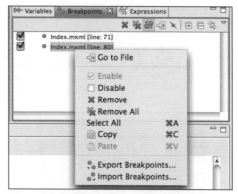

Figure 4-12: The Breakpoints view of the Debugging perspective.

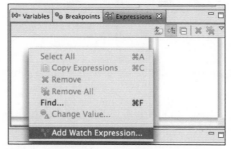

Figure 4-13: The Expressions view of the Debugging perspective.

Introducing Flash CS3

Flash CS3 is the newest development tool in the Flash product line released from Adobe. Flash CS3 is the most advanced tool yet for creating rich interactive content for the Web as well as mobile devices.

Flash CS3 is the first product in the Flash lineup to include the new ActionScript 3, which was first introduced in 2006 within the Flex 2 product line. This is significant as it allows the two product lines to interact by sharing a native language.

The Flash IDE is made up of many views; here is a description of some of the most used views.

The Stage

The *stage* is the main visual workspace when working on the design elements of a Flash project. By default, the timeline is attached, but it can be turned off independently from the stage. See Figure 4-14.

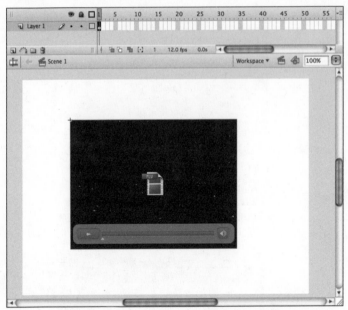

Figure 4-14: The Flash CS3 stage with a single component added.

The Components window as shown in Figure 4-15 allows for easy drag and drop of the components onto the stage. The components are grouped into categories, and different categories are available depending on what version of the application you're building, ActionScript 2 versus 3.

Figure 4-15: The Components window.

Flash CS3 has full ActionScript capabilities utilizing the Actions window. The Actions window includes a script assistant, syntax checker, code formatter, code collapse, and debugging tools. Figure 4-16 shows the Actions window.

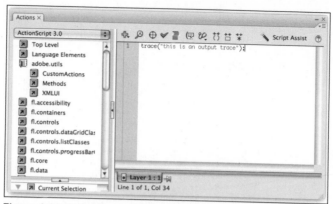

Figure 4-16: Example showing the Actions window.

When running/debugging your application, the Output window is the place where you will see debug information as well as any trace statements that you have included in your code. This is an invaluable part of Flash development. Figure 4-17 shows the results of the trace statement that was shown in Figure 4-16.

Figure 4-17: The Output window and a sample trace statement.

When a component is selected while on the stage, the Properties window will show some of the common properties associated with the component. This allows for easy editing of the component properties. Figure 4-18 shows the properties of the FLVPlayback component that was shown on stage in Figure 4-14. These properties as well as additional properties not shown in the Properties window can be set directly within ActionScript.

Figure 4-18: The Properties window.

The Library window shows details about all of the components that are currently part of your application. It also contains the component assets and lets you open up each asset piece for custom skinning. The Library window shown in Figure 4-19 contains the FLVPlayback component as well as a Button component. The assets folder has been expanded to show the skins.

**Figure 4-19: The Library window
with the assets folder expanded.**

There are many additional windows that serve a variety of functions. This overview is simply to show the most common and most widely used windows within the Flash development environment.

The AIR/Flash CS3 Updater

Adobe has provided an updater for Flash CS3 to allow for testing and packaging of AIR projects using the Flash development environment. Thus whether you are building a complete AIR application with Flash CS3 or just building pieces that will eventually become a part of a Flex application compiled to AIR, Flash CS3 makes this a very simple process.

The extension distributed by Adobe is a simple self-installing update. Just download it from Adobe.com and follow the installer's directions.

The minimum system requirements for the Adobe AIR update for Flash CS3 are as follows.

Windows

❑   Windows XP sp2

❑   Windows Vista Home Premium, Business, Ultimate, or Enterprise (certified for 32-bit) editions

❑   Flash CS3 Professional

Macintosh

❑   Mac OS X 10.4.x (Intel or PPC)

❑   Flash CS3 Professional

Earlier versions of Flash are not supported with this update.

For more information and demonstrations on how to use the Flash CS3 AIR plug-in, please refer to Chapter 5.

Introducing Dreamweaver CS3

Dreamweaver CS3 is the latest update to the Dreamweaver product family and has many new features that are pertinent to AIR applications. The most important of these is the inclusion of the Spry framework tools. The Spry framework is an Ajax library that allows for the development of dynamic user interfaces. Spry effects add visual transitions like grow, shrink, fade, and highlight. Spry widgets are a set of tools like menus, lists, tables, and repeaters. Spry data allow for easy integration of XML data or mash-ups with RSS data. These Spry features, along with full control over layouts via CSS, make it very easy to create rich user interfaces using only HTML/JavaScript. These applications can then be easily compiled to desktop applications using the Dreamweaver AIR extension.

Since Dreamweaver is also a CS3 product, the Dreamweaver interface shares some commonality with the Flash CS3 interface that was demonstrated above in this chapter. The following are some of the more commonly used windows and components that make up the Dreamweaver development environment.

Code/Design View

Dreamweaver CS3's main workspace includes three different views of the content being developed. First, there is a *Code view*, which shows the full source code of the document being edited, with full code highlighting and code hinting for HTML and JavaScript that are used in AIR applications as well as many other languages. There is also a *Design view*, which shows a preview of what the code will look like and also allows for WYSIWYG ("what you see is what you get") editing. The Design view also uses the Properties view for easy editing of many standard text options. Finally, there is a *Split view*, which combines both the Code view and the Design view into one workspace. In this view, the source code can be edited by altering the code or by editing the design section. Figure 4-20 shows the Split view of a sample application that is covered in the next chapter.

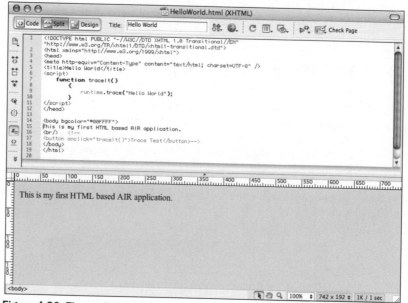

Figure 4-20: The main workspace of Dreamweaver CS3 in Split view.

The *File window* is the main interaction with files within your project. Your application files are stored in a nested folder system and displayed in a tree menu within the File window. Figure 4-21 shows the File window and the assets of a Dreamweaver site named *HelloWorld*, which will be created in the next chapter.

The *Properties window* allows for easy editing of many text properties including standard formatting of text as well as the ability to use CSS to format text and layouts. Figure 4-22 shows the Properties window.

Figure 4-21: The Dreamweaver CS3
File window.

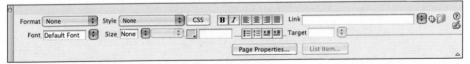

Figure 4-22: The Dreamweaver CS3 Properties window.

The main toolbar of the Dreamweaver development environment is a tabbed toolbar. It includes the *Common tab*, which is made up of objects like images, links, tables, and the like. The *Layout tab* includes traditional divs, tables, and frames but also includes the Spry menu, accordion, tabbed, and collapsible panels. The *Forms tab* includes all of the standard form objects as well as Spry form validation objects. The *Data tab* includes many tools to connect to application servers as well as tools for working with Spry data sets. The *Spry tab* includes all the previously mentioned Spry tools in a single toolbar, and finally the *Text tab* includes all the tools to alter text fonts and sizes. Figure 4-23 shows the Spry tab within the Dreamweaver main toolbar.

Figure 4-23: Dreamweaver's main toolbar showing the
Spry tools.

The AIR/Dreamweaver CS3 Extension

Adobe has provided an extension for Dreamweaver CS3 that makes it very easy to create, test, and package HTML-based AIR applications using the Dreamweaver development environment. The Dreamweaver extension is distributed as an MXP file and is easily installed using the Adobe Extension Manager.

The minimum system requirements for the Dreamweaver CS3 extension for Adobe AIR are

Windows

- ❑ Windows XP
- ❑ Windows Vista
- ❑ Dreamweaver CS3

Macintosh

- ❑ Mac OS 10.4.x (Intel or PPC)
- ❑ Dreamweaver CS3

Earlier versions of Dreamweaver are not supported with this extension.

For more information and demonstrations on how to use the Dreamweaver CS3 AIR extension, refer to Chapter 5.

Summary

This chapter offered an outline and demonstration of some of the key features and tools of Flex Builder 3, Flash CS3, and Dreamweaver CS3. Chapter 5 will demonstrate how to create projects within these development environments. It will then demonstrate how to test and package AIR applications within Flex Builder 3, Flash CS3, and Dreamweaver CS3. It will also demonstrate how to use the AIR SDK to test and package AIR applications using a console.

5

Building an Application

There are several tools and technologies for testing and creating AIR applications. Depending on which technology you're using, AIR applications can be tested or compiled using the Flex Builder 3, Flash CS3, or Dreamweaver CS3 development environments.

Flex Builder 3 is used to build Flex-based AIR applications, Flash CS3 is used to build Flash-based applications, and Dreamweaver CS3 is used to build HTML-based applications.

All the different technologies can also be tested or compiled to AIR using the free AIR SDK.

This chapter demonstrates how to test and debug AIR applications. Please refer to Chapter 6 for information on compiling AIR applications.

Create Your First AIR Flex Application

Flex-based AIR applications may consist of MXML code, ActionScript code, or both. Since Flex-based AIR applications consist of source code that can be edited with any basic text editor, Flex Builder 3 is not necessary to write the application code. Although you may write the source code with an editor as simple as Notepad or TextEdit, you will still need a compiler to test the application. Flex Builder 3 makes testing very easy. The following examples demonstrate how to test AIR applications using Flex Builder and the AIR SDK.

Testing with Flex Builder

Open Flex Builder and create a new AIR project called *HelloWorld*. Please review Chapter 3 for information on creating AIR projects within Flex Builder. Once you have created this project, you should see a navigator window that resembles Figure 5-1.

**Figure 5-1: The HelloWorld
AIR project in Flex Builder 3.**

Update the new HelloWorld.mxml file so that the code looks like Listing 5-1.

Listing 5-1: HelloWorld.mxml sample code

```
<?xml version="1.0" encoding="utf-8"?>
<mx:WindowedApplication
        xmlns:mx="http://www.adobe.com/2006/mxml"
        layout="absolute">
        <mx:Label text="Hello World!"
                horizontalCenter="0"
                verticalCenter="0"/>
</mx:WindowedApplication>
```

To test this project with Flex Builder, you will simply need to click the green Play button in the top tool-bar. Flex Builder will launch a test version of the application, which should look like Figure 5-2.

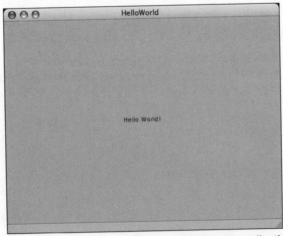

Figure 5-2: The test version of the HelloWorld application.

Debugging with Flex Builder

To test your application with the debugger, you'll first need to add some trace statements to see within the debugger. Trace statements are the easiest way to output data to the console when debugging Flex applications. A trace statement has the following signature:

```
trace('Debug Test');
```

Update the code of your HelloWorld.mxml file by adding a Button, which includes a trace statement within the Button's click handler. The mx:Button should look like this.

```
<mx:Button label="Debug Test" click="trace('Debug Test')"
       verticalCenter="28" horizontalCenter="0"/>
```

The full HelloWorld.mxml file should now contain the code shown in Listing 5-2.

Listing 5-2: The HelloWorld.mxml sample code with a trace statement

```
<?xml version="1.0" encoding="utf-8"?>
<mx:WindowedApplication
       xmlns:mx="http://www.adobe.com/2006/mxml"
       layout="absolute">
       <mx:Label text="Hello World!"
           horizontalCenter="0"
           verticalCenter="0"/>
  <mx:Button label="Debug Test" click="trace('Debug Test')"
           verticalCenter="28" horizontalCenter="0"/>
</mx:WindowedApplication>
```

To test this file in the Flex debugger, simply click on the Debugger button. The application will then open as it did before. However, when you click the Debug Test button, you will see output to the console that will look like Figure 5-3.

Figure 5-3: The debugger output in the Flex Builder 3 console view.

Testing with SDK

To run this application in the Terminal window with the AIR SDK, you will first need to create the HelloWorld-app.xml file in the same folder as the HelloWorld.html file. Here is a sample -app.xml file. For more information on the properties of this XML file, refer to Chapter 6.

Listing 5-3: HelloWorld-app.xml configuration file

```
<?xml version="1.0" encoding="UTF-8"?>
<application xmlns="http://ns.adobe.com/air/application/1.0">
    <id>com.everythingflex.beginningAIR.helloWorldFlex</id>
    <filename>HelloWorld</filename>
    <version>v1</version>
    <initialWindow>
        <content>HelloWorld.swf</content>
    </initialWindow>
    <name>HelloWorld</name>
</application>
```

Assuming that you have your Mac or Windows environment set up correctly as described in Chapter 1, open up your Terminal window, navigate to the folder containing the HelloWorld.mxml and the HelloWord-app.xml files and Mac, and run the following code:

```
adl HelloWorld-app.xml
```

This will generate a test version of the HelloWorld application, and you should see something similar to Figure 5-2.

Debugging with the SDK

When testing the application with the SDK, you will notice that the same trace statements that were appearing in the console view of Flex Builder 3 are now showing in the Terminal window as shown in Figure 5-4.

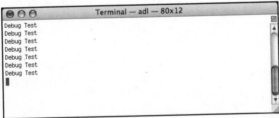

Figure 5-4: Debug information within the Terminal window.

Create Your First AIR HTML Application

So far, we have explored AIR applications that have been created using Flex with MXML and ActionScript or Flash using ActionScript with the Flash CS3 IDE. However, AIR applications can also consist of HTML or HTML with JavaScript. This application can be compiled using either the AIR SDK or the Dreamweaver CS3 AIR plug-in (at the time of this writing, the Dreamweaver CS3 AIR plug-in was in beta testing and available at http://labs.adobe.com).

Testing with Dreamweaver CS3

After installing the Dreamweaver CS3 AIR plug-in, open Dreamweaver CS3 and create a new site. Do this by clicking on the Site menu and selecting New Site, as shown in Figure 5-5, and then entering the site name, as shown in Figure 5-6.

Figure 5-5: Creating a New Site in Dreamweaver CS3.

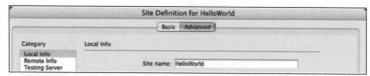

Figure 5-6: Setting the Site name in Dreamweaver CS3.

Now, create a new file by selecting File and the New from the top menu. Then with Blank Page, HTML, and <none> selected, click the Create button. A new window will open containing the new file you have created. After switching the view to Code, you should see something that looks like Figure 5-7.

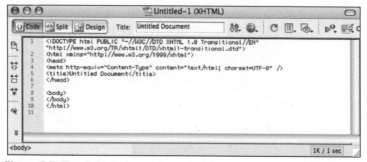

Figure 5-7: The default document created in the newly created site.

Now, update the title to be HelloWorld, and add some content within the body tag, or just copy the code from Listing 5-4.

Listing 5-4: The contents of HelloWorld.html

```
<!DOCTYPE html PUBLIC "-//W3C//DTD XHTML 1.0 Transitional//EN"
"http://www.w3.org/TR/xhtml1/DTD/xhtml1-transitional.dtd"><html
xmlns="http://www.w3.org/1999/xhtml">
<head>
<meta http-equiv="Content-Type" content="text/html; charset=UTF-8" />
<title>Hello World</title>
</head>
<body bgcolor="#0066FF">
This is my first HTML based AIR application.
</body>
</html>
```

Save the file by selecting File and then Save from the top menu. Name the file *HelloWorld.html* as shown in Figure 5-8.

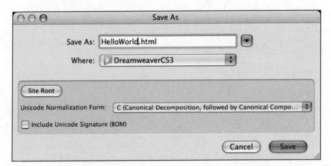

Figure 5-8: Setting the file name for the new HelloWorld.html file.

To test this new HTML page as an AIR application, you'll need to click *Ctrl (Command)+Shift+F12*. This will compile the application to a test version, and the results should be similar to what is seen in Figure 5-9.

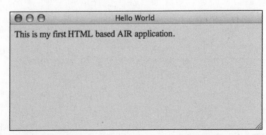

Figure 5-9: The test version of the HelloWorld application.

Testing Your Applications with the SDK

To run this application in the Terminal window with the AIR SDK, you will first need to create the HelloWorld-app.xml file in the same folder as the HelloWorld.html file. Listing 5-5 is a sample -app.xml file. For more information on the properties of this XML file, please refer to Chapter 6.

Listing 5-5: The -app.xml file for the HelloWorld.html file

```xml
<?xml version="1.0" encoding="UTF-8"?>
<application xmlns="http://ns.adobe.com/air/application/1.0">
    <id>com.everythingflex.beginningAIR.helloWorldHTML</id>
    <filename>HelloWorld</filename>
    <version>v1</version>
    <initialWindow>
        <content>HelloWorld.html</content>
    </initialWindow>
    <name>HelloWorld</name>
</application>
```

Assuming that you have your Mac or Windows environment set up correctly as described in Chapter 1, open up your Terminal window, navigate to the folder containing the HelloWorld.html file and Mac, and run the following code:

```
adl HelloWorld-app.xml
```

This will generate a test version of the HelloWorld application, and you should see something similar to Figure 5-9.

Debugging with the SDK

To see debug information within the Terminal window when testing with the SDK, you can use the `runtime.trace()` statement within a script block. Building on the previous test from Listing 5-4, add the following JavaScript block to the head of the document:

```javascript
<script>
    function traceIt() {
        runtime.trace("Hello World");
    }
</script>
```

Also add the following button to the body of the document:

```html
<button onclick="traceIt()">Trace Test</button>
```

The full contents of the HelloWorld.html document should now look like Listing 5-6.

Listing 5-6: Updated version of HelloWorld.html, including a JavaScript trace statement

```
<!DOCTYPE html PUBLIC "-//W3C//DTD XHTML 1.0 Transitional//EN"
"http://www.w3.org/TR/xhtml1/DTD/xhtml1-transitional.dtd">
<html xmlns="http://www.w3.org/1999/xhtml">
<head>
<meta http-equiv="Content-Type" content="text/html; charset=UTF-8" />
<title>Hello World</title>
<script>
    function traceIt(){
runtime.trace("Hello World");
    }
</script>
</head>
<body bgcolor="#0066FF">
This is my first HTML based AIR application.
<br/>
<button onclick="traceIt()">Trace Test</button>
</body>
</html>
```

Now, open your Terminal window and navigate to the folder containing the HelloWorld.html and HelloWorld-app.xml file. Run the following statement:

```
adl HelloWorld-app.xml
```

You should now see the application created, and it should look like Figure 5-10.

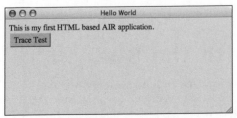

Figure 5-10: The updated HelloWorld application with the Trace Test button.

Clicking on the Trace Test button a few times will show the trace statements within the Terminal window as shown in Figure 5-11.

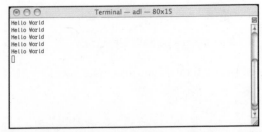

Figure 5-11: The Terminal window with the output of trace statements.

Create Your First AIR Flash Application

To create your first AIR Flash application, you must have the AIR/Flash CS3 updater installed. For more information on this, please refer to Chapter 4.

Begin by opening the Flash CS3 development environment and clicking the File menu and selecting New as shown in Figure 5-12. Next choose Flash File (ActionScript 3.0) from the new file dialog box shown in Figure 5-13, and click OK. In order to set up the AIR application settings, you will need to save this new file. Choose File ⇨ Save As, and enter **FirstFlashAIR.fla** as the file name.

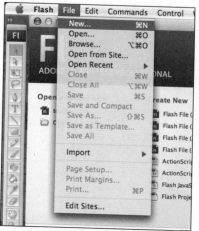

Figure 5-12: Example showing the first step in creating an AIR Flash application.

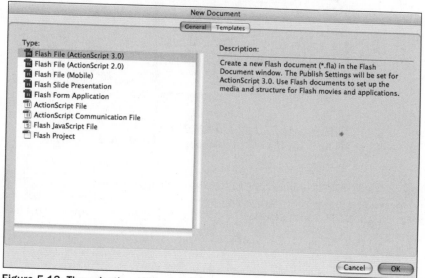

Figure 5-13: The selection of Flash File (ActionScript 3.0).

Now that you have saved the file, you can update the publish settings to include the needed settings for AIR. Choose File ➪ Publish Settings as shown in Figure 5-14 to open the Settings dialog. Select Flash from the top menu, then switch the `Version` property to Adobe AIR 1.0 as shown in Figure 5-15 and click OK.

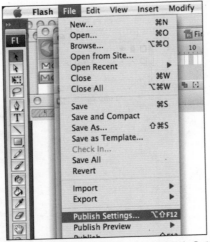

Figure 5-14: The selection of Publish Settings from the File menu.

Figure 5-15: The switch to Adobe AIR 1.0 as the Version type.

Now, when you select File ➪ Publish or *Ctrl (Command)+Enter*, you will notice that the application opens within an `adl` window as shown in Figure 5-16. Any trace statements that are included within your Flash application will show as debug info within the Flash Output window just like any other Flash application.

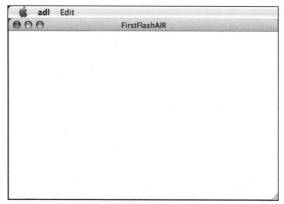

Figure 5-16: The FirstFlashAIR opening with `adl` **from Flash CS3.**

That is it — you have now successfully created an AIR application with Flash CS3. The only thing left to do is to package this new application into an AIR distribution package. This will be covered within the next chapter in the section titled "Packaging with Flash CS3."

Summary

This chapter demonstrated how to create applications within three different tools. Flex Builder 3 was used to build Flex-based AIR applications, Flash CS3 was used to build Flash-based applications, and Dreamweaver CS3 was used to build HTML-based applications.

The next chapter will demonstrate how to configure and package applications to AIR distribution files using Flex Builder, AIR SDK, Dreamweaver CS3, and Flash CS3.

Packaging the AIR

AIR applications are distributed and installed using a package achieved with the .air extension. Chapter 5 had two examples in which an AIR configuration file was used for testing out applications, using the SDK with the `adl` command. In this chapter, we'll examine further the settings of this configuration file and show ways to alter how the compiled AIR file is generated.

The AIR Configuration File

The *AIR configuration file* is an XML file that contains all the settings that determine the way an AIR application is packaged for distribution. There are many required and optional properties available in this file, and the first part of this chapter will focus on each setting and how it affects the package that is generated.

<application/>

The `<application>` tag is the root tag of the AIR configuration file. Its only property is the `xmlns` that defines the version of the AIR runtime needed to install and run the application.

```
<application xmlns="http://ns.adobe.com/air/application/1.0">
```

<id/>

The `<id>` tag is a child of the `<application>` tag. The id is a unique identifier to your application and should be specific to the application. It is recommended that an id consist of a domain namespace to ensure uniqueness. For example, the following example is an application named *ConfigureIt*, thus the id I chose to use was `com.everythingflex.beginningAIR.configureIt`.

```
<id>com.everythingflex.beginningAIR.configureIt</id>
```

The <version> tag is a child of the <application> tag. The version property alerts the AIR installer to prompt the user when the new version is different from the currently installed version. It does not know if the installed version is newer or older than the one being installed; it simply notices the difference and alerts the user. See Figures 6-1 and 6-2, which demonstrate version 1.as the installed version of our test application and the installer attempting to install two different versions.

```
<version>version 1</version>
```

Figure 6-1: Version 1 as the installed version and 2 in current installer.

Figure 6-2: Version 1 as the installed version and .9 in current installer.

The <name> tag is a child of the <application> tag. The name can be set to whatever you wish and will be shown within the installation process (Figure 6-3) as well as the application info within the Mac Finder and the program menu on Windows.

```
<name>ConfigureIt</name>
```

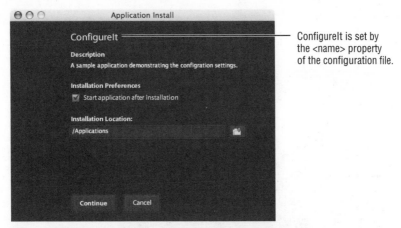

Figure 6-3: The name *ConfigureIt* during installation process.

<filename/>

The `<filename>` tag is a child of the `<application>` tag. This filename is displayed during the installation process, as shown in Figure 6-4.

```
<filename>ConfigureIt</filename>
```

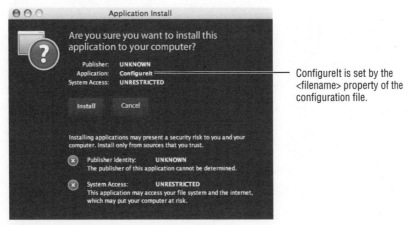

Figure 6-4: The filename during installation.

<description/>

The `<description>` tag is a child of the `<application>` tag. This description is displayed during the installation process, as shown in Figure 6-5.

```
<description> A sample application demonstrating the configuration
settings.</description>
```

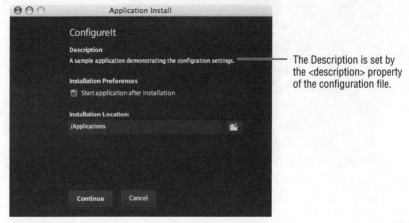

Figure 6-5: The description as shown during installation.

<copyright/>

The `<copyright>` tag is a child of the `<application>` tag. This title is displayed in the About menu on Mac OS X. This is shown in Figure 6-6.

```
<copyright>Copyright 2007 EverythingFlex.com</copyright>
```

Figure 6-6: The Mac OS X About menu displaying a custom icon, the filename, and copyright.

<icon/>

Four sizes of icons can be included in the AIR application. These are 16 × 16, 32 × 32, 48 × 48, and 128 × 128. The acceptable format for icons is PNG. In the following sample code, I have created an assets folder right under the main project folder that contains the assorted PNGs.

```
<icon>
        <image16x16>assets/e16.png</image16x16>
        <image32x32>assets/e32.png</image32x32>
        <image48x48>assets/e48.png</image48x48>
        <image128x128>assets/e128.png</image128x128>
</icon>
```

When packaging the application, be sure to include these image files, either within the wizard dialog of Flex Builder (see Figure 6-7) or the `adt` command statement with the SDK. Refer to the "Packaging with the SDK" section of this chapter for information on packaging with `adt`.

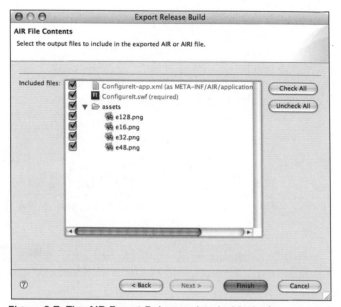

Figure 6-7: The AIR Export Release wizard with the icon assets included.

The application icons will then appear in place of the default AIR icons in many places. Figures 6-8 through 6-13 show a few examples of icon placements on Windows XP and Mac OS X.

Figure 6-8: The custom icon in the Alt–Tab interface on the Mac.

Figure 6-9: The application with two different-sized icons within the Finder on the Mac.

Figure 6-10: The application within the dock on the Mac.

Figure 6-11: The application window in the WindowsXP taskbar.

Figure 6-12: The icon within the WindowsXP application window.

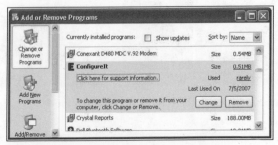

Figure 6-13: The icon within the WindowsXP Add or Remove Programs window.

There are several properties that can be set within the `<initialWindow>` tag, which is a child of the `<application>` tag. With the exception of the `<content>` tag, all these are optional settings for the compiler. This section covers these properties.

```
<initialWindow>
    <content></content>
    <title></title>
    <systmChrome></systemChrome>
    <transparent></transparent>
    <visible></visible>
    <minimizable></minimizable>
    <maximizable></maximizable>
    <resizable></resizable>
    <width></width>
    <height></height>
    <x></x>
    <y></y>
    <minSize></minSize>
    <MaxSize></maxSize>
</initialWindow>
```

The `<content>` tag is a child of the `<initialWindow>` tag, which is a child of the `<application>` tag. If you are compiling your application within the AIR SDK, you will need to set the contents of the `<content>` tag to the root content of your application. This can be an `.swf` or an `.html` file. If you are using Flex Builder, Dreamweaver CS3, or Flash CS3, this value will be set for you when you compile your application.

```
<content>ConfigureIt.swf</content>
```

<title/>

The `<title>` tag is a child of the `<initialWindow>` tag, which is a child of the `<application>` tag. The value set within this tag will be the title of the main application window.

```
<title>ConfigureIt</title>
```

<transparent/> and

Application transparency can be set within the `<transparent>` tag, which is a child of the `<initialWindow>` tag, which is a child of the `<application>` tag. The available options are True or False.

```
<transparent>true</transparent>
<systmChrome>none</systemChrome>
```

System Chrome is set within the `<systemChrome>` tag, which is a child of the `<initialWindow>` tag, which is a child of the `<application>` tag. The available options for `systemChrome` are Standard and None. When the `systemChrome` is set to Standard, the AIR application will use the operating system's native controls for the application window (close, minimize, restore). When `systemChrome` is set to None in an HTML application, there will be no controls for the application. In a Flex application, there will be an alternate set of controls that will handle close, minimize, and restore, as this is a built-in functionality of the <mx:WindowedApplication> tag. To disable these controls, you must set the showFlexChrome property of the <mx:WindowedApplication> tag to False.

Note that transparent can only be set to True if systemChrome is set to None. If transparent is set to True and systemChrome is set to Standard, there will be a compiler error, as shown in Figure 6-14.

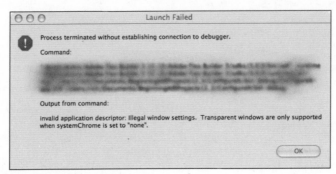

Figure 6-14: A compiler error.

The visibility of the AIR application can be set within the <visible> node of the <initialWindow> tag, which is a child of the <application> tag. The default is True; however, it can be set to False initially and then updated to True within the AIR application after it has launched.

```
<visible>false</visible>
```

, , and

The , , and tags are all children of the <initialWindow> tag, which is a child of the <application> tag. They all default to True but can be set to False to disable the functionality of how your AIR application can be sized by its user.

```
<minimizable>false</minimizable>
<maximizable>false</maximizable>
<resizable>false</resizable>
```

and

The and tags are all children of the <initialWindow> tag, which is a child of the <application> tag. These are optional, but setting them will force your application to launch at the specified height and width properties.

```
<height>600</height>
<width>800</width>
```

<x/> and <y/>

The <x/> and <y/> tags are all children of the <initialWindow> tag, which is a child of the <applica-tion> tag. These are optional, but setting them will force your application to launch at the specified x and y positions.

```
<x>100</x>
<y>200</y>
```

<minSize/> and <maxSize/>

The <maxSize/> and <minSize/> tags are all children of the <initialWindow> tag, which is a child of the <application> tag. These are optional, but setting them will limit the minimum and maximum sizes that your application can be resized to. They are entered as a paired value of width and height values:

```
<minSize>640 480</minSize>
<maxSize>800 600</maxSize>
```

<installFolder/>

The <installFolder> tag is a child of the <application> and is optional. Adding a folder path will append the added path to the default install directory. Figure 6-15 shows the default install path.

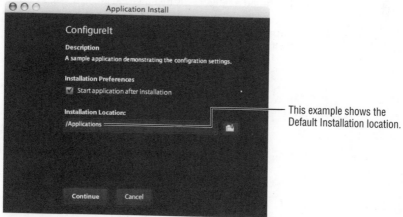

Figure 6-15: Example of a default install path.

The following example of the <installFolder> node will result in the installation location shown in Figure 6-16:

```
<installFolder>AIRApps/</installFolder>
```

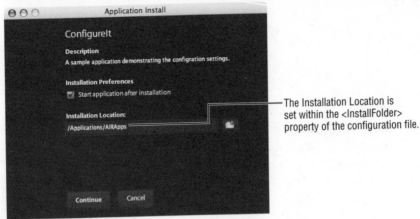

Figure 6-16: The custom install path set within the `<installFolder>` **node.**

`<customUpdateUI/>`

The `<customUpdateUI>` tag is a child of the `<application>`. Setting this value to True will alert the application that, once it is installed, it will be up to the application itself to do any further updates. This means that even if you were to download a newer AIR installer package, it will not update the installed application. When the user attempts to install, the currently installed application will open, and it will be the responsibility of the installed application to handle the update. Do not set this to True unless you have built your application to handle updates.

```
<customUpdateUI>true</customUpdateUI>
```

`<allowBrowserInvocation>`

The `<allowBrowserInvocation>` tag is a child of the `<application>`. Setting this to `True` will allow the application to be installed using the seamless badge install process from within a web browser.

```
<allowBrowserInvocation>true</allowBrowserInvocation>
```

`<programMenuFolder/>`

The `<programMenuFolder>` tag is a child of the `<application>`. Setting the contents of this tag will alert the installer of the folder to create the shortcut to within the Windows start menu.

```
<programMenuFolder>EverythingFlex</programMenuFolder/>
```

`<fileTypes/>`

The `<fileTypes>` tag is a child of the `<application>`. This node can hold one or many sets of `<fileType>` tags. Each can define a file type to be associated with the AIR application. The `<fileType>`

node holds children tags defining the name, extension, description, `contentType`, and icon that will be associated with the file type. This example associates files with the extension of .test with the AIR application and assigns the icons as well. The description and `contentType` are optional child tags and have been omitted in this example. Figure 6-17 shows a file named `myfile.test` being associated with the `ConfigureIt.app`.

```
<fileTypes>
    <fileType>
        <name>Test</name>
        <extension>test</extension>
        <icon>
            <image16x16>assets/e16.png</image16x16>
            <image32x32>assets/e32.png</image32x32>
            <image48x48>assets/e48.png</image48x48>
            <image128x128>assets/e128.png</image128x128>
        </icon>
    </fileType>
</fileTypes>
```

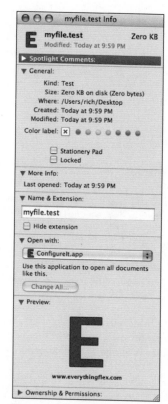

Figure 6-17: myfile.test is associated with ConfigureIt.app.

Packaging to AIR

There are many ways to package your application to an AIR package. For Flex projects, the options are Flex Builder 3 or the free SDK. For HTML projects, the options are Dreamweaver CS3 or the free SDK, and for Flash projects the options are Flash CS3 or the free SDK. The following examples demonstrate how to package to AIR using Flex Builder 3, Dreamweaver CS3, Flash CS3, and the AIR SDK.

Packaging with Flex Builder 3

To package your AIR project to an AIR package within Flex Builder 3, with the project you wish to export selected, select File ⇨ Export ⇨ Release Build (see Figure 6-18).

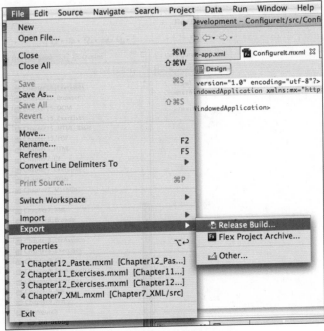

Figure 6-18: The Export AIR package button.

This will launch the Export Release Build wizard, which will guide you through the creation of the distributable AIR package. Step 1 of this process, shown in Figure 6-19, asks you to select the project and main application file that you wish to package as well as the location where the package will be created.

After completing Step 1 and clicking next, you will arrive at Step 2, shown in Figure 6-20. This is where you will define the certificate that will be used to sign your application. If you have purchased a commercial certificate or already created a self-signed certificate, you can browse to it and enter your password and move on to Step 3. If not, click the Create button, which will open the form shown in Figure 6-21. Fill in the appropriate information and click OK to save your new certificate.

Figure 6-22 shows Step 2 of the Export Release Build wizard after a certificate has been selected.

Click the next button and move on to Step 3, which is where you will select the assets you wish to compile into your application. This is shown in Figure 6-23.

Now, just click finish, and the new AIR package will be created in the location you specified. Figure 6-24 shows the AIR package being created to the default location.

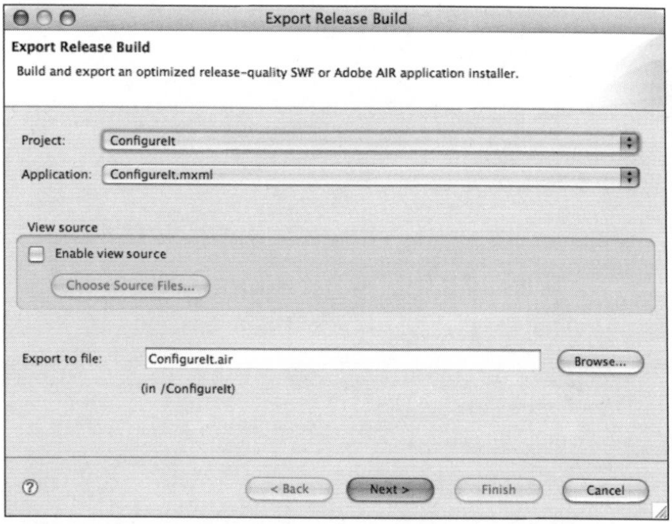

Figure 6-19: The Flex Builder 3 Export AIR Package wizard.

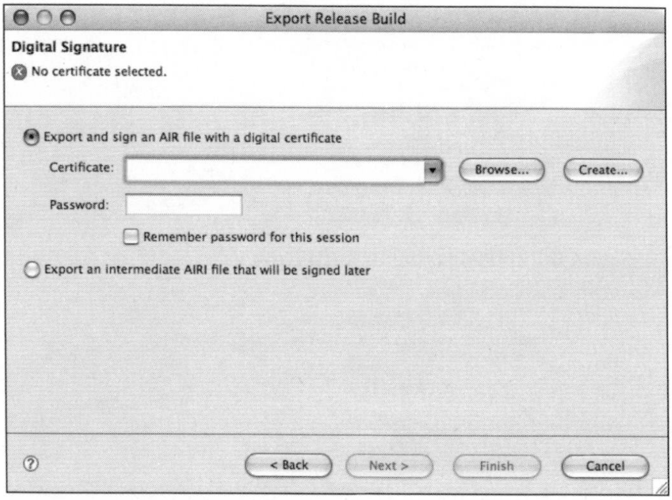

Figure 6-20: Export Release Build wizard Step 2.

Figure 6-21: Creating a self-signed certificate.

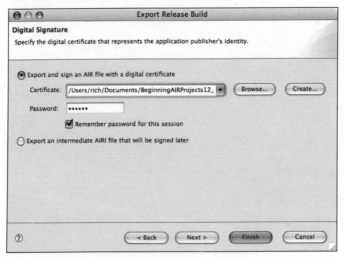

Figure 6-22: Using a digital certificate.

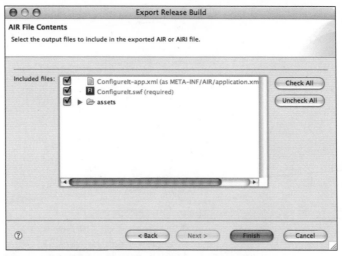

Figure 6-23: Export Release Build wizard Step 3.

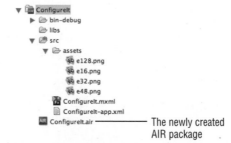

The newly created
AIR package

Figure 6-24: The newly created .air file.

Packaging with Dreamweaver CS3

To package an HTML application to AIR within Dreamweaver CS3, select "Site" and the "Create AIR File" from the top menu, as shown in Figure 6-25.

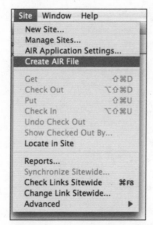

Figure 6-25: Creating an AIR File from
the Site menu in Dreamweaver CS3.

Next, fill in the form within the AIR Application and Installer Settings. The required fields are File name, ID, Initial content, and Digital signature. The optional fields are Description, Copyright, and so forth (see Figure 6-26). For definitions of all the fields on this form, refer to the beginning of this chapter.

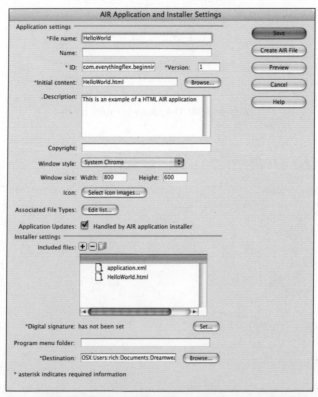

Figure 6-26: The Dreamweaver AIR Application and Installer Settings.

Clicking the Select icon images button will launch an Application Icon wizard as pictured in Figure 6-27. This is an optional step. If you do not provide custom icons, the default AIR icons will be used.

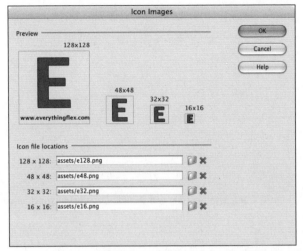

Figure 6-27: The Dreamweaver CS3 AIR icon-selection tool.

Next, you will need to define a "Digital signature" file. As with Flex Builder, you can create a self-signed security certificate from Dreamweaver CS3. Click the Set button to launch the Digital Signature window shown in Figure 6-28. Either browse to an existing certificate or click the Create button to create a new certificate. The Create button will launch the Self-Signed Digital Certificate window, shown in Figure 6-29.

Finally, click the Create AIR File button in the AIR Application and Installer Settings window or click the Site menu and Create AIR File from the top menu to create the AIR package. The results are shown in Figure 6-30.

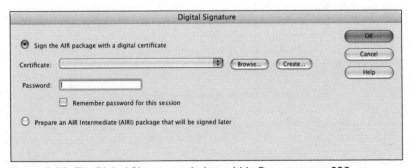

Figure 6-28: The Digital Signature window within Dreamweaver CS3.

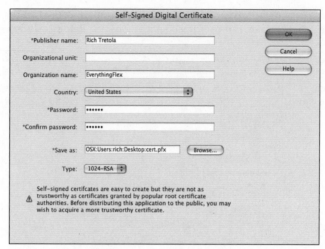

Figure 6-29: The Self-Signed Digital Certificate window within Dreamweaver CS3.

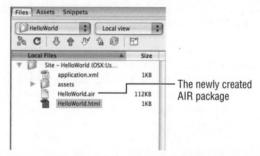

Figure 6-30: The newly created HelloWorld.air package.

Packaging with Flash CS3

To package a Flash CS3 application to an AIR file, you will need to be sure first to set the publish settings of the Flash application to Adobe AIR. If you need help with this, please refer to the section on creating your first Flash CS3 AIR application in Chapter 5.

Choose Commands ➪ "AIR - Application and Installer Settings" as shown in Figure 6-31 to open the settings dialog window. The "AIR - Application & Installer Settings" window as shown in Figure 6-32 allows you to edit the information that will be packaged into the application.xml file when the AIR file is created. This window also has an additional dialog to set the application icons. Clicking the Select Icon Images button will open the "AIR - Icon Images" window as shown in Figure 6-33. Once this window is open, you will be able to browse your local file system to select the icon images you wish to package with your AIR file.

Next, you will need to click the Set button to add a digital certificate. This will open the "Digital signature" window shown in Figure 6-34, where you can browse to a certificate file or create a new one by clicking the Create button.

Clicking the Create button within the "Digital signature" window will open the "Create Self-Signed Digital Certificate" window shown in Figure 6-35.

Now that you have completed the "AIR - Application & Installer Settings" window, you can click the "Publish AIR File" button at the bottom of the window to create the new AIR package. You can also click OK to close this window and create the new AIR package by clicking the Commands ➪ "AIR - Create AIR File" menu as shown in Figure 6-36.

Figure 6-31: Steps needed to open the settings dialog window.

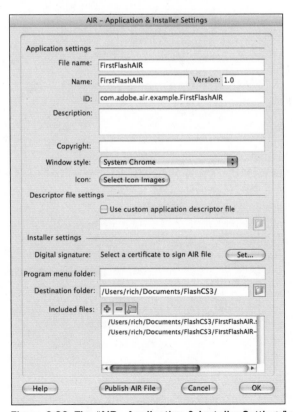

Figure 6-32: The "AIR - Application & Installer Settings" window.

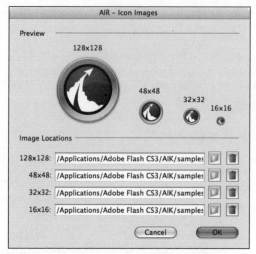

Figure 6-33: The AIR Icon Images window.

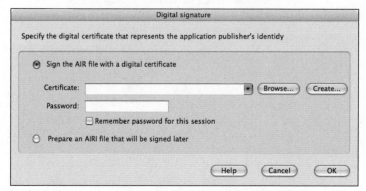

Figure 6-34: The "Digital signature" window within Flash CS3.

Figure 6-35: The Self-Signed Digital Certificate window within Flash CS3.

Figure 6-36: Shortcut to creating an
AIR package.

Packaging with the SDK

Both SWF- and HTML-based applications can be packaged to AIR using the AIR SDK. The only difference is the main file that is set within the `<content>` tag, which is a child of the `<initialWindow>` tag
of the AIR configuration file. For example, the `<content>` tag could look like this for a SWF-based
application:

```
<content>HelloWorld.swf</content>
```

or like this for an HTML-based application:

```
<content>HelloWorld.html</content>
```

Once you have all of the configuration file settings the way you want them, the next step is to open a
Terminal window and navigate to the directory containing the configuration file. The following command will create a new AIR package named *HelloWorld.air*. The signature of the `adt` command is

```
adt -package SIGNING_OPTIONS <air-file> <app-desc> FILE_ARGS
```

If you do not have a certificate, you can use `adt` to create a self-signed certificate. The signature for creating a self-signed certificate looks like this:

```
adt -certificate -cn name [-ou org_unit][-o org_name][-c country] key_type pfx_file
password
```

An actual example would be

```
adt -certificate -cn SelfSign -ou QE -o "EverythingFlex" -c US 1024-RSA mycert.pfx
3air78w
```

Once you have a certificate, you can compile your application to an AIR package.

A sample command to compile an HTML application to an AIR package would be

```
adt -package -storetype pkcs12 -keystore mycert.pfx HelloWorld.air
application.xml HelloWorld.html
```

or to compile an SWF application to an AIR package:

```
adt -package -storetype pkcs12 -keystore mycert.pfx HelloWorld.air
application.xml HelloWorld.swf
```

A sample that includes additional files (in this case the icon PNGs) in the package would look like this:

```
adt -package -storetype pkcs12 -keystore mycert.pfx HelloWorld.air
application.xml HelloWorld.swf assets/e16.png assets/e32.png assets/e48.png
assets/e128.png
```

A shortcut would just include the entire assets folder in one line like this:

```
adt -package -storetype pkcs12 -keystore mycert.pfx HelloWorld.air
application.xml HelloWorld.swf /assets
```

Summary

This chapter covered all the possible configuration settings that may be needed when packaging an AIR application and also demonstrated how to do this using different techniques including Flex Builder, Dreamweaver CS3, Flash CS3, and the AIR SDK.

The next chapter will demonstrate how to work with remote data within an AIR application. The techniques that will be covered include AMF remoting via ColdFusion, Restful data services, and web services.

Part II
Adding Data

Chapter 7: Working with Remote Data

7

Working with Remote Data

Although an AIR application is meant to run on the desktop and there are a variety of ways to store local data, there will certainly be times when it's beneficial to work with remote data sources. Whether the data are being supplied through middleware like ColdFusion, restful data services like XML or JSON, or through web services, AIR makes it easy to connect and retrieve data. This chapter will demonstrate how to work with remote data using AMF via the Flex RPC (Remote Procedure Call) services, XML and JSON via Flex HTTPServices, and SOAP via Flex WebServices.

AMF/Remoting

ActionScript Message Format (AMF) is a data format that transfers data as binary, which is smaller and faster than other data transfer formats. AMF is a proprietary format created by Macromedia and now owned by Adobe and used in many of their product lines including ColdFusion, which will be demonstrated in this chapter.

ColdFusion

Starting with version 7.02, *ColdFusion* has supported the ability of a *CFC (ColdFusion Component)* to be called directly from Flex, with data transport occurring over the very speedy AMF format. The following example demonstrates how to connect to a ColdFusion server from AIR via the `<mx:RemoteObject>` tag using *RPC (Remote Procedure Calls)*. For this example, you will need a ColdFusion server. A free developer version can be downloaded from Adobe.com.

This example includes two ColdFusion components. The first is the main access point in which AIR will communicate, and the second is a value object, which will demonstrate how server-side ColdFusion objects can be mapped to ActionScript objects. Please follow these steps to get the backend ColdFusion files created.

1. Create a new directory directly under the root of your ColdFusion 7.02 or later server, and name it *beginningAIR*. Within that folder, create a new directory named *business*. So far your directory structure should look like Figure 7-1.

Figure 7-1: The directory structure under the root of the ColdFusion server.

2.   Now create a new file within the business directory, and name it *Delegate.cfc*. Open the new file and copy in the contents of Listing 7-1. This ColdFusion component has a single method named `helloWorld()`. This method will be accessed from AIR using the `RemoteObject` class.

Listing 7-1: The Delegate.cfc ColdFusion file

```
<cfcomponent>
    <cffunction name="helloWorld" returntype="string" access="remote">
        <cfreturn "Hello From ColdFusion">
    </cffunction>
</cfcomponent>
```

3.   Create a new AIR project named *Chapter7_CF*, and name the main file *Chapter7_CF.mxml*. Copy the contents of Listing 7-2 into this file. Notice that this file is using the `<mx:RemoteObject>` tag to create a connection to the ColdFusion server. Please note that the endpoint property may be different, depending on the setup of your ColdFusion server. The file also contains an `<mx:Button>` that calls the `helloWorld()` function. This function adds an eventListener to the cfService and then calls the ColdFusion Delegate with the line that says `cfService.helloWorld()`. The result handler function named helloWorldResult launches an Alert that shows the returned data by calling `event.result.toString()`. The results of this function can be seen in Figure 7-2.

Listing 7-2: The contents of Chapter7_CF.mxml

```
<?xml version="1.0" encoding="utf-8"?>
<mx:WindowedApplication xmlns:mx="http://www.adobe.com/2006/mxml">
    <mx:Script>
      <![CDATA[
      import mx.rpc.events.ResultEvent;
      import mx.controls.Alert;

      private function helloWorld():void{
        cfService.addEventListener(ResultEvent.RESULT,helloWorldResult);
        cfService.helloWorld();
      }
      private function helloWorldResult(event:ResultEvent):void{
        Alert.show(event.result.toString(),"Result");
      }
      ]]>
    </mx:Script>

    <mx:RemoteObject
        destination="ColdFusion"
        id="cfService"
        endpoint="http://localhost:8500/flex2gateway/"
        showBusyCursor="true"
```

```
        source="beginningAIR.business.Delegate"
        concurrency="last"/>

    <mx:Button label="Hello World" click="helloWorld()"/>

</mx:WindowedApplication>
```

Figure 7-2: The data being returned from ColdFusion.

The previous example demonstrated how to return a simple string from ColdFusion to AIR. ColdFusion also has the ability to return objects that can be automatically translated to ActionScript objects. To demonstrate this, please create a new directory named *vo* within the beginningAIR directory under the ColdFusion server root. Once this directory has been created, the file structure should look like Figure 7-3.

Figure 7-3: The updated directory structure under the root of the ColdFusion server.

Within the vo directory, create a new file named *Person.cfc*, and copy in the contents of Listing 7-3. Person.cfc is a value object that has two properties, `firstName` and `lastName`. Next we must add a new function to the Delegate.cfc file to return a Person object to our application. The `getPerson()` function that is listed in Listing 7-4 creates a new Person object, sets a few properties, and returns that object. Add this function to the Delegate.cfc file below the `helloWorld()` function.

Listing 7-3: The Person.cfc ColdFusion value object

```
<cfcomponent output="false">
    <cfproperty name="firstName" type="string" />
    <cfproperty name="lastName" type="string" />
    <!--- Initialize vars --->
    <cfscript>
        variables.instance["firstName"]="";
        variables.instance["lastName"]="";
    </cfscript>

    <!--- Populate data --->
    <cffunction name="init" output="false" access="public"
```

(Continued)

91

Listing 7-3: The Person.cfc ColdFusion value object (continued)

```
            returntype="beginningAIR.vo.Person">
        <cfargument name="firstName" type="string" required="yes">
        <cfargument name="lastName" type="string" required="yes">
        <!--- Save it all --->
        <cfscript>
            setFirstName(arguments.firstName);
            setLastName(arguments.lastName);
        </cfscript>
        <cfreturn this>
    </cffunction>

    <cffunction name="getFirstName" output="false" access="public"
        returntype="string">
        <cfreturn variables.instance.firstName>
    </cffunction>
    <cffunction name="setFirstName" output="false" access="public"
        returntype="void">
        <cfargument name="val" required="true" type="string">
        <cfset variables.instance.firstName=arguments.val>
    </cffunction>

    <cffunction name="getLastName" output="false" access="public"
        returntype="string">
        <cfreturn variables.instance.lastName>
    </cffunction>
    <cffunction name="setLastName" output="false" access="public"
        returntype="void">
        <cfargument name="val" required="true" type="string">
        <cfset variables.instance.lastName=arguments.val>
    </cffunction>
</cfcomponent>
```

Listing 7-4: The `getPerson` **function that is added to the Delegate.cfc file**

```
    <cffunction name="getPerson" returntype="beginningAIR.vo.Person"
        access="remote">

        <cfscript>
        var person = createObject("component","beginningAIR.vo.Person");
            person.setFirstName("Rich");
            person.setLastName("Tretola");
        </cfscript>
        <cfreturn person/>
    </cffunction>
```

That takes care of the server side of this sample. Now we need to update the AIR application to use the getPerson() function. Add the following to the `<mx:Script>` block of Chapter7_CF.mxml:

```
private function getPerson():void{
    removeAllListeners();
```

```
        cfService.addEventListener(ResultEvent.RESULT,getPersonResult);
        cfService.getPerson();
    }
    private function getPersonResult(event:ResultEvent):void{
        var person:Person = event.result as Person;
        Alert.show(person.toString(),"Result");
    }
```

You will also need to add an import statement for the Person class. Add `import beginningAIR.vo.Person;` to the Chapter7_CF.mxml file.

Next update the `helloWorld()` function by adding a call to the new `removeAllListeners()` function, which will remove the existing listeners so that the same service may be used for both examples. The updated function should look like this:

```
    private function helloWorld():void{
        removeAllListeners();
        cfService.addEventListener(ResultEvent.RESULT,helloWorldResult);
        cfService.helloWorld();
    }
```

Now add the new `removeAllListeners()` function.

```
    private function removeAllListeners():void{
        cfService.removeEventListener(ResultEvent.RESULT,helloWorldResult);
        cfService.removeEventListener(ResultEvent.RESULT,getPersonResult);
    }
```

Finally add a new button to call the service's new function.

```
    <mx:Button label="Get Person" click="getPerson()"/>
```

If you take a look at the new `getPersonResult()` handler function, you will notice that the returned variable is being set as a Person object, which currently does not exist, nor do the directories to hold the `Person` class. This directory structure needs to match the directory structure that was previously created under the ColdFusion root. To create this new class, first create a directory within the AIR project named *beginningAIR* and then another directory named *vo* within the beginningAIR folder. Now create a new `ActionScript` class named `Person.as` within the vo directory. Paste the contents of Listing 7-5 into this new file.

Listing 7-5: The `Person.as` class

```
    package beginningAIR.vo
    {
        [RemoteClass(alias="beginningAIR.vo.Person")]
        public class Person
        {
            public var firstName:String;
            public var lastName:String;

            public function toString():String{
                return firstName + " " + lastName;
```

(Continued)

Listing 7-5: The `Person.as` **class** *(continued)*

```
            }
        }
    }
```

Notice that the `Person.as` class has the same two properties as the Person.cfc object. It also includes a `[RemoteClass]` metadata tag, which is what creates the relationship between the `ActionScript` class and ColdFusion component. The `Person.as` class also has an additional method named `toString()`, which is what is used to Alert the data in the example application. When you now run this application, you should see what is shown in Figure 7-4.

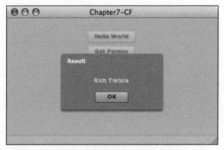

Figure 7-4: The results of the
`cfService.getPerson()` **method.**

In addition to returning objects, ColdFusion can also return arrays of data to AIR. To demonstrate this, add the following function to the Delegate.cfc file. This new function creates an array of two person objects and returns the array.

```
<cffunction name="getPeople" returntype="array">
    <cfscript>
    var people = ArrayNew(1);
    var person1 = createObject("component","beginningAIR.vo.Person");
    var person2 = createObject("component","beginningAIR.vo.Person");
        person1.setFirstName("Rich");
        person1.setLastName("Tretola");
        person2.setFirstName("Coral");
        person2.setLastName("Skye");
        arrayAppend(people,person1);
        arrayAppend(people,person2);
    </cfscript>
    <cfreturn people/>
</cffunction>
```

To use this new ColdFusion function, we will again need to update the Chapter7_CF.mxml file. Please follow these steps:

1. Add two new functions to get data from ColdFusion and handle the data when it is received. The functions below will first remove all active event listeners and then create a new listener to handle the results of the `getPeople()` function. This listener receives the data and sets it to the dataProvider of a DataGrid.

```
private function getPeople():void{
    removeAllListeners();
    cfService.addEventListener(ResultEvent.RESULT,getPeopleResult);
    cfService.getPeople();
}
private function getPeopleResult(event:ResultEvent):void{
    dataGrid.dataProvider = event.result;
}
```

2. Next, update the `removeAllListeners()` function by adding another line to remove the new listener. The function should now look like this:

```
private function removeAllListeners():void{
    cfService.removeEventListener(ResultEvent.RESULT,helloWorldResult);
    cfService.removeEventListener(ResultEvent.RESULT,getPersonResult);
    cfService.removeEventListener(ResultEvent.RESULT,getPeopleResult);
}
```

Now, add a data grid to show the results of the `getPeople()` function and a button to call this new function.

```
<mx:Button label="Get People" click="getPeople()"/>
<mx:DataGrid id="dataGrid">
    <mx:columns>
        <mx:DataGridColumn headerText="First Name"
            dataField="firstName"/>
        <mx:DataGridColumn headerText="Last Name"
            dataField="lastName"/>
    </mx:columns>
</mx:DataGrid>
```

If you have done everything correctly, your results should look like Figure 7-5.

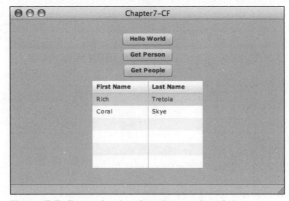

Figure 7-5: Example showing the results of the `cfService.getPeople()` **method.**

REST

REST stands for *Representational State Transfer* and is defined as a very simple interface for exchanging data over HTTP without the complexities of web services. SOAP.REST is accessed using either an HTTP get or post, depending on whether you wish to read or write data. Systems that are using REST are often referred to as RESTFul or as a RESTFul data service. The next two examples, using JSON and XML with the Flex `<mx:HTTPService>` component, illustrate use of a RESTFul data service.

JSON

JSON, which stands for *JavaScript Object Notation*, is a lightweight data format that is in plaintext and human readable (as opposed to a binary format like AMF). Being lightweight, it is a faster data transport than XML but not as fast as a binary format. JSON is based on a subset of the JavaScript Programming Language, Standard ECMA-262, 3rd edition. JSON can be used for data storage both local to the AIR application or on a remote server. This chapter will focus on reading JSON data from a remote server by using the `<mx:HTTPSevice>` tag. To work with local data in JSON format, please refer to the file reading and writing examples in Chapter 8. If you read the file in via `FileStream`, you can run the same parsing function to extract data into an ActionScript array. To save the data back to the file system, you would simply use the `encode()` static method of the `JSON` class.

Listing 7-6 is an example of a JSON file.

Listing 7-6: Example showing people.json

```
[{"lastName":"Tretola","firstName":"Rich"},{"lastName":"Tretola","firstName":"Kim"}
,{"lastName":"Tretola","firstName":"Skye"},{"lastName":"Tretola","firstName":"Coral
"}]
```

To demonstrate how to use JSON as a data source, create a new AIR project named *Chapter7_JSON*. To parse the JSON files, you will need the help of some third-party classes. These classes are part of the as3corelib project hosted on Google code at `http://code.google.com/p/as3corelib/`. Download this library and add the SWC to your new project. Now copy the contents of Listing 7-7 into Chapter7_JSON.mxml. You will also need to create the people.json file shown in Listing 7-6 and place it in the root of your package. Your file structure should now look like Figure 7-6.

Listing 7-7: Contents of the complete Chapter7_JSON.mxml file

```
<?xml version="1.0" encoding="utf-8"?>
<mx:WindowedApplication xmlns:mx="http://www.adobe.com/2006/mxml">

    <mx:Script>
      <![CDATA[
      import mx.rpc.events.ResultEvent;
      import com.adobe.serialization.json.JSON;

      private function onLoad(event:ResultEvent):void{
        var rawData:String = String(event.result);
        dataGrid.dataProvider = (JSON.decode(rawData) as Array);
      }
      ]]>
```

```
        </mx:Script>

        <mx:HTTPService
            id="httpService"
            resultFormat="text"
            url="people.json"
            result="onLoad(event);" />

        <mx:DataGrid id="dataGrid">
          <mx:columns>
            <mx:DataGridColumn headerText="First Name"
              dataField="firstName"/>
            <mx:DataGridColumn headerText="Last Name"
              dataField="lastName"/>
          </mx:columns>
        </mx:DataGrid>
        <mx:Button label="Load JSON Data"  click="httpService.send()"/>
      </mx:WindowedApplication>
```

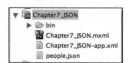

Figure 7-6: The file
structure of the
Chapter7_JSON project.

While examining the contents of Listing 7-7, you will notice that there is not much to it. It starts by importing a few classes, the ResultEvent class, which is needed for the signature of the onLoad() function, and the JSON class, which is part of the coreLib and needed to parse the JSON file into an array. Although in this sample, the <mx:HTTPService> is pointing to a local URL (people.json), this file could be located at any HTTP address. Once the file is loaded and the result event is fired, the event-result data are cast as a string named *rawData* and then converted to an array using the static JSON.decode method. The results can be seen in Figure 7-7.

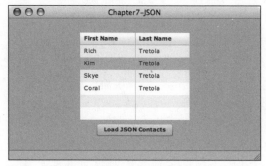

Figure 7-7: The results of the HTTPService call to
the people.json data file.

XML

XML, which stands for *Extensible Markup Language*, is a tag-based language that is an industry standard for data exchange. *RSS (Really Simple Syndication)* and *ATOM (Atom Syndication Format)* are popular examples of XML, being used for data transport of syndication feeds for all types of data, including news, entertainment, and blog posts. XML can also be used for data storage both local to the AIR application or on a remote server. This chapter will focus on reading XML data from a remote server by using the `<mx:HTTPSevice>` tag. To work with local data in XML format, please refer to the file reading and writing examples in Chapter 8. If you read the file via `FileStream`, you can run the same parsing function to extract data into an XML object. To save the data back to the file system, you would simply create the XML string using the built-in XML classes.

Listing 7-8 is an example of an XML file. Listing 7-9 shows the contents of Chapter7_XML.mxml.

Listing 7-8: Example showing `people.xml`

```
<?xml version="1.0" encoding="utf-8"?>
<people>
    <person firstName="Rich" lastName="Tretola"/>
    <person firstName="Kim" lastName="Tretola"/>
    <person firstName="Skye" lastName="Tretola"/>
    <person firstName="Coral" lastName="Tretola"/>
</people>
```

Listing 7-9: Contents of Chapter7_XML.mxml

```
<?xml version="1.0" encoding="utf-8"?>
<mx:WindowedApplication xmlns:mx="http://www.adobe.com/2006/mxml">

    <mx:Script>
      <![CDATA[
        import mx.rpc.events.ResultEvent;

        private function onLoad(event:ResultEvent):void{
          var xml:XML = event.result as XML;
          dataGrid.dataProvider = xml.person;
        }

      ]]>
    </mx:Script>

    <mx:HTTPService
      id="httpService"
      url="people.xml"
      resultFormat="e4x"
      result="onLoad(event)"/>

    <mx:DataGrid id="dataGrid" width="100%">
      <mx:columns>
        <mx:DataGridColumn headerText="First Name"
          dataField="@firstName"/>
```

```
            <mx:DataGridColumn headerText="Last Name"
              dataField="@lastName"/>
          </mx:columns>
        </mx:DataGrid>
        <mx:Button label="Load XML" click="httpService.send()"/>
</mx:WindowedApplication>
```

To demonstrate how to use XML as a data source, create a new AIR project named *Chapter7_XML*. Now copy the contents of Listing 7-9 into Chapter7_XML.mxml. You will also need to create the people.xml file shown in Listing 7-8 and place it in the root of your package. Your file structure should now look like Figure 7-8.

Figure 7-8: The file structure of the Chapter7_XML project.

While examining the contents of Listing 7-9, we can see that it starts by importing only one class, the ResultEvent class, which is needed for the signature of the onLoad() function. Although in this sample, the <mx:HTTPService> is pointing to a local URL (people.xml), this file could be located at any HTTP address. Once the file is loaded and the result event is fired, the event-result data are cast as an XML object named *xml* and then set as the dataProvider of the DataGrid. The dataProvider is pointed directly to the <person> node, and the DataGrid looks at the firstName and lastName attributes using the @ symbol within the dataField property of the DataGrid column definitions. The results can be seen in Figure 7-9.

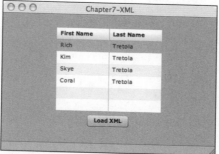

Figure 7-9: The results of the HTTPService call to the people.xml data file.

Web Services

A web service is a way of exchanging data between servers with a request and response metaphor. Flex and AIR make invoking web services very easy by managing all of the SOAP packet generation. For a definition of a SOAP packet, please see below. Calling a web service is done by using the <mx:WebService> tag. As previously stated, this tag will handle the creation and parsing of the SOAP packets that are sent and received from the remote server. The example in this section uses a free web service from webservicesx.net.

SOAP

SOAP stands for *Simple Object Access Protocol* and is a protocol for data exchange in XML format. When data are sent to the remote server invoking a web service, they're sent as a SOAP packet. The results returned from the server are also in a SOAP packet. Here is an example of the SOAP packets that will be used in the example later in this section. Listing 7-10 is an example of a SOAP request, and Listing 7-11 is an example of a SOAP response.

Listing 7-10: Example of a SOAP request

```
POST /stockquote.asmx HTTP/1.1
Host: www.webservicex.net
Content-Type: text/xml; charset=utf-8
Content-Length: length
SOAPAction: "http://www.webserviceX.NET/GetQuote"

<?xml version="1.0" encoding="utf-8"?>
<soap:Envelope xmlns:xsi="http://www.w3.org/2001/XMLSchema-instance"
xmlns:xsd="http://www.w3.org/2001/XMLSchema"
xmlns:soap="http://schemas.xmlsoap.org/soap/envelope/">
  <soap:Body>
    <GetQuote xmlns="http://www.webserviceX.NET/">
      <symbol>string</symbol>
    </GetQuote>
  </soap:Body>
</soap:Envelope>
```

Listing 7-11: Example of a SOAP response

```
HTTP/1.1 200 OK
Content-Type: text/xml; charset=utf-8
Content-Length: length

<?xml version="1.0" encoding="utf-8"?>
<soap:Envelope xmlns:xsi="http://www.w3.org/2001/XMLSchema-instance"
xmlns:xsd="http://www.w3.org/2001/XMLSchema"
 xmlns:soap="http://schemas.xmlsoap.org/soap/envelope/">
  <soap:Body>
    <GetQuoteResponse xmlns="http://www.webserviceX.NET/">
      <GetQuoteResult>string</GetQuoteResult>
    </GetQuoteResponse>
  </soap:Body>
</soap:Envelope>
```

WSDL

WSDL stands for *Web Services Description Language* and is an XML format file, which describes a set of network services. Fortunately, many tools, including Flex Builder 3, use the WSDL file for introspection, which interprets the WSDL file. The last section of this chapter demonstrates how the new Flex Builder 3 Import Web Service wizard works for doing introspection on a web service. Listing 7-12 shows an example of a WSDL file that will be used to supply data to an application later in this section.

Listing 7-12 is an example of the WSDL file that will be used in the example later in this section.

Listing 7-12: WSDL file from `www.webservicex.net/stockquote.asmx?wsdl`

```xml
<?xml version="1.0" encoding="utf-8"?>
<wsdl:definitions xmlns:http="http://schemas.xmlsoap.org/wsdl/http/"
    xmlns:soap="http://schemas.xmlsoap.org/wsdl/soap/"
    xmlns:s="http://www.w3.org/2001/XMLSchema"
    xmlns:soapenc="http://schemas.xmlsoap.org/soap/encoding/"
    xmlns:tns="http://www.webserviceX.NET/"
    xmlns:tm="http://microsoft.com/wsdl/mime/textMatching/"
    xmlns:mime="http://schemas.xmlsoap.org/wsdl/mime/"
    targetNamespace="http://www.webserviceX.NET/"
    xmlns:wsdl="http://schemas.xmlsoap.org/wsdl/">
  <wsdl:types>
    <s:schema elementFormDefault="qualified"
targetNamespace="http://www.webserviceX.NET/">
      <s:element name="GetQuote">
        <s:complexType>
          <s:sequence>
            <s:element minOccurs="0" maxOccurs="1" name="symbol" type="s:string" />
          </s:sequence>
        </s:complexType>

      </s:element>
      <s:element name="GetQuoteResponse">
        <s:complexType>
          <s:sequence>
            <s:element minOccurs="0" maxOccurs="1" name="GetQuoteResult"
type="s:string" />
          </s:sequence>
        </s:complexType>
      </s:element>
      <s:element name="string" nillable="true" type="s:string" />

    </s:schema>
  </wsdl:types>
  <wsdl:message name="GetQuoteSoapIn">
    <wsdl:part name="parameters" element="tns:GetQuote" />
  </wsdl:message>
  <wsdl:message name="GetQuoteSoapOut">
    <wsdl:part name="parameters" element="tns:GetQuoteResponse" />
  </wsdl:message>
  <wsdl:message name="GetQuoteHttpGetIn">

    <wsdl:part name="symbol" type="s:string" />
  </wsdl:message>
  <wsdl:message name="GetQuoteHttpGetOut">
    <wsdl:part name="Body" element="tns:string" />
  </wsdl:message>
  <wsdl:message name="GetQuoteHttpPostIn">
    <wsdl:part name="symbol" type="s:string" />
  </wsdl:message>
  <wsdl:message name="GetQuoteHttpPostOut">
```

(Continued)

```
      <wsdl:part name="Body" element="tns:string" />
  </wsdl:message>
  <wsdl:portType name="StockQuoteSoap">
    <wsdl:operation name="GetQuote">
      <documentation xmlns="http://schemas.xmlsoap.org/wsdl/">Get Stock quote for a
company Symbol</documentation>
      <wsdl:input message="tns:GetQuoteSoapIn" />
      <wsdl:output message="tns:GetQuoteSoapOut" />
    </wsdl:operation>

  </wsdl:portType>
  <wsdl:portType name="StockQuoteHttpGet">
    <wsdl:operation name="GetQuote">
      <documentation xmlns="http://schemas.xmlsoap.org/wsdl/">Get Stock quote for a
company Symbol</documentation>
      <wsdl:input message="tns:GetQuoteHttpGetIn" />
      <wsdl:output message="tns:GetQuoteHttpGetOut" />
    </wsdl:operation>
  </wsdl:portType>

  <wsdl:portType name="StockQuoteHttpPost">
    <wsdl:operation name="GetQuote">
      <documentation xmlns="http://schemas.xmlsoap.org/wsdl/">Get Stock quote for a
company Symbol</documentation>
      <wsdl:input message="tns:GetQuoteHttpPostIn" />
      <wsdl:output message="tns:GetQuoteHttpPostOut" />
    </wsdl:operation>
  </wsdl:portType>
  <wsdl:binding name="StockQuoteSoap" type="tns:StockQuoteSoap">

    <soap:binding transport="http://schemas.xmlsoap.org/soap/http" style="document" />
    <wsdl:operation name="GetQuote">
      <soap:operation soapAction="http://www.webserviceX.NET/GetQuote"
style="document" />
      <wsdl:input>
        <soap:body use="literal" />
      </wsdl:input>
      <wsdl:output>
        <soap:body use="literal" />
      </wsdl:output>

    </wsdl:operation>
  </wsdl:binding>
  <wsdl:binding name="StockQuoteHttpGet" type="tns:StockQuoteHttpGet">
    <http:binding verb="GET" />
    <wsdl:operation name="GetQuote">
      <http:operation location="/GetQuote" />
      <wsdl:input>
        <http:urlEncoded />
      </wsdl:input>

      <wsdl:output>
```

```
        <mime:mimeXml part="Body" />
      </wsdl:output>
    </wsdl:operation>
  </wsdl:binding>
  <wsdl:binding name="StockQuoteHttpPost" type="tns:StockQuoteHttpPost">
    <http:binding verb="POST" />
    <wsdl:operation name="GetQuote">
      <http:operation location="/GetQuote" />

      <wsdl:input>
        <mime:content type="application/x-www-form-urlencoded" />
      </wsdl:input>
      <wsdl:output>
        <mime:mimeXml part="Body" />
      </wsdl:output>
    </wsdl:operation>
  </wsdl:binding>
  <wsdl:service name="StockQuote">

    <wsdl:port name="StockQuoteSoap" binding="tns:StockQuoteSoap">
      <soap:address location="http://www.webservicex.net/stockquote.asmx" />
    </wsdl:port>
    <wsdl:port name="StockQuoteHttpGet" binding="tns:StockQuoteHttpGet">
      <http:address location="http://www.webservicex.net/stockquote.asmx" />
    </wsdl:port>
    <wsdl:port name="StockQuoteHttpPost" binding="tns:StockQuoteHttpPost">
      <http:address location="http://www.webservicex.net/stockquote.asmx" />
    </wsdl:port>

  </wsdl:service>
</wsdl:definitions>
```

Now that you know the parts of the web service, it's time to demonstrate how easy it is to use a web service from AIR. As stated above, you don't need to create the SOAP packet to send to the remote server, and you don't need to parse the SOAP packet that is returned, since the `<mx:WebService>` class will do this for you. Let's start by creating a new AIR project named *Chapter7_WebService* and copy the contents of Listing 7-13 into the new Chapter7_WebService.mxml file.

Listing 7-13: The contents of Chapter7_WebService.mxml

```
<?xml version="1.0" encoding="utf-8"?>
<mx:WindowedApplication xmlns:mx="http://www.adobe.com/2006/mxml">

  <mx:Script>
    <![CDATA[
    import mx.controls.Alert;
    import mx.rpc.events.ResultEvent;

    private function onLoad(event:ResultEvent):void{
      Alert.show(event.result.toString(),"WebService Results");
    }
```

(Continued)

Listing 7-13: The contents of Chapter7_WebService.mxml *(continued)*

```
    ]]>
  </mx:Script>

  <mx:WebService id="webService"
      wsdl="http://www.webservicex.net/stockquote.asmx?wsdl"
      result="onLoad(event);" />
  <mx:TextInput id="symbol" text="adbe"/>
  <mx:Button label="Call WebService"
      click="webService.GetQuote(symbol.text)"/>
</mx:WindowedApplication>
```

If we examine the code in Listing 7-13, we can see that there isn't really much involved in interacting with a remote server by invoking a web service. The `<mx:WebService>` tag has a few properties defined. First, it is given an `id`, next it is assigned a `wsdl`, and finally it is told what to do with the result. Please note that a best practice would also be to assign a function to the `fault` property for handling errors that may occur when the web service is invoked. The `onLoad()` function accepts the `ResultEvent` and, in this case, simply shows an Alert with the response. A real-world example would parse the resulting XML string to gain access to the data. To see an example of these data being parsed, please see the MashUp example at the end of this chapter. Finally, there is a button to invoke the web service by passing in a single argument from the `<mx:TextInput>` component. So when the button is clicked, it calls the `webService.GetQuote()` method, passing in the value of `symbol.text` from the `<mx:TextInput>` component. The results can be seen in Figure 7-10.

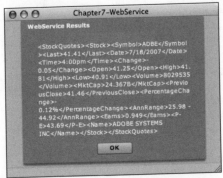

Figure 7-10: The results of the web service call.

MashUps

A *MashUp* is defined as an application that utilizes data from more than one source and combines them into a single user experience. The following example will utilize two data services to supply different types of data about the same stock symbol. First, it will use the same web service as was used in Listing 7-13 to get pricing information on the stock symbol. And then it will also use a RESTful service to get news information from Yahoo about the stock symbol.

The components being used are `<mx:WebService>` to connect to the stock data service and `<mx:HTTPService>` to connect to the Yahoo news service.

To create this MashUp application, start by creating a new AIR application named *Chapter7_MashUp*. Copy the code from Listing 7-14 into the Chapter7_MashUp.mxml file. A further step using an item renderer is shown in Listing 7-15.

Listing 7-14: The complete code for Chapter7_MashUp.mxml

```
<?xml version="1.0" encoding="utf-8"?>
<mx:WindowedApplication xmlns:mx="http://www.adobe.com/2006/mxml"
    layout="absolute"
    width="500" height="500">

    <mx:Script>
        <![CDATA[
            import mx.rpc.events.ResultEvent;
            import mx.controls.Alert;
            [Bindable]
            private var stockInfo:XML;

            private function getStockData():void{
                stockInfo = null;
                news.dataProvider = null;
                webService.GetQuote(symbol.text);
                httpService.send();
            }

            private function webServiceOnLoad(event:ResultEvent):void{
                stockInfo = new XML(event.result);
            }
            private function httpServiceOnLoad(event:ResultEvent):void{
                news.dataProvider = event.result.rss.channel.item;
            }
        ]]>
    </mx:Script>
    <mx:WebService
        id="webService"
        wsdl="http://www.webservicex.net/stockquote.asmx?wsdl"
        result="webServiceOnLoad(event)"
        fault="Alert.show(event.fault.toString(),'GetQuote Error')"/>

    <mx:HTTPService
        id="httpService"
        url="http://finance.yahoo.com/rss/headline?s={symbol.text}"
        result="httpServiceOnLoad(event)"
        fault="Alert.show(event.fault.toString(),'Yahoo Error')"/>

    <mx:Label x="134.5" y="12" text="Symbol" fontWeight="bold"/>
    <mx:TextInput id="symbol" text="adbe" x="193.5"
        y="10" width="50" enter="getStockData()"/>
    <mx:Button label="Get Stock Data"
```

(Continued)

Listing 7-14: The complete code for Chapter7_MashUp.mxml *(continued)*

```
              click="getStockData()"
              x="251.5" y="10"/>

     <mx:Label x="24" y="44" text="Company Name:"
         fontWeight="bold"/>
     <mx:Label x="130" y="44"
         text="{stockInfo.Stock.Name} "
         width="343"/>

     <mx:Label x="24" y="70" text="Quote" fontWeight="bold"/>
     <mx:Label x="67.5" y="70"
         text="{stockInfo.Stock.Last}  {stockInfo.Stock.Change}"
         width="164.5"/>
     <mx:Label x="240" y="70"
         text="{stockInfo.Stock.Date} {stockInfo.Stock.Time}"/>

     <mx:List id="news" width="450" rowHeight="160"
         itemRenderer="NewsRenderer"  x="24" y="96" height="368"/>
</mx:WindowedApplication>
```

Listing 7-15: The NewsRenderer.mxml item renderer used within the `<mx:List>`

```
<?xml version="1.0" encoding="utf-8"?>
<mx:VBox xmlns:mx="http://www.adobe.com/2006/mxml" height="154">
    <mx:Script>
        <![CDATA[
            private function goToFullStory():void{
                var u:URLRequest = new URLRequest(data.link);
                navigateToURL(u,"_blank");
            }
        ]]>
    </mx:Script>
    <mx:DateFormatter id="dateFormat"/>
    <mx:Label text="{data.title}" width="400" fontWeight="bold"/>
    <mx:Label text="{dateFormat.format(data.pubDate)}"/>
    <mx:TextArea text="{data.description}"
        borderStyle="none" editable="false"
        backgroundAlpha="0" width="400" height="75"/>
    <mx:LinkButton label="Read More" click="goToFullStory()"
        rollOverColor="#FFFFFF"/>
</mx:VBox>
```

Let's examine the code in Listing 7-14. As mentioned above, there are two different services involved. First, there is the call to the `GetQuote()` function of the `www.webservicex.net/stockquote.asmx?wsdl` web service, followed by a call to `http://finance.yahoo.com/rss/headline?s={symbol.text}`, where the stock symbol is being bound from the `<mx:TextInput>` with the id symbol's text value via an HTTPService. The results of the web service are parsed by the `webServiceOnLoad()` function into the separate Flex display components to show company name, quote value, increase/decrease, and quote data/time. The results of the HTTPService are parsed by the `httpServiceOnLoad()` function and displayed within an `<mx:List>` component using an item renderer named *NewsRenderer.mxml* that can be seen in Listing 7-15. This renderer displays the article name, date, small description, and link to the full story.

This application, which doesn't contain a very large amount of code, demonstrates how easy it is to build a data-rich application using multiple sources of data. The results of this application can be seen in Figure 7-11.

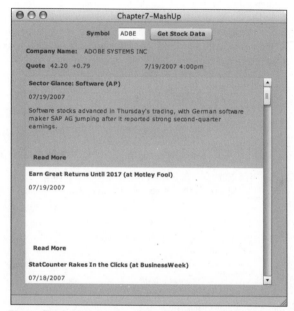

Figure 7-11: The results of the Chapter7_MashUp application.

Import Web Service (WSDL)

Flex Builder 3 has a built-in introspection wizard that reads the remote WSDL file and automatically creates the client-side code needed to invoke the web service. This wizard creates ActionScript classes that will return typed objects that can be easily used within your application. If you are using Flex Builder 3, the WSDL Introspection wizard will certainly make it easier to use web services within your application. To demonstrate how to use the wizard, create a new AIR project named *Chapter7_Introspection*.

1. To launch the wizard, select the Data menu and choose Import Web Service (WSDL) to launch the WSDL Introspection wizard (see Figure 7-12).

2. Next, select a source folder, which will be the location where the new ActionScript classes will be generated, and click the Next button (see Figure 7-13).

This sample will use the same stock quote web service that was previously used.

3. Enter `www.webservicex.net/stockquote.asmx?wsdl` for the WSDL URI in the next step, which is shown in Figure 7-14.

4. Click Next and you may see an error that says SOAP 1.1 is the only supported protocol. To remedy this, select StockQuoteSOAP from the Port dropdown menu. This is shown in Figure 7-15.

5. Now click the Finish button, and the ActionScript classes will be generated.

Figure 7-16 shows the generated classes. To use this service, you now can simply create a new StockQuote object and call methods as you would any other object. The newly created classes will handle the call out to the remote service. The exercise at the end of this chapter will ask you to use the classes we just generated to retrieve stock quote information.

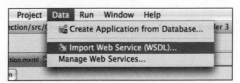

Figure 7-12: Select Import Web Service to launch the Introspection wizard.

Figure 7-13: Select a source folder for the class generation.

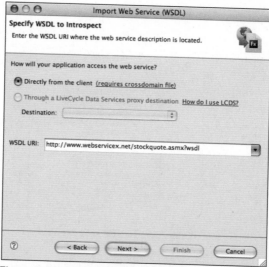

Figure 7-14: Enter the WSDL address.

Figure 7-15: Select a valid SOAP 1.1 service.

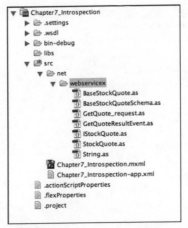

Figure 7-16: The classes created by the WSDL Import wizard.

Summary

This chapter demonstrated many ways to consume data from remote data sources. It showed connections to remote confusion servers using RPC (Remote Procedure Calls), RESTFul data like XML and JSON using HTTPServices, and traditional WSDLs via the invocation of web services. Finally, it demonstrated how to combine multiple services in a MashUp.

The next chapter will explore the Windowing API included in AIR. We will demonstrate how to create desktop windows with different options enabled or disabled including transparency.

Exercise

Use the project created in the Import Web Service section of this chapter to duplicate the functionality that was demonstrated in Listing 7-13 and Figure 7-10. Instead of calling the WSDL directly as demonstrated in Listing 7-13, use the ActionScript classes created by the WSDL Import wizard.

Part III
AIR APIs

Accessing the File System

This chapter will cover an AIR application's file system access. The features covered include creating directories, moving directories, copying directories, deleting a directory, listing directory contents, creating files, writing and updating file contents, moving files, copying files, deleting files, and temporary files and directories.

File System Security

AIR applications enjoy all the privileges of traditional desktop applications, which means that you must work with extreme caution when accessing the local file system. There are no restrictions built in to prevent an AIR application from moving or deleting a resource on the file system. This type of access is a privilege but can also be a double-edged sword, since giving control to an application to have full file system access can be useful but also dangerous.

Working with the File System

AIR has made it easy to work with the local file system of the client machine. Once an application is installed and has the required permissions, then creating, updating, moving, and deleting files or directories is done through an API. This is an important fact since, because the commands are issued through an API, the AIR runtime ensures that the file system change requests will work on whatever operating system/version the application is installed on.

Directories

The following examples demonstrate how to use the File API to make changes to the file system. These examples use the `flash.filesystem.File` class for interactions with the file system. The next group of samples will work with the same project and build on it with each new piece of functionality. To get started, create a new AIR project and name it *Chapter8_Dir*. You should now have an empty file named `Chapter8_Dir.mxml` that looks like Listing 8-1. Please note that the completed source code for `Chapter8_Dir.mxml` is available in Listing 8-3.

Listing 8-1: Empty `Chapter8_Dir.mxml` **file used for the next set of examples**

```
<?xml version="1.0" encoding="utf-8"?>
<mx:WindowedApplication xmlns:mx="http://www.adobe.com/2006/mxml"
    layout="absolute">

</mx:WindowedApplication>
```

Creating a Directory

The first set of functionality that we will explore will be the creation of a new directory. To create a new directory, you must first add an `<mx:Script>` block to the `Chapter8_Dir.mxml`. Next add an import statement and import the `flash.filesystem.File` class. Now, add a new function named `createDirectory()` that returns void and declares a var named `newDirectory` of type File and set it equal to `File.desktopDirectory.resolvePath("MyNewDirectory")`. Now add an additional statement to the `createDirectory` function that says `newDirectory.createDirectory()`. Now simply add an `<mx:Button>` to the file calling the new function with the `click` property, and you will have a sample application that will create a new directory on your desktop named *MyNewDirectory*.

If you have followed along correctly, your `Chapter8_Dir.mxml` should now look like Listing 8-2.

Listing 8-2: The updated `Chapter8_Dir.mxml` **file**

```
<?xml version="1.0" encoding="utf-8"?>
<mx:WindowedApplication xmlns:mx="http://www.adobe.com/2006/mxml"
    layout="absolute">

    <mx:Script>
    <![CDATA[
    import mx.controls.Alert;
    import flash.filesystem.File;

    private function createDirectory():void{
        var newDirectory:File =
        File.desktopDirectory.resolvePath("MyNewDirectory");
        newDirectory.createDirectory();
        Alert.show(newDirectory.nativePath);
    }

    ]]>
    </mx:Script>
    <mx:Button label="Create New Directory"
        click="createDirectory()" y="10" horizontalCenter="0"/>
</mx:WindowedApplication>
```

You may have noticed that the File class had a built-in property named desktopDirectory that gave a reference to the desktop of the user's machine. This is a convenient shortcut that AIR has provided to make it easy to navigate to the user's desktop without even knowing what operating system is being used. AIR provides four other shortcut properties. Try any of the following in place of desktopDirectory and see what kind of results you get:

❑ applicationResourceDirectory is a reference to the application install path /Contents/ Resources directory. For example, using applicationResourceDirectory to create the directory in this example will create the MyNewDirectory folder at /Users/rich/Applications/ Chapter8File-API.app/Contents/Resources/MyNewDirectory on Mac or C:\Documents and Settings\rich\Local Settings\Application Data\Chapter8-FileAPI\ MyNewDirectory on Windows.

❑ applicationStorageDirectory is a reference to the default storage location for the application. For example, on a Mac it will create the directory at /Users/rich/Library/Preferences/ Chapter8-FileAPI/Local Store/MyNewDirectory, while on Windows it will create the folder at C:\Documents and Settings\rich\Application Data\Chapter8-FileAPI\ Local Store\MyNewDirectory.

❑ desktopDirectory is a reference to the users desktop directory. For example, on a Mac it will create the directory at /Users/rich/Desktop/MyNewDirectory, while on Windows it will create the directory at C:\Documents and Settings\rich\Desktop\MyNewDirectory.

❑ documentsDirectory is a reference to the users documents directory. For example, on a Mac it will create the directory at /Users/rich/Documents/MyNewDirectory, while on Windows it will create the directory at C:\Documents and Settings\rich\My Documents\MyNewDirectory.

❑ userDirectory is a reference to the user directory. For example, on a Mac it will create the directory at /Users/rich/MyNewDirectory, while on Windows it will create the directory at C:\Documents and Settings\rich\MyNewDirectory.

Moving a Directory

To demonstrate how to move a directory, we will need to add a new function to the test application. Moving a directory is made easy using the moveTo method of the File class. To test this, add the following new function to the script block of the Chapter8_Dir.mxml file:

```
private function moveDirectory():void{
  var originalLoc:File = File.desktopDirectory.resolvePath("MyNewDirectory");
  var newLoc:File = File.desktopDirectory.resolvePath("MovedDirectory");
  originalLoc.moveTo(newLoc);
}
```

Now add another button to the file below the original button.

```
<mx:Button label="Move Directory"
    click="moveDirectory()" y="40" horizontalCenter="0"/>
```

When you test the updated application, be sure to create the directory first before attempting to move it or you will wind up with an error. (Error #3003: File or directory does not exist.)

Copy a Directory

To demonstrate how to copy a directory, we will need to add a new function to the test application. To copy a directory, we will use the copyTo method of the File class. To demonstrate this, add the following new function to the script block of the Chapter8_Dir.mxml file:

```
private function copyDirectory():void{
  var originalLoc:File = File.desktopDirectory.resolvePath("MyNewDirectory");
  var copyLoc:File = File.desktopDirectory.resolvePath("MyNewDirectory copy");
  originalLoc.copyTo(copyLoc);
}
```

Now add another button to the file below the original button.

```
<mx:Button label="Copy Directory"
    click="copyDirectory()" y="70" horizontalCenter="0"/>
```

When you test the updated application, be sure to create the directory first before attempting to copy it or you will wind up with an error. (Error #3003: File or directory does not exist.)

Delete a Directory

To demonstrate how to delete a directory, we will need to add a new function to the test application. The File class has a deleteDirectory method that makes it easy to delete a folder. The following new function added to the script block of the Chapter8_Dir.mxml file will demonstrate how to delete a directory:

```
private function deleteDirectory():void{
  var newDirectory:File=File.desktopDirectory.resolvePath("MyNewDirectory");
  newDirectory.deleteDirectory();
}
```

Now add another button to the file below the original button.

```
<mx:Button label="Delete Directory"
    click="deleteDirectory()" y="100" horizontalCenter="0"/>
```

When you test the updated application, be sure to create the directory first before attempting to move it to the trash or you will wind up with an error. (Error: Error #3003: File or directory does not exist.)

The deleteDirectory method within the File class takes an optional argument of type Boolean. This argument will determine whether a directory that is not empty will be deleted or throw the same error, Error #3003: File or directory does not exist. To test this, run the application and click the Create Directory button, then without closing the application go to your desktop and add something to the "MyNewDirectory." Now go back to the application and click the Delete Directory button, and you will get a runtime Error #3003: File or directory does not exist.

Close the application and update the source code to say newDirectory.deleteDirectory(true);. Run through the steps again (create directory, add something to it, and then attempt delete), and you will see that this time it was deleted successfully.

Move a Directory to Trash

A safer way to handle file deletes would be to move them to the trash instead of deleting them permanently. To demonstrate how to move a directory to the trash, we will need to add a new function to the test application. Add the following new function to the script block of the Chapter8_Dir.mxml file:

```
private function moveDirToTrash():void{
   var newDirectory:File=File.desktopDirectory.resolvePath("MyNewDirectory");
   newDirectory.moveToTrash();
}
```

Now add another button to the file below the original button.

```
<mx:Button label="Move Dir to Trash"
    click="moveDirToTrash()" y="130" horizontalCenter="0"/>
```

When you test the updated application, be sure to create the directory first before attempting to move it to the trash or you will wind up with an error. (Error #3003: File or directory does not exist.)

List Directory Contents

To list a directory's contents, you can use the getDirectoryListing() method of the File class to set the directory's contents into an Array, which you can then loop through to output the contents of the directory. Here is an example:

```
private function listDirectory():void{
   var newDirectory:File=File.desktopDirectory.resolvePath("MyNewDirectory");
   var dirContents:Array = newDirectory.getDirectoryListing();
   for(var i:int=0; i<dirContents.length; i++){
    log.text += dirContents[i].name + " " + dirContents[i].size + " bytes\n";
   }
}

<mx:Button label="List Directory"
    click="listDirectory()" y="160" horizontalCenter="0"/>
<mx:TextArea id="log" y="190" horizontalCenter="0"
    height="125" width="400"/>
```

To test this example, open the application and click the Create Directory button. Now go to your desktop and add some files to the directory. Go back to the application and click the List Directory button, and you should see something like what is shown in Figure 8-1.

Many other properties are available in addition to the name and size properties that are shown in the example above. Here is the complete list:

creationDate

creator

exists

icon

isDirectory

modificationDate

name

nativePath

parent

size

type

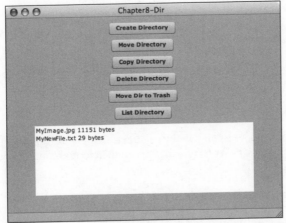

Figure 8-1: Contents of a directory after calling listDirectory().

Listing 8-3: The completed Chapter8_Dir.mxml **file**

```
<?xml version="1.0" encoding="utf-8"?>
<mx:WindowedApplication xmlns:mx="http://www.adobe.com/2006/mxml"
    layout="absolute">

  <mx:Script>
    <![CDATA[
    import mx.controls.Alert;
    import flash.filesystem.File;

    /*
    Create a new directory
    */
    private function createDirectory():void{
        var newDirectory:File =
File.desktopDirectory.resolvePath("MyNewDirectory");
        newDirectory.createDirectory();
        Alert.show(newDirectory.nativePath);
    }
```

```
/*
Move a directory
NOTE: Be sure to create the "MyNewDirectory"
first before attempting to move
*/
private function moveDirectory():void{
    var originalLoc:File =
File.desktopDirectory.resolvePath("MyNewDirectory");
    var newLoc:File = File.desktopDirectory.resolvePath("MovedDirectory");
    originalLoc.moveTo(newLoc);
}
/*
Copy a directory
NOTE: Be sure to create the "MyNewDirectory"
first before attempting to copy
*/
private function copyDirectory():void{
    var originalLoc:File = File.desktopDirectory.resolvePath("MyNewDirectory");
    var copyLoc:File = File.desktopDirectory.resolvePath("MyNewDirectory copy");
    originalLoc.copyTo(copyLoc);
}
/*
Delete a directory
NOTE: Be sure to create the "MyNewDirectory"
first before attempting to delete it
*/
private function deleteDirectory():void{
    var newDirectory:File =
File.desktopDirectory.resolvePath("MyNewDirectory");
    newDirectory.deleteDirectory();
}
/*
Move a directory to Trash
NOTE: Be sure to create the "MyNewDirectory"
first before attempting to move it to Trash
*/
private function moveDirToTrash():void{
    var newDirectory:File =
File.desktopDirectory.resolvePath("MyNewDirectory");
    newDirectory.moveToTrash();
}
/*
List a directory
*/
private function listDirectory():void{
    var newDirectory:File =
File.desktopDirectory.resolvePath("MyNewDirectory");
    var dirContents:Array = newDirectory.getDirectoryListing();
    for(var i:int=0; i<dirContents.length; i++){
        log.text += dirContents[i].name + " " + dirContents[i].size +
        "bytes\n";
    }
```

(Continued)

Listing 8-3: The completed `Chapter8_Dir.mxml` **file** *(continued)*

```
        }

    ]]>
    </mx:Script>

    <mx:Button label="Create Directory"
        click="createDirectory()" y="10" horizontalCenter="0"/>
    <mx:Button label="Move Directory"
        click="moveDirectory()" y="40" horizontalCenter="0"/>
    <mx:Button label="Copy Directory"
        click="copyDirectory()" y="70" horizontalCenter="0"/>
    <mx:Button label="Delete Directory"
        click="deleteDirectory()" y="100" horizontalCenter="0"/>
    <mx:Button label="Move Dir to Trash"
        click="moveDirToTrash()" y="130" horizontalCenter="0"/>
    <mx:Button label="List Directory"
        click="listDirectory()" y="160" horizontalCenter="0"/>
    <mx:TextArea id="log" y="190" horizontalCenter="0"
        height="125" width="400"/>

</mx:WindowedApplication>
```

Files

Working with files is very similar to working with directories, with the addition of the `flash.filesystem` `.FileStream` class for interactions with the contents of an individual file and the `flash.filesystem` `.FileMode` class for opening a file with specific permissions (read, write, etc.). The next group of samples will work with the same project and build upon it with each new piece of functionality. To get started, create a new AIR project and name it *Chapter8_File*. You should now have an empty file named `Chapter8_File.mxml` that looks like Listing 8-4. Please note that the completed code for `Chapter8_File.mxml` is shown in Listing 8-5.

Listing 8-4: Empty `Chapter8_File.mxml` **file used for the next example set**

```
<?xml version="1.0" encoding="utf-8"?>
<mx:WindowedApplication xmlns:mx="http://www.adobe.com/2006/mxml"
    layout="absolute">

    </mx:WindowedApplication>
```

In addition to the READ constant of the `FileMode` class, the class also has WRITE, UPDATE, and APPEND constants. The definitions of these constants are as follows:

❑ `FileMode.READ` will open a file for read only. The file must exist to avoid a File I/O error.

❑ `FileMode.WRITE` will open a file with full Write permissions. If the file does not exist, it will be created. If the file does exist, its contents will be overwritten.

❑ `FileMode.APPEND` will open a file with full append access. If the file does not exist, it will be created. If the file does exist, any additions will occur at the end of any existing contents, and no data will be overwritten.

❑ `FileMode.UPDATE` will open a file with read and write access. If the file does not exist, it will be created. Only changed data will be overwritten when a file is open with UPDATE.

Create a File

Creating a new file is the same process as creating a directory. The following sample will create a new file by getting a reference with the File class and then opening the file with Write permissions using the `FileStream` and `FileMode` classes. Finally, the file is written out using the `writeUTFBytes` method, and the stream is closed. Starting with the empty `Chaper8_file.mxml` file, add the following `<mx:Script>` block:

```
<mx:Script>
  <![CDATA[
  import flash.filesystem.FileMode;
  import flash.filesystem.FileStream;
  import flash.filesystem.File;

  private function createFile():void{
      var newFile:File = File.desktopDirectory.resolvePath("MyNewFile.txt");
      var fileStream:FileStream = new FileStream();
      fileStream.open(newFile, FileMode.WRITE);
      fileStream.writeUTFBytes("Beginning air");
      fileStream.close();
  }
  ]]>
</mx:Script>
```

Now add the following button:

```
<mx:Button label="Create File"
        click="createFile()" y="10" horizontalCenter="0"/>
```

The results can be seen in Figure 8-2.

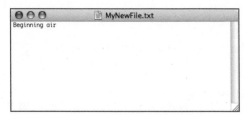

Figure 8-2: The newly created text file.

Read a File

To read the file we just created back in, you will need to open the `FileStream` with the `FileMode.READ` constant. To demonstrate this, simply add the following function:

```
private function readFile():void{
    var myFile:File = File.desktopDirectory.resolvePath("MyNewFile.txt");
    var fileStream:FileStream = new FileStream();
    fileStream.open(myFile, FileMode.READ);
    Alert.show(fileStream.readUTFBytes(fileStream.bytesAvailable),"Read File");
    fileStream.close();
}
```

Since this example uses an Alert to show the results of the file read, you will also need to add an import statement.

```
import mx.controls.Alert;
```

Finally add another button to trigger the new function.

```
<mx:Button label="Read File"
        click="readFile()" y="40" horizontalCenter="0"/>
```

Be sure to create the file before attempting to read the file to avoid a file error. (Error #3003: File or directory does not exist.)

The results of the file read will look like Figure 8-3.

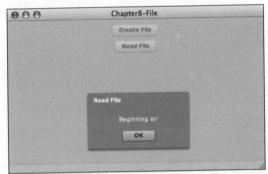

Figure 8-3: Example showing the `File Read` function.

Update a File

Updating a file requires that it is opened in UPDATE mode. The following example will open a file in UPDATE mode and write a new chunk of data at a specific position in the file:

```
private function updateFile():void{
    var myFile:File = File.desktopDirectory.resolvePath("MyNewFile.txt");
    var fileStream:FileStream = new FileStream();
    fileStream.open(myFile, FileMode.UPDATE);
    fileStream.position = 10;
    fileStream.writeUTFBytes("AIR");
    fileStream.close();
}

<mx:Button label="Update File"
        click="updateFile()" y="70" horizontalCenter="0"/>
```

To test this, run the application and create the file using the Create File button. Next, click the Read File button and you should see something similar to Figure 8-3. Now, click the Update File button and then again click the Read File button, and you should now see something similar to Figure 8-4.

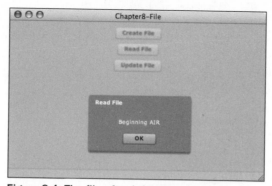

Figure 8-4: The file after it has been updated.

Append to a File

To append to a file, you should open the file with FileMode.APPEND. The following function will open the file in APPEND mode and will append some data to the file:

```
private function appendFile():void{
  var myFile:File = File.desktopDirectory.resolvePath("MyNewFile.txt");
  var fileStream:FileStream = new FileStream();
  fileStream.open(myFile, FileMode.APPEND);
  fileStream.writeUTFBytes(" by Rich Tretola");
  fileStream.close();
}

<mx:Button label="Append File"
        click="appendFile()" y="100" horizontalCenter="0"/>
```

To test this, run the application and create the file using the Create File button. Next, click the Read File button and you should see something similar to Figure 8-3. Now, click the Update File button and then again click the Read File button, and you should see something similar to Figure 8-4. Finally, click the Append File button to append some text, and then hit the Read File button again. You should now see something similar to Figure 8-5.

Figure 8-5: The file after it has been appended.

Move a File

To move a file, use the `moveTo` method of the `File` class. Add the following function and button to the `Chapter8_File.mxml` file:

```
private function moveFile():void{
    var originalLoc:File = File.desktopDirectory.resolvePath("MyNewFile.txt");
    var newLoc:File = File.desktopDirectory.resolvePath("MovedFile.txt");
    originalLoc.moveTo(newLoc);
}

<mx:Button label="Move File"
        click="moveFile()" y="130" horizontalCenter="0"/>
```

Be sure to create the file before attempting to move the file to avoid a file error. (Error #3003: File or directory does not exist.)

Copy a File

To copy a file, use the `copyTo` method of the File class. Add the following function and button to the `Chapter8_File.mxml` file:

```
private function copyFile():void{
    var originalLoc:File = File.desktopDirectory.resolvePath("MyNewFile.txt");
    var copyLoc:File = File.desktopDirectory.resolvePath("MyNewFileCopy.txt");
    originalLoc.copyTo(copyLoc);
}

<mx:Button label="Copy File"
        click="copyFile()" y="160" horizontalCenter="0"/>
```

Be sure to create the file before attempting to copy the file to avoid a file error. (Error #3003: File or directory does not exist.)

Delete a File

To copy a file, use the `deleteFile` method of the File class. Add the following function and button to the `Chapter8_File.mxml` file:

```
private function deleteFile():void{
    var newFile:File = File.desktopDirectory.resolvePath("MyNewFile.txt");
    newFile.deleteFile ();
}

<mx:Button label="Delete File"
        click="deleteFile()" y="190" horizontalCenter="0"/>
```

Be sure to create the file before attempting to delete the file to avoid a file error. (Error #3003: File or directory does not exist.)

Move a File to Trash

To copy a file, use the `moveToTrash` method of the `File` class. Add the following function and button to the `Chapter8_File.mxml` file:

```
private function moveFileToTrash():void{
  var newFile:File = File.desktopDirectory.resolvePath("MyNewFile.txt");
  newFile.moveToTrash();
}

<mx:Button label="Move File to Trash"
        click="moveFileToTrash()" y="220" horizontalCenter="0"/>
```

Be sure to create the file before attempting to move a file to the trash to avoid a file error. (Error #3003: File or directory does not exist.) The completed code for Chapter8_File.mxml is shown in Listing 8-5.

Listing 8-5: The completed `Chapter8_File.mxml`

```
<?xml version="1.0" encoding="utf-8"?>
<mx:WindowedApplication xmlns:mx="http://www.adobe.com/2006/mxml"
    layout="absolute">
    <mx:Script>
      <![CDATA[
      import flash.filesystem.FileMode;
      import flash.filesystem.FileStream;
      import flash.filesystem.File;
      import mx.controls.Alert;
      /*
      Create a new file
      */
      private function createFile():void{
        var newFile:File = File.desktopDirectory.resolvePath("MyNewFile.txt");
        var fileStream:FileStream = new FileStream();
        fileStream.open(newFile, FileMode.WRITE);
        fileStream.writeUTFBytes("Beginning air");
        fileStream.close();
      }
      /*
      Read in a file
      Note: Be sure to create the file first
      */
      private function readFile():void{
        var myFile:File = File.desktopDirectory.resolvePath("MyNewFile.txt");
        var fileStream:FileStream = new FileStream();
        fileStream.open(myFile, FileMode.READ);
        Alert.show(fileStream.readUTFBytes(fileStream.bytesAvailable),"Read File");
        fileStream.close();
      }
      /*
      Update a file
      */
```

(Continued)

Listing 8-5: The completed Chapter8_File.mxml *(continued)*

```
    private function updateFile():void{
       var myFile:File = File.desktopDirectory.resolvePath("MyNewFile.txt");
       var fileStream:FileStream = new FileStream();
       fileStream.open(myFile, FileMode.UPDATE);
       fileStream.position = 10;
       fileStream.writeUTFBytes("AIR");
       fileStream.close();
    }
    /*
    Append to a file
    */
    private function appendFile():void{
       var myFile:File = File.desktopDirectory.resolvePath("MyNewFile.txt");
       var fileStream:FileStream = new FileStream();
       fileStream.open(myFile, FileMode.APPEND);
       fileStream.writeUTFBytes(" by Rich Tretola");
       fileStream.close();
    }
    /*
    Move a file
    NOTE: Be sure to create the file
    first before attempting to move
    */
    private function moveFile():void{
       var originalLoc:File = File.desktopDirectory.resolvePath("MyNewFile.txt");
       var newLoc:File = File.desktopDirectory.resolvePath("MovedFile.txt");
       originalLoc.moveTo(newLoc);
    }
    /*
    Copy a file
    NOTE: Be sure to create the file
    first before attempting to copy
    */
    private function copyFile():void{
       var originalLoc:File = File.desktopDirectory.resolvePath("MyNewFile.txt");
       var copyLoc:File = File.desktopDirectory.resolvePath("MyNewFileCopy.txt");
       originalLoc.copyTo(copyLoc);
    }
    /*
    Delete a file
    NOTE: Be sure to create the file
    first before attempting to delete it
    */
    private function deleteFile():void{
        var newFile:File = File.desktopDirectory.resolvePath("MyNewFile.txt");
        newFile.deleteFile();
    }
    /*
    Move a directory to Trash
    NOTE: Be sure to create the file
    first before attempting to move it to Trash
    */
```

```
    private function moveFileToTrash():void{
        var newFile:File = File.desktopDirectory.resolvePath("MyNewFile.txt");
        newFile.moveToTrash();
    }
    ]]>
</mx:Script>
<mx:Button label="Create File"
    click="createFile()" y="10" horizontalCenter="0"/>
<mx:Button label="Read File"
    click="readFile()" y="40" horizontalCenter="0"/>
<mx:Button label="Update File"
    click="updateFile()" y="70" horizontalCenter="0"/>
<mx:Button label="Append File"
    click="appendFile()" y="100" horizontalCenter="0"/>
<mx:Button label="Move File"
    click="moveFile()" y="130" horizontalCenter="0"/>
<mx:Button label="Copy File"
    click="copyFile()" y="160" horizontalCenter="0"/>
<mx:Button label="Delete File"
    click="deleteFile()" y="190" horizontalCenter="0"/>
<mx:Button label="Move File to Trash"
    click="moveFileToTrash()" y="220" horizontalCenter="0"/>
</mx:WindowedApplication>
```

Asynchronous versus Synchronous

The examples given so far have concentrated on synchronous methods. Calling a method *synchronously* means that while the call is being made the application pauses until the method call has completed. For example, let's say that you would like to read in file information for 1,000 images that exist in an image folder. Doing this as a synchronous method would mean that the application would be unusable while it is reading in the image files. A better way to do this would be to use an *asynchronous method,* which would allow the user to continue to use the application while the asynchronous method executes. While the asynchronous method is executing, you can receive updates of its progress by setting up event listeners.

There are asynchronous versions of many of the `File` class methods. Here is the complete list:

Directories

```
copyToAsync()

deleteDirectoryAsync()

getDirectoryListingAsync()

moveToAsync()

moveToTrashAsync()
```

Files

```
copyToAsync()

deleteFileAsync()
```

```
moveToAsync()

moveToTrashAsync()
```

FileStream

```
openAsync()
```

The following examples will demonstrate how to use the `deleteDirectoryAsync()` method of the `File` class as well as the `openAsync()` method of the `FileStream` class. The same principles can be used for all of the other asynchronous methods as well.

To test the example in Listing 8-6, create a directory first by clicking on the Create Directory button, and then delete the directory asynchronously by clicking on the Delete Directory button. The results can be seen in Figure 8-6.

Listing 8-6: Source code for `Chapter8_DirAsynch.mxml`

```xml
<?xml version="1.0" encoding="utf-8"?>
<mx:WindowedApplication xmlns:mx="http://www.adobe.com/2006/mxml"
    layout="absolute">
    <mx:Script>
      <![CDATA[
      import flash.filesystem.File;
      import mx.events.FileEvent;
      import mx.controls.Alert;

      /*
      Create a new directory
      */
      private function createDirectory():void{
        var newDirectory:File=File.desktopDirectory.resolvePath("MyNewDirectory");
        newDirectory.createDirectory();
      }
      /*
      Delete directory Asynchronously
      */
      private function deleteDirectory():void{
        var directory:File = File.desktopDirectory.resolvePath("MyNewDirectory");
        directory.addEventListener(Event.COMPLETE,completeHandler);
        directory.deleteDirectoryAsync();
      }
      private function completeHandler(event:Event):void {
        Alert.show("Directory deleted","Complete Handler");
      }

      ]]>
    </mx:Script>
    <mx:Button label="Create Directory"
      click="createDirectory()" y="10" horizontalCenter="0"/>
    <mx:Button label="Delete Directory"
      click="deleteDirectory()" y="40" horizontalCenter="0"/>
</mx:WindowedApplication>
```

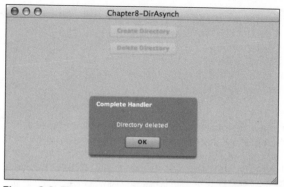

Figure 8-6: The complete handler triggered when Delete event is completed.

The example in Listing 8-7 demonstrates how to use the openAsynch method of the FileStream class. To test this, create a file by clicking on the Create File button, and then read the file asynchronously by clicking on the Read File Asynchronously button. The results can be seen in Figure 8-7.

Listing 8-7: Source code for Chapter8_FileAsynch.mxml

```
<?xml version="1.0" encoding="utf-8"?>
<mx:WindowedApplication xmlns:mx="http://www.adobe.com/2006/mxml"
    layout="absolute">

    <mx:Script>
    <![CDATA[
    import mx.controls.Alert;
    import mx.events.FileEvent;
    import flash.filesystem.FileMode;
    import flash.filesystem.FileStream;
    import flash.filesystem.File;

    private var fileContents:String;
    /*
    Create a new file
    */
    private function createFile():void{
      var newFile:File = File.desktopDirectory.resolvePath("MyNewFile.txt");
      var fileStream:FileStream = new FileStream();
      fileStream.open(newFile, FileMode.WRITE);
      fileStream.writeUTFBytes("Beginning AIR by Rich Tretola");
      fileStream.close();
    }
    /*
    Read in a file
    Note: Be sure to create the file first
    */
    private function readFileAsynch():void{
      var resourceFile:File = File.desktopDirectory.resolvePath("MyNewFile.txt");
      var fileStream:FileStream = new FileStream();
      fileStream.openAsync(resourceFile, FileMode.READ);
```

(Continued)

Listing 8-7: Source code for `Chapter8_FileAsynch.mxml` *(continued)*

```
          fileStream.addEventListener(Event.CLOSE,completeHandler);
          fileStream.addEventListener(IOErrorEvent.IO_ERROR,errorHandler);
          fileContents = fileStream.readUTFBytes(fileStream.bytesAvailable);
          fileStream.close();
      }

      private function completeHandler(event:Event):void {
          Alert.show("File read completed","Complete Handler");
      }
      private function errorHandler(event:IOErrorEvent):void {
          Alert.show("Error " + event.text,"errorHandler");
      }

      ]]>
      </mx:Script>

      <mx:Button label="Create File"
          click="createFile()" y="10" horizontalCenter="0"/>
      <mx:Button label="Read File Asynchronously"
          click="readFileAsynch()" y="40" horizontalCenter="0"/>
  </mx:WindowedApplication>
```

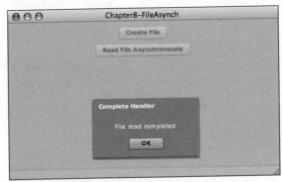

Figure 8-7: The complete handler triggered when
`File Read` is completed.

Creating Temporary Files and Directories

There may be occasions when you would like to have local file storage for temporary files and directories. AIR has included methods within the File API to create temporary directories and files. After importing the File class, a temporary (temp) directory can be created by calling the `createTempDirectory()` method on the `File` class, and a temp file can be created by calling the `createTempFile()` method. Listing 8-8 shows how to create a temporary directory and a temp file.

Listing 8-8: Sample file for creating temp directories and files

```
<?xml version="1.0" encoding="utf-8"?>
<mx:WindowedApplication xmlns:mx="http://www.adobe.com/2006/mxml"
```

```
  layout="absolute">

<mx:Script>
<![CDATA[
import mx.controls.Alert;
import flash.filesystem.File;

private function createTempDirectory():void{
 var tempDirectory:File = File.createTempDirectory();
 Alert.show("nativePath = " + tempDirectory.nativePath +
 "\n\nisDirectory = " + tempDirectory.isDirectory,
 "tempDirectory");
 }

private function createTempFile():void{
 var tempFile:File = File.createTempFile();
  Alert.show("nativePath = " + tempFile.nativePath +
 "\n\nisDirectory = " + tempFile.isDirectory,
 "tempFile");
 }

 ]]>
</mx:Script>

<mx:Button label="Create Temp Directory"
 click="createTempDirectory()" horizontalCenter="0"
 y="10"/>
<mx:Button label="Create Temp File"
 click="createTempFile()" horizontalCenter="0"
 y="40"/>
</mx:WindowedApplication>
```

The results can be see in Figures 8-8 and 8-9. Notice that the output of the `isDirectory` property in each figure shows that the temp directory is recognized as a directory, while the temp file is not. If you are running this sample on a Windows machine, your expected outcome would be a file path similar to `C:\Documents and Settings\rich\Local Settings\Temp\fla28F.tmp`.

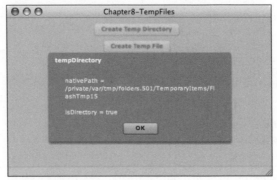

Figure 8-8: The `nativePath` and `isDirectory` **property of a temp directory created on Mac OS X.**

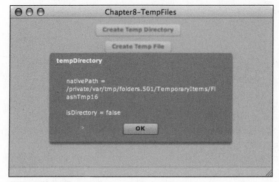

Figure 8-9: The `nativePath` and `isDirectory` **properties of a temp file created on Mac OS X.**

Browse for Files

The last section of this chapter demonstrates how to allow users to select a file or a directory by browsing their file systems with their native operating system's browse dialog. The sample code in Listing 8-9 shows two methods for opening the native browse dialog. The first uses the `browseForOpen` function of the `File` class, which is supplied a single argument for the label of the dialog box. A second argument to limit the browse dialog to specific file types is also available as an optional argument. An `eventListener` has been added to show the user's selection. The results can be seen in Figures 8-10 and 8-11. The second example uses the `browseForDirectory` function of the `File` class, which accepts a single argument for the browse dialog label. The results of this can be seen in Figures 8-12 and 8-13.

Listing 8-9: Code for using the operating system's native browse dialog within AIR

```
<?xml version="1.0" encoding="utf-8"?>
<mx:WindowedApplication xmlns:mx="http://www.adobe.com/2006/mxml"
    layout="absolute">
    <mx:Script>
    <![CDATA[
    import flash.filesystem.File;
    import mx.controls.Alert;
    // Allows user to select a file
    private function browseForOpen():void{
      var file:File = new File();
      file.addEventListener(Event.SELECT,openHandler);
      file.browseForOpen("Select a File");
    }
     private function openHandler(event:Event):void{
       Alert.show(event.target.nativePath,"Selected File");
    }
    // Allows user to select a directory
    private function browseForDirectory():void{
      var file:File = new File();
      file.addEventListener(Event.SELECT,openDirHandler);
```

```
            file..browseForDirectory("Select a Directory");
        }
        private function openDirHandler(event:Event):void{
            Alert.show(event.target.nativePath,"Selected Directory");
        }

        ]]>
    </mx:Script>
    <mx:Button label="Browse for File"
        click="browseForOpen()" y="10" horizontalCenter="0"/>
    <mx:Button label="Browse for Directory"
        click="browseForDirectory()" y="40" horizontalCenter="0"/>
</mx:WindowedApplication>
```

Figure 8-10: Dialog from `browseForOpen` with label of "Select a File."

Figure 8-11: The selected file.

Figure 8-12: Dialog from `browseForDirectory` with label of "Select a Directory."

Figure 8-13: The selected directory.

This chapter demonstrated how to interact with the file system from an AIR application by using the `File`, `FileMode`, and `FileStream` classes. The next chapter will cover AIR windows and the windowing API.

Summary

This chapter demonstrated AIR's ability to interact with the operating system's file system. It showed how to create, edit, and delete files and folders. It also offered samples showing how to use the built-in file browse controls to browse and select files and folders.

The next chapter will offer examples of how to build applications that use multiple windows. It will also show how to add NativeMenus to the main application window on Mac OS X.

Exercise

Create a new file on the desktop named *Today.txt*, and set its contents to be "Today is *(insert the date using the Date class)* and I have created my first file from AIR."

The Windowing API

Windows have been a part of traditional desktop applications for many years. If you have ever opened a Help window or a preferences window of a desktop application, you have experienced a multi-window application. AIR has given us the ability to create windows as part of AIR desktop applications as well. Each window is a full-fledged system window and can act independently of the additional windows; it can even persist after the main application window has been closed. If you are operating a computer running Microsoft Windows, you will see each window appear in the taskbar as you would with any other desktop application.

Creating Windows

Creating windows with AIR is an extremely simple process. There are two different types of AIR application windows. The `NativeWindow` is a lightweight window class that falls under the flash class path and can only add children that are under the flash class path. The `mx:Window` component is a full window component that falls under the `mx` namespace and therefore can include any component under the `mx` namespace.

NativeWindow

Since `NativeWindow` falls under the `flash.display` package, it can be used in any Flex, Flash, or HTML AIR project. `NativeWindows` have many properties that can alter their functionality and look. The following example will create a basic `NativeWindow` and build on the same file, creating different versions of the `NativeWindow`.

Start by creating a new AIR project named *Chapter9_NW*, which will create a new application file named *Chapter9_NW.mxml*. This will look like Listing 9-1.

Listing 9-1: The newly created Chapter9_NW.mxml file

```
<?xml version="1.0" encoding="utf-8"?>
<mx:WindowedApplication xmlns:mx="http://www.adobe.com/2006/mxml"
layout="absolute">
</mx:WindowedApplication>
```

Now add a new script block by adding the code from Listing 9-2. This function will create a default new `NativeWindow` object by passing a new `NativeWindowInitOptions()` object into the constructor. Next the title, width, and height are set. A new `TextField` is created and added to the `NativeWindow` by calling the `stage.addChild()` method. The contents of the `NativeWindow` are then aligned to the top left and set to not scale. Finally, the `activate()` method is called to create the window. To call the `createNativeWindow()` function, add the button from Listing 9-3. Run the application, and you should see something similar to Figure 9-1 or 9-2.

Listing 9-2: The `createNativeWindow()` **function**

```
<mx:Script>
    <![CDATA[
    private var nw1:NativeWindow;

    private function createNativeWindow():void{
        nw1 = new NativeWindow(new NativeWindowInitOptions());
        nw1.title = "Native Window";
        nw1.width = 400;
        nw1.height = 200;
        var tf:TextField = new TextField();
        tf.text="A NativeWindow";
        tf.wordWrap=true;
        tf.name="winText";
        nw1.stage.addChild(tf);
        nw1.stage.align = StageAlign.TOP_LEFT;
        nw1.stage.scaleMode = StageScaleMode.NO_SCALE;
        nw1.activate();
    }

    ]]>
</mx:Script>
```

Listing 9-3: The button used to call the `createNativeWindow()` **function**

```
<mx:Button label="Native Window" click="this.createNativeWindow()"
    horizontalCenter="0" y="10"/>
```

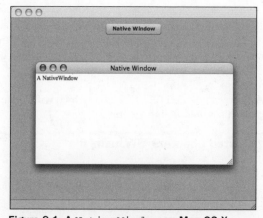

Figure 9-1: A `NativeWindow` **on Mac OS X.**

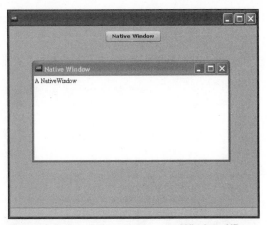

Figure 9-2: A `NativeWindow` on **WindowsXP**.

Building on the same example, we will add a property to keep the NativeWindow in front of the application window. Simply add `nw1.alwaysInFront = true;` right above `nw1.activate();`. To demonstrate how to access the controls of the `NativeWindow`, add the contents of Listing 9-4 to the Chapter9_NW.mxml file. There are four button components, each accessing a different method of the `NativeWindow`. These controls demonstrate how you can minimize, maximize, restore, and close a `NativeWindow`. Also, there is a TextInput component, which will update the contents of the TextField within the `NativeWindow`. Run the application and, after launching the `NativeWindow`, test each of the buttons and then type into the TextInput to see the contents of the `NativeWindow`'s TextField get updated. The application should now look like Figure 9-3 or 9-4.

Listing 9-4: Components to access the controls of the NativeWindow

```
<mx:Button click="nw1.minimize()" label="Minimize" x="77.5" y="40"/>
<mx:Button click="nw1.maximize()" label="Maximize" x="160.5" y="40"/>
<mx:Button click="nw1.restore()" label="Restore" x="247.5" y="40"/>
<mx:Button click="nw1.close()" label="Close" x="326.5" y="40"/>
<mx:Label x="120" y="72" text="Set Text"/>
<mx:TextInput  id="t1" x="180" y="70"
    change="TextField(nw1.stage.getChildByName('winText')).text = t1.text "/>
```

Figure 9-3: This shows the button controls and
the TextField being updated on Mac OS X.

Figure 9-4: The button controls and the TextField
are shown being updated on WindowsXP.

NativeWindowInitOptions

For even more control over the NativeWindow object, we will now explore the NativeWindowInitOptions class. If you recall from Listing 9-2, we passed a new NativeWindowInitOptions object into the NativeWindow constructor. By creating an instance of this class, we can set some properties before passing it into the NativeWindow constructor.

Start by updating the first line of the createNativeWindow() function from

```
nw1 = new NativeWindow(new NativeWindowInitOptions());
```

to

```
var nwio:NativeWindowInitOptions = new NativeWindowInitOptions();
nw1 = new NativeWindow(nwio);
```

This change alone will not result in any difference when you run the application; however, it will now allow us to experiment with some of the NativeWindowInitOptions properties.

Titlebar Buttons and Resize Settings

The NativeWindowInitOptions class includes properties to disable the maximize and the minimize buttons, as well as the resize handles. To disable these features, add the code from Listing 9-5 right below the nwio variable so that your createNativeWindow() function now looks like Listing 9-6. The results, showing the Close button enabled and the Resize handle gone from the lower right corner, are shown in Figure 9-5 or 9-6.

Listing 9-5: The properties to disable the Window controls

```
nwio.maximizable = false;
nwio.minimizable = false;
nwio.resizable = false;
```

Listing 9-6: The updated version of the createNativeWindow() function

```
private function createNativeWindow():void{
    var nwio:NativeWindowInitOptions = new NativeWindowInitOptions();
        nwio.maximizable = false;
    nwio.minimizable = false;
    nwio.resizable = false;
    nw1 = new NativeWindow(nwio);
    nw1.title = "Native Window";
    nw1.width = 400;
    nw1.height = 200;
    var tf:TextField = new TextField();
    tf.text="A NativeWindow";
    tf.wordWrap=true;
    tf.name="winText";
    nw1.stage.addChild(tf);
    nw1.stage.align = StageAlign.TOP_LEFT;
    nw1.stage.scaleMode = StageScaleMode.NO_SCALE;
    nw1.alwaysInFront = true;
    nw1.activate();
    }
```

Figure 9-5: Only the Close button is enabled and the Resize handle is gone on Mac OS X.

Figure 9-6: Only the Close button is enabled and the Resize handle is gone on WindowsXP.

NativeMenus

Depending on the operating system, NativeWindows may allow NativeMenus. The following example code will compile on both Mac and Windows but will only show the NativeMenu on Windows, as Mac does not allow NativeMenus on subwindows. For more information on NativeMenus, please refer to Chapter 12. To add a NativeMenu, add the code from Listing 9-7 right above the line that says nw1.activate();. If we examine the code, you will see that the NativeWindow.supportsMenu will return True or False depending on the operating system. This will only add the NativeMenu if it is allowed. The results can be seen in Figure 9-7 if you are using WindowsXP.

Listing 9-7: The code to add a NativeMenu **to the** NativeWindow

```
var nativeMenu:NativeMenu = new NativeMenu();
var menuRoot:NativeMenuItem = new NativeMenuItem();
var menuItem1:NativeMenuItem = new NativeMenuItem("Menu Item 1");
var menuItem2:NativeMenuItem = new NativeMenuItem("Menu Item 2");
nativeMenu.addItem (menuItem1);
nativeMenu.addItem(menuItem2);
menuRoot.submenu = nativeMenu;
if(NativeWindow.supportsMenu){
   nw1.menu = nativeMenu;
}
```

NativeWindowType

NativeWindows can take on a few different appearances. The type property on the NativeWindowInitOptions class accepts a static property from the NativeWindowType class. These include NativeWindowType.LIGHTWEIGHT, NativeWindowType.MODAL, NativeWindowType.NORMAL, and `NativeWindowType.UTILITY`. To demonstrate the use of the `NativeWindowInitOptions` type property, add the following line right below the line that says `nwio.resizable = false;`:

```
nwio.type = NativeWindowType.UTILITY;
```

Running this sample code will give the window a new look, taking on the operating system's utility window chrome. The results will look like Figure 9-8 or 9-9. It is also important to note that a window of type Utility will not show as a true independent window within the operating system's taskbar.

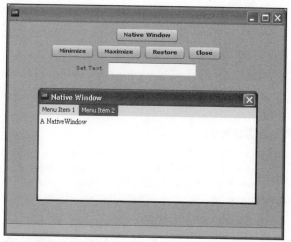

Figure 9-7: The `NativeMenu` being displayed on WindowsXP.

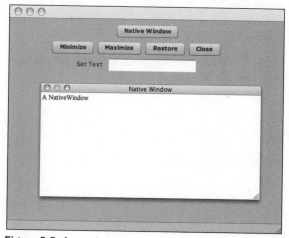

Figure 9-8: A `NativeWindow` of type Utility on Mac OS X.

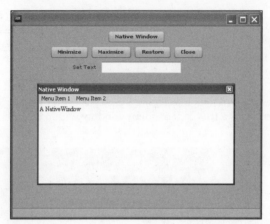

Figure 9-9: A `NativeWindow` of type Utility on WindowsXP.

NativeWindowSystemChrome

`NativeWindows` also allow you the ability to remove the system chrome completely, allowing you to create a custom-looking window and manage it with your own custom controls. Before we change the chrome, you will need to remove or comment out the `NativeMenu` code that was added in Listing 9-7, as windows without chrome cannot have a `NativeMenu` and will throw an error.

To avoid having the new window get stuck as the only open window, let's add some code to make sure that we close the `NativeWindow` when the application closes. To close all windows when closing the main application window, add `closing="NativeApplication.nativeApplication.exit(0)"` to the `mx:WindowedApplication` tag. This will make sure that a window that no longer has chrome and therefore no Close button will close upon exit of the application.

To demonstrate how to remove the chrome, try adding `nwio.systemChrome = NativeWindowSystemChrome` `.NONE;` right below `var nwio.type = NativeWindowType.UTILITY;`, and you will see something like Figure 9-10 or 9-11. Notice that there is now no system chrome or controls, thus you will need to use the buttons on the main application file to manage this window.

Figure 9-10: A `NativeWindow` with no system chrome on Mac OS X.

Figure 9-11: A `NativeWindow` **with no system chrome on WindowsXP.**

Now to make the window transparent, try adding `nwio.transparent = true;` right below `nwio.systemChrome = NativeWindowSystemChrome.NONE;`, and you will see the words "A NativeWindow" floating over the main application window, as the rest of the NativeWindow is now completely transparent.

Window (mx:Window)

The Window component is a component of the Flex framework that resides under the `mx.core` package, which means that it may contain children of any Flex component type. Creating a Window component is just as easy as creating any other Flex component. Listing 9-8 shows an example of a Window component with a single Label component included. You will notice that it is a simple container tag that lays out its children like any other layout control (Canvas, HBox, etc.).

To demonstrate how to create windows with `mx:Window`, start by creating a new AIR project named *Chapter9_Win*. Now create a new file named *BasicWindow.mxml* and copy in the code from Listing 9-8. Next simply copy the code from Listing 9-9 to the new Chapter9_Win.mxml file. In examining the code from Listing 9-9, you will see that a variable named `win` or type BasicWindow is instantiated. Then within the button's click handler method, the `open()` method is called on the `win` instance. The results can be seen in Figure 9-12 or 9-13.

Listing 9-8: A sample `mx:Window` **component**

```
<?xml version="1.0" encoding="utf-8"?>
<mx:Window xmlns:mx="http://www.adobe.com/2006/mxml"
    layout="absolute"
    width="300" height="200">

 <mx:Label horizontalCenter="0" y="58"
    text="A Sample Window" id="lbl"/>

</mx:Window>
```

Listing 9-9: The contents of Chapter9_Win.mxml

```xml
<?xml version="1.0" encoding="utf-8"?>
<mx:WindowedApplication
    xmlns:mx="http://www.adobe.com/2006/mxml"
    layout="absolute">
    <mx:Script>
    <![CDATA[
        private var win:BasicWindow = new BasicWindow ();

        private function createWindow():void{
            win.open();
        }
    ]]>
    </mx:Script>
    <mx:Button label="Create Window" click="createWindow()"
        horizontalCenter="0" y="10"/>
</mx:WindowedApplication>
```

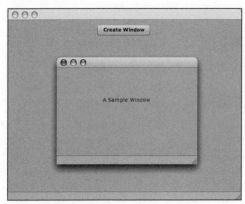

Figure 9-12: The new instance of the BasicWindow class on Mac OS X.

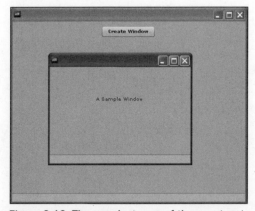

Figure 9-13: The new instance of the BasicWindow class on WindowsXP.

Titlebar Buttons and Resize Settings

To control the window from the main application window, we will use the same controls that we previously used in the NativeWindow example. To demonstrate this, add the code from Listing 9-10 to the Chapter9_Win.mxml file. The results can be seen in Figure 9-14 or 9-15.

Listing 9-10: The components to control the window from the main file

```
<mx:Button click="win.minimize()" label="Minimize" x="77.5" y="40"/>
<mx:Button click="win.maximize()" label="Maximize" x="160.5" y="40"/>
<mx:Button click="win.restore()" label="Restore" x="247.5" y="40"/>
<mx:Button click="win.close()" label="Close" x="326.5" y="40"/>
<mx:Label x="120" y="72" text="Set Text"/>
<mx:TextInput  id="t1" x="180" y="70"
     change="win.lbl.text = t1.text "/>
```

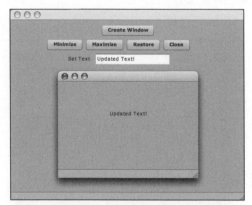

Figure 9-14: The text being updated from the TextInput on the main file on Mac OS X.

Figure 9-15: The text being updated from the TextInput on the main file on WindowsXP.

The Window component has properties to disable the maximize, minimize, and resize controls as well as a property to keep the window in front of other windows. Listing 9-11 shows an updated version of the Window component with these additional properties. Figures 9-16 and 9-17 show the results of these additional properties being set.

Listing 9-11: The Window component with additional properties

```
<?xml version="1.0" encoding="utf-8"?>
<mx:Window xmlns:mx="http://www.adobe.com/2006/mxml"
    layout="absolute"
    width="300" height="200"
    maximizable="false"
    minimizable="false"
    resizable="false"
    alwaysInFront="true">

  <mx:Label horizontalCenter="0" y="58"
        text="A Sample Window" id="lbl"/>

</mx:Window>
```

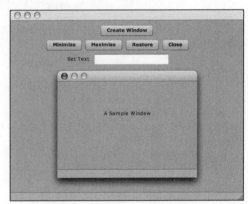

Figure 9-16: The window on Mac OS X, with only the Close button enabled and no Resize handle.

Figure 9-17: The window on WindowsXP, with only the Close button enabled and no Resize handle.

NativeMenus

A NativeMenu can be added to a window by assigning it to the underlying nativeWindow.menu property of the mx:Window component as shown in Listing 9-12. When the new window is created, the creationComplete event is fired, which then calls the init() function. The init function creates the new NativeMenu and then assigns the menu only if the NativeWindow.supportMenu property returns True. As with the section on NativeMenu in the beginning of this chapter, NativeMenus will only show within Window components when running the application on Microsoft Windows as shown in Figure 9-18. For more information on NativeMenus, please refer to Chapter 12.

Listing 9-12: The NativeMenu being added to the nativeMenu.menu property

```xml
<?xml version="1.0" encoding="utf-8"?>
<mx:Window xmlns:mx="http://www.adobe.com/2006/mxml"
    layout="absolute"
    width="300" height="200"
    creationComplete="init()">

    <mx:Script>
        <![CDATA[
            private var nativeMenu:NativeMenu = new NativeMenu();

            private function init():void{
                var menuRoot:NativeMenuItem = new NativeMenuItem();
                var menuItem1:NativeMenuItem = new NativeMenuItem("Menu Item 1");
                var menuItem2:NativeMenuItem = new NativeMenuItem("Menu Item 2");
                nativeMenu.addItem (menuItem1);
                nativeMenu.addItem(menuItem2);
                menuRoot.submenu = nativeMenu;
                 if(NativeWindow.supportsMenu){
                    this.nativeWindow.menu = nativeMenu;
                 }
            }
        ]]>
    </mx:Script>

    <mx:Label horizontalCenter="0" y="58"
        text="A Sample Window" id="lbl"/>

</mx:Window>
```

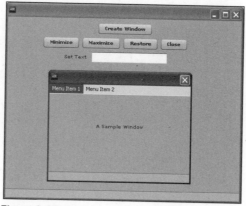

Figure 9-18: A NativeMenu **within an** mx:Window **on WindowsXP.**

NativeWindowType

As with the `NativeWindow` object previously discussed, Window also has a type property, which allows for the setting of the style of the window. Setting the NativeWindowType is as easy as adding a type property to an `mx:Window` tag. Listing 9-13 shows an example of a updated `mx:Window` tag applied to the same code from Listing 9-12. The results of this updated example can be seen in Figures 9-19 and 9-20.

Listing 9-13: An example of a Utility window

```xml
<?xml version="1.0" encoding="utf-8"?>
<mx:Window xmlns:mx="http://www.adobe.com/2006/mxml"
    layout="absolute"
    width="300" height="200"
    type="utility">

    <mx:Label horizontalCenter="0" y="58"
        text="A Sample Window" id="lbl"/>

</mx:Window>
```

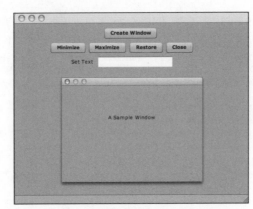

Figure 9-19: A Utility window on Mac OS X.

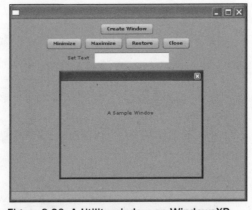

Figure 9-20: A Utility window on WindowsXP.

Window Icons

AIR 1.0 window title icons will show on Mac OS X and Microsoft Windows when systemChrome is set to None and flexChrome becomes the default chrome. With subsequent versions of AIR, it will be possible to assign a custom icon to each window when the application is run on Windows. To assign an icon to the window, you will simply need to embed an instance of an image file as of object type Class and make it Bindable. This is demonstrated within Listing 9-14 and Figure 9-21.

NativeWindowSystemChrome

As with the NativeWindow object previously discussed, Window also has a systemChrome property, which allows for the setting of the style of the window. Before experimenting with the systemChrome property, let's add some code to make sure that we close the NativeWindow when the application closes. To close all windows when closing the main application window, add closing="NativeApplication .nativeApplication.exit(0)" to the mx:WindowedApplication tag in the Chapter9_Win.mxml file. This will make sure that a window that no longer has chrome and therefore no Close button will close upon exit of the application.

Now, we will simply add systemChrome="none" borderStyle="solid" to the root tag of our window. An example of this can be seen in Listing 9-14. This will remove the system chrome and show the default flex chrome, which will look the same on Mac and Windows. This can be seen in Figures 9-21 and 9-22.

Listing 9-14: An example of a window using the flex chrome

```
<?xml version="1.0" encoding="utf-8"?>
<mx:Window xmlns:mx="http://www.adobe.com/2006/mxml"
    layout="absolute"
    width="300" height="200"
    titleIcon="{myIcon}"
    systemChrome="none"
    borderStyle="solid">

  <mx:Script>
      <![CDATA[
          [Embed(source="e16.png")]
          [Bindable]
          public var myIcon:Class;
            ]]>
  </mx:Script>

  <mx:Label horizontalCenter="0" y="58"
      text="A Sample Window" id="lbl"/>

</mx:Window>
```

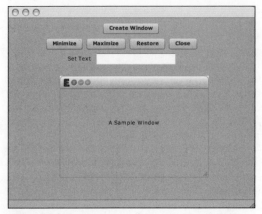

Figure 9-21: Here, `systemChrome` is set to None, which defaults to `flexChrome` on Mac OS X.

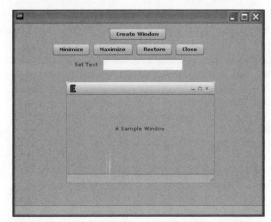

Figure 9-22: Here, `systemChrome` is set to None, which defaults to `flexChrome` on WindowsXP.

To remove the `flexChrome`, you will need to set `showFlexChrome` to False as is shown in Listing 9-14. As long as `systemChrome` is still set to None, you will wind up with something that looks like Figures 9-23 and 9-24. Note that removing the flex chrome means that you will need to create a way for the user to manage the window.

Listing 9-14: An example of a window with no chrome

```
<?xml version="1.0" encoding="utf-8"?>
<mx:Window xmlns:mx="http://www.adobe.com/2006/mxml"
    layout="absolute"
    width="300" height="200"
    systemChrome="none"
```

```
        borderStyle="solid"
        showFlexChrome="false">

    <mx:Label horizontalCenter="0" y="58"
        text="A Sample Window" id="lbl"/>

  </mx:Window>
```

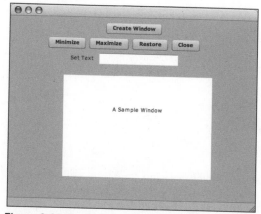

Figure 9-23: A window with `systemChrome` set to None and `showFlexChrome` set to False on Mac OS X.

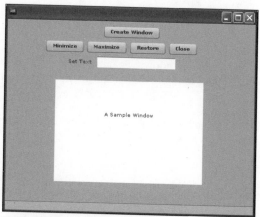

Figure 9-24: A window with `systemChrome` set to None and `showFlexChrome` set to False on WindowsXP.

Transparency

To make a window completely transparent, you will need to set the `systemChrome` to None and `showFlexChrome` to False as was demonstrated in the previous section, and you will also need to set transparent to True. Listing 9-15 shows an example of a transparent window.

Listing 9-15: A transparent window

```
<?xml version="1.0" encoding="utf-8"?>
<mx:Window xmlns:mx="http://www.adobe.com/2006/mxml"
    layout="absolute"
    width="300" height="200"
    systemChrome="none"
    borderStyle="solid"
    showFlexChrome="false"
    transparent="true">

    <mx:Label horizontalCenter="0" y="58"
        text="A Sample Window" id="lbl"/>

</mx:Window>
```

Summary

This chapter has demonstrated how to use and configure properties of the NativeWindow class. We also discussed how to create windows using the mx:Window class and demonstrated how to use systemChrome, NativeMenus, and titleBar icons.

In the next chapter, we will discuss how to use system tray and dock icons with menus. The chapter will also show how to use context menus within AIR applications.

Exercise

Create an application that creates two windows. The first window should have a TextInput component, and the second should have a Label component that shows the current contents of the TextInput in the first window.

Be sure to create the windows as instances of the main class and pass a reference of the main application into each window. Then you can reference them by instance name.

Interacting with the O.S.

AIR can interact with the underlying operating system by utilizing some of its existing features, including dock icons on Mac OS X, system tray icons on Microsoft Windows, and context right-click menus. The dock icons and system tray icons can also contain menus.

Dock Icons

Mac OS X has a dock that is mounted either at the right side, left side, or bottom of the screen. The dock contains shortcuts to open installed applications and also shows currently running applications. Chapter 6 demonstrated how to create custom icons for the installer. This icon would be the one shown in the dock when an application launches. AIR also gives us the ability to change the dock icon while the application is running. This can be very useful to display information to the user. Changing the icon is a simple process and simply requires the creation of a `flash.display` `.BitmapData` object. This can be created from an existing image displayed within the application or can be created from an embedded image class.

To get started, please create a new AIR project named *Chapter10_Dock*, which will create a new file named *Chapter10_Dock.mxml*. You will also need an image file to use as the dock icon. The source code that is part of this book has four PNG files representing four different-sized icons that I created. The image sizes are 16×16, 32×32, 48×48, and 128×128. As you will see shortly, the dock icon accepts an array of images of various sizes and then uses the best image to fit the situation; you can get away with using just one mid-sized image, which will be scaled accordingly.

We'll now proceed to the source code for adding a dock icon. Enter the code from Listing 10-1 into the newly created Chapter10_Dock.mxml file. If you only have one icon image that is 128×128, you could alternatively use the code from Listing 10-2, but the quality may not be acceptable when it is scaled to meet all the system requirements.

The code in Listing 10-1 first embeds four image files and types them as class objects. Next, on creationComplete of the application, the `init()` function is called where four new BitMap objects are created from the embedded images. Finally, the `NativeApplication.nativeApplication` `.icon.bitmaps` is set using the `bitMapData` properties from the BitMap objects.

The results of this can be seen in Figures 10-1 and 10-2. Figure 10-1 shows the image being used as the dock icon image, and Figure 10-2 shows the image being used within the Alt-Tab menu.

This section will provide additional code to add a dock icon menu and bounce functionality to the dock icon. The complete code for this section can be seen in Listing 10-5.

Listing 10-1: An example of a dock icon with four image files being created on Mac OS X

```
<?xml version="1.0" encoding="utf-8"?>
<mx:WindowedApplication xmlns:mx="http://www.adobe.com/2006/mxml"
    layout="absolute" creationComplete="init()">

    <mx:Script>
        <![CDATA[
            [Embed(source="e16.png")]
            [Bindable]
            private var Icon16:Class;
            [Embed(source="e32.png")]
            [Bindable]
            private var Icon32:Class;
            [Embed(source="e48.png")]
            [Bindable]
            private var Icon48:Class;
            [Embed(source="e128.png")]
            [Bindable]
            private var Icon128:Class;

            private function init():void{
                var bitmap16:Bitmap = new Icon16();
                var bitmap32:Bitmap = new Icon32();
                var bitmap48:Bitmap = new Icon48();
                var bitmap128:Bitmap = new Icon128();
                NativeApplication.nativeApplication.icon.bitmaps =
                                    [bitmap16.bitmapData,
                                     bitmap32.bitmapData,
                                     bitmap48.bitmapData,
                                     bitmap128.bitmapData];

            }

        ]]>
    </mx:Script>
</mx:WindowedApplication>
```

Listing 10-2: An example of a dock icon with one image being created on Mac OS X

```
<?xml version="1.0" encoding="utf-8"?>
<mx:WindowedApplication xmlns:mx="http://www.adobe.com/2006/mxml"
    layout="absolute" creationComplete="init()">

    <mx:Script>
        <![CDATA[
```

```
[Embed(source="e128.png")]
[Bindable]
private var Icon128:Class;

private function init():void{
    var bitmap128:Bitmap = new Icon128();
    NativeApplication.nativeApplication.icon.bitmaps =
[bitmap128.bitmapData];
    }

    ]]>

</mx:Script>
</mx:WindowedApplication>
```

Figure 10-1: The dock icon on Mac OS X.

Figure 10-2: The Alt-Tab menu with the new icon.

Menu

Dock icons also support the addition of *custom menus*. Adding a custom menu is very similar to adding a NativeMenu or a ContextMenu. You will simply need to build a NativeMenu object and then apply it to the DockIcon object. For more information on NativeMenus, please take a look at Chapter 12.

To add a menu to the dock icon, add the two functions from Listing 10-3 to the Chapter10_Dock.mxml file's script block. If you examine these functions, you will see that there is a createMenu() function and a handleMenuClick() function. The createMenu() function first creates a NativeMenu object and then creates four NativeMenuItem objects. Each NativeMenuItem has an event listener added and assigned the handleMenuClick() function, the function that will be called when the menu is selected. The NativeMenuItem items are then added to the NativeMenu object, and finally, if the NativeApplication .supportsDockIcon returns True, the NativeApplication.nativeApplication.icon is cast as a DockIcon and the menu is set.

When a NativeMenuItem is selected, the handleMenuClick() function is called and the appropriate action is taken.

The last thing you need to do is add a call to the createMenu() function within the Chapter10_Dock.mxml's init() function. The results can be seen in Figure 10-3.

Listing 10-3: The `createMenu()` **and** `handleMenuClick()` **functions**

```
private function createMenu():void{
    var dockMenu:NativeMenu = new NativeMenu();
    var minimizeMenu:NativeMenuItem = new NativeMenuItem("Minimize");
    var maximizeMenu:NativeMenuItem = new NativeMenuItem("Maximize");
    var restoreMenu:NativeMenuItem = new NativeMenuItem("Restore");
    var closeMenu:NativeMenuItem = new NativeMenuItem("Close");
    minimizeMenu.addEventListener(Event.SELECT, handleMenuClick);
    maximizeMenu.addEventListener(Event.SELECT, handleMenuClick);
    restoreMenu.addEventListener(Event.SELECT, handleMenuClick);
    closeMenu.addEventListener(Event.SELECT, handleMenuClick);
    dockMenu.addItem(minimizeMenu);
    dockMenu.addItem(maximizeMenu);
    dockMenu.addItem(restoreMenu);
    dockMenu.addItem(closeMenu);
    if(NativeApplication.supportsDockIcon) {
        DockIcon(NativeApplication.nativeApplication.icon).menu = dockMenu;
    }
}

private function handleMenuClick(e:Event):void{
    var menuItem:NativeMenuItem = e.target as NativeMenuItem;
    if(menuItem.label == "Minimize") this.minimize();
    if(menuItem.label == "Maximize") this.maximize();
    if(menuItem.label == "Restore") this.restore();
    if(menuItem.label == "Close") this.close();
}
```

Figure 10-3: The DockIcon menu.

Bounce

When an application is running but not currently in focus and wants to get the user's attention, the application will instruct the dock icon to *bounce*. AIR has added this functionality and provides two options. The icon can be set to bounce only once, or it can be set to bounce until the user interacts with it. The default is for the icon to bounce once only. Normally, you would want to set the dock icon to bounce when something changes within the application and the application is not currently in focus. In this example, we will mimic this situation by setting the icon to bounce after a 10-second delay.

Add the functions within Listing 10-4 to the script block on the Chapter10_Dock.mxml file. There are two methods. The first, called `bounceTimer()`, will create a Timer object that will run one time after waiting 10 seconds. When it runs, it will call the `timerHandler()` function, which will test to see if the `NativeApplication.supportsDockIcon` is true and then cast the `NativeApplication.nativeApplication.icon` as a DockIcon and call the `bounce()` method. In this case, the `bounce()` method is being passed the static `NotificationType.CRITICAL` property, which will cause the icon to bounce until the user interacts with it. If the `bounce()` method were passed nothing or `NotificationType.INFORMATIONAL`, the icon would bounce only one time.

Before testing this, you will need to add a call to the `bounceTimer()` function within the Chapter10_Dock.mxml `init()` function. Once you have done this, run the application, and then click on any other application so that the Chapter10_Dock application is no longer in focus. The icon will begin to bounce 10 seconds after the launch of the application.

Listing 10-4: The sample code to cause the icon to bounce

```
private function bounceTimer():void{
    var myTimer:Timer = new Timer(10000, 1);
    myTimer.addEventListener("timer", timerHandler);
    myTimer.start();
}


public function timerHandler(event:TimerEvent):void {
    if(NativeApplication.supportsDockIcon){

DockIcon(NativeApplication.nativeApplication.icon).bounce(NotificationType.CRITICAL
);
    }
}
```

Listing 10-5: The final full source for the dock icon examples including menu and bounce

```
<?xml version="1.0" encoding="utf-8"?>
<mx:WindowedApplication xmlns:mx="http://www.adobe.com/2006/mxml"
    layout="absolute" creationComplete="init()">

    <mx:Script>
        <![CDATA[
            [Embed(source="e16.png")]
            [Bindable]
            private var Icon16:Class;
            [Embed(source="e32.png")]
            [Bindable]
            private var Icon32:Class;
            [Embed(source="e48.png")]
            [Bindable]
            private var Icon48:Class;
            [Embed(source="e128.png")]
            [Bindable]
            private var Icon128:Class;
```

(Continued)

Listing 10-5: The final full source for the dock icon examples including menu and bounce
(continued)

```
private function init():void{
    var bitmap16:Bitmap = new Icon16();
    var bitmap32:Bitmap = new Icon32();
    var bitmap48:Bitmap = new Icon48();
    var bitmap128:Bitmap = new Icon128();
    NativeApplication.nativeApplication.icon.bitmaps =
                            [bitmap16.bitmapData,
                             bitmap32.bitmapData,
                             bitmap48.bitmapData,
                             bitmap128.bitmapData];

    createMenu();
    bounceTimer();
}

private function createMenu():void{
    var dockMenu:NativeMenu = new NativeMenu();
    var minimizeMenu:NativeMenuItem = new NativeMenuItem("Minimize");
    var maximizeMenu:NativeMenuItem = new NativeMenuItem("Maximize");
    var restoreMenu:NativeMenuItem = new NativeMenuItem("Restore");
    var closeMenu:NativeMenuItem = new NativeMenuItem("Close");
    minimizeMenu.addEventListener(Event.SELECT, handleMenuClick);
    maximizeMenu.addEventListener(Event.SELECT, handleMenuClick);
    restoreMenu.addEventListener(Event.SELECT, handleMenuClick);
    closeMenu.addEventListener(Event.SELECT, handleMenuClick);
    dockMenu.addItem(minimizeMenu);
    dockMenu.addItem(maximizeMenu);
    dockMenu.addItem(restoreMenu);
    dockMenu.addItem(closeMenu);
    if(NativeApplication.supportsDockIcon) {
        DockIcon(NativeApplication.nativeApplication.icon).menu = dockMenu;
    }
}

private function handleMenuClick(e:Event):void{
    var menuItem:NativeMenuItem = e.target as NativeMenuItem;
    if(menuItem.label == "Minimize") this.minimize();
    if(menuItem.label == "Maximize") this.maximize();
    if(menuItem.label == "Restore") this.restore();
    if(menuItem.label == "Close") this.close();
}

private function bounceTimer():void{
    var myTimer:Timer = new Timer(10000, 1);
    myTimer.addEventListener("timer", timerHandler);
    myTimer.start();
}157

public function timerHandler(event:TimerEvent):void {
    if(NativeApplication.supportsDockIcon){
        DockIcon(NativeApplication.nativeApplication.icon)
.bounce(NotificationType.CRITICAL);
```

```
            }
        }

    ]]>
    </mx:Script>
</mx:WindowedApplication>
```

System Tray Icons

The Windows system tray is located within the taskbar at the bottom right of the screen. This is the area where applications can have a small presence with the ability to provide controls and notifications to the user about the status of the application. Adding a system tray icon is the same as adding a dock icon on the Mac.

Let's start by creating a new AIR project named *Chapter10_SysTray*, which will create a new file named *Chapter10_SysTray.mxml*. Now enter the contents of Listing 10-6 into the Chapter10_SysTray.mxml file. Note that this listing is the same as Listing 10-1 but will change as we add features in the next few sections. As with the dock icon example, this example has four PNG files being used as icons. You can use a single image; however, the quality may not be acceptable when the image is scaled to meet all the system requirements.

The code in Listing 10-6 first embeds four image files and types them as class objects. Next, on creationComplete of the application, the init() function is called where four new BitMap objects are created from the embedded images. Finally, the NativeApplication.nativeApplication.icon .bitmaps is set using the bitMapData properties from the BitMap objects. The results can be seen in Figure 10-4.

This section will add additional code to add a system tray icon menu and tool-tip functionality to the system tray icon. The complete code for this section can be seen in Listing 10-9.

Listing 10-6: Example of a system tray icon with four image files being created on WindowsXP

```xml
<?xml version="1.0" encoding="utf-8"?>
<mx:WindowedApplication xmlns:mx="http://www.adobe.com/2006/mxml"
    layout="absolute" creationComplete="init()">

    <mx:Script>
        <![CDATA[
            [Embed(source="e16.png")]
            [Bindable]
            private var Icon16:Class;
            [Embed(source="e32.png")]
            [Bindable]
            private var Icon32:Class;
            [Embed(source="e48.png")]
            [Bindable]
            private var Icon48:Class;
            [Embed(source="e128.png")]
            [Bindable]
            private var Icon128:Class;
```

(Continued)

Listing 10-6: Example of a system tray icon with four image files being created on WindowsXP *(continued)*

```
        private function init():void{
            var bitmap16:Bitmap = new Icon16();
            var bitmap32:Bitmap = new Icon32();
            var bitmap48:Bitmap = new Icon48();
            var bitmap128:Bitmap = new Icon128();
            NativeApplication.nativeApplication.icon.bitmaps =
                            [bitmap16.bitmapData,
                             bitmap32.bitmapData,
                             bitmap48.bitmapData,
                             bitmap128.bitmapData];
        }

    ]]>
    </mx:Script>
</mx:WindowedApplication>
Tooltip
```

Figure 10-4: The system tray icon
on WindowsXP.

The `SystemTrayIcon` class also supports tool tips. Adding a tool tip is very simple and requires only one line of code. Listing 10-7 shows a function to add the tool tip to the system tray icon. It first needs to check to see if the `NativeApplication.supportsSystemTrayIcon` is true, and if so it casts the `NativeApplication.nativeApplication.icon` to a SystemTrayIcon object and then applies the tool tip using the `toolTip` property. Add the function shown in Listing 10-7 to the script block of Chapter10_SysTray.mxml, and then also add a call to the `createToolTip()` function to the `init()` function. The results can be seen in Figure 10-5.

Listing 10-7: The code needed to add a tool tip to the system tray icon

```
private function createToolTip():void{
    if(NativeApplication.supportsSystemTrayIcon){
        SystemTrayIcon(NativeApplication.nativeApplication.icon).tooltip =
"Sample Tooltip";
    }
}
```

Figure 10-5: The system tray icon with
tool tip.

Menu

As was the case with dock icons, system tray icons also support menus. These menus are launched with a right click in the same manner that context menus are launched on Windows. To add a menu to the system tray icon, add the two functions from Listing 10-8 to the script block on Chapter10_SysTray.mxml. You will also need to add a call to the createMenu() function within the init() function.

The createMenu() function first creates a NativeMenu object; next it creates four NativeMenuItem objects. Each NativeMenuItem has an event listener added and assigned the handleMenuClick() function, the function that will be called when the menu is selected. The NativeMenuItem items are then added to the NativeMenu object, and finally, if the NativeApplication.supportsSystemTrayIcon returns True, the NativeApplication.nativeApplication.icon is cast as a SystemTrayIcon and the menu is set. The results can be seen in Figure 10-6.

Figure 10-6: The system tray icon
with menu.

Listing 10-8: Functions needed to create and handle system tray menu functionality

```
private function createMenu():void{
    var trayMenu:NativeMenu = new NativeMenu();
    var minimizeMenu:NativeMenuItem = new NativeMenuItem("Minimize");
    var maximizeMenu:NativeMenuItem = new NativeMenuItem("Maximize");
    var restoreMenu:NativeMenuItem = new NativeMenuItem("Restore");
    var closeMenu:NativeMenuItem = new NativeMenuItem("Close");
    minimizeMenu.addEventListener(Event.SELECT, handleMenuClick);
    maximizeMenu.addEventListener(Event.SELECT, handleMenuClick);
    restoreMenu.addEventListener(Event.SELECT, handleMenuClick);
    closeMenu.addEventListener(Event.SELECT, handleMenuClick);
    trayMenu.addItem(minimizeMenu);
    trayMenu.addItem(maximizeMenu);
    trayMenu.addItem(restoreMenu);
    trayMenu.addItem(closeMenu);
    if(NativeApplication.supportsSystemTrayIcon){
        SystemTrayIcon(NativeApplication.nativeApplication.icon).menu = trayMenu;
    }
}

private function handleMenuClick(e:Event):void{
    var menuItem:NativeMenuItem = e.target as NativeMenuItem;
    if(menuItem.label == "Minimize") this.minimize();
    if(menuItem.label == "Maximize") this.maximize();
    if(menuItem.label == "Restore") this.restore();
    if(menuItem.label == "Close") this.close();
}
```

Listing 10-9: The final version of Chapter10_SysTray.mxml

```
<?xml version="1.0" encoding="utf-8"?>
<mx:WindowedApplication xmlns:mx="http://www.adobe.com/2006/mxml"
    layout="absolute" creationComplete="init()">

    <mx:Script>
        <![CDATA[
            [Embed(source="e16.png")]
            [Bindable]
            private var Icon16:Class;
            [Embed(source="e32.png")]
            [Bindable]
            private var Icon32:Class;
            [Embed(source="e48.png")]
            [Bindable]
            private var Icon48:Class;
            [Embed(source="e128.png")]
            [Bindable]
            private var Icon128:Class;

            private function init():void{
                var bitmap16:Bitmap = new Icon16();
                var bitmap32:Bitmap = new Icon32();
                var bitmap48:Bitmap = new Icon48();
                var bitmap128:Bitmap = new Icon128();
                NativeApplication.nativeApplication.icon.bitmaps =
                                    [bitmap16.bitmapData,
                                     bitmap32.bitmapData,
                                     bitmap48.bitmapData,
                                     bitmap128.bitmapData];

                createToolTip();
                createMenu();
            }

            private function createToolTip():void{
                if(NativeApplication.supportsSystemTrayIcon){

SystemTrayIcon(NativeApplication.nativeApplication.icon).tooltip =
"Sample Tooltip";
                }
            }

            private function createMenu():void{
                var trayMenu:NativeMenu = new NativeMenu();
                var minimizeMenu:NativeMenuItem = new NativeMenuItem("Minimize");
                var maximizeMenu:NativeMenuItem = new NativeMenuItem("Maximize");
                var restoreMenu:NativeMenuItem = new NativeMenuItem("Restore");
                var closeMenu:NativeMenuItem = new NativeMenuItem("Close");
                minimizeMenu.addEventListener(Event.SELECT, handleMenuClick);
                maximizeMenu.addEventListener(Event.SELECT, handleMenuClick);
```

```
        restoreMenu.addEventListener(Event.SELECT, handleMenuClick);
        closeMenu.addEventListener(Event.SELECT, handleMenuClick);
        trayMenu.addItem(minimizeMenu);
        trayMenu.addItem(maximizeMenu);
        trayMenu.addItem(restoreMenu);
        trayMenu.addItem(closeMenu);
        if(NativeApplication.supportsSystemTrayIcon){
            SystemTrayIcon(NativeApplication.nativeApplication.icon).menu =
trayMenu;
        }
    }

    private function handleMenuClick(e:Event):void{
        var menuItem:NativeMenuItem = e.target as NativeMenuItem;
        if(menuItem.label == "Minimize") this.minimize();
        if(menuItem.label == "Maximize") this.maximize();
        if(menuItem.label == "Restore") this.restore();
        if(menuItem.label == "Close") this.close();
    }

    ]]>
  </mx:Script>
</mx:WindowedApplication>
```

Context Menus

Context Menus, otherwise known as *Ctrl-Click menus* on Mac or *right-click menus* on Windows, are an important part of traditional desktop applications. AIR gives us the ability to add context menus on any object, which extends `flash.display.InteractiveObject`. This means that not only can you add a context menu to your application windows, but you can also add context menus to almost all of your visible components.

A context menu is of type `NativeMenu`, thus creating a context menu is the same as creating a `NativeMenu`, which is also covered in Chapter 12.

To demonstrate how to use context menus, please start by creating a new AIR project within Flex Builder 3 named *Chapter10_ContextMenu*, which will automatically create the main application file named *Chapter10_ContextMenu.mxml*. Now add the contents of Listing 10-10 to Chapter10_ContextMenu.mxml file.

If we examine Listing 10-10, you will see that upon `creationComplete` of the application, the `createMainMenu()` function is called. Within this function, a `NativeMenu` object is created, and four `NativeMenuItems` are also created. The `NativeMenuItems` are all assigned the same event listener so that when they are selected, the `handleMenuClick` function is called. This function evaluates the menu item that was selected and then calls the corresponding method on the application to minimize, maximize, restore, or close the application. The results can be seen in Figure 10-7.

The final version of this file can be seen in Listing 10-12.

Listing 10-10: How to create a context menu

```xml
<?xml version="1.0" encoding="utf-8"?>
<mx:WindowedApplication xmlns:mx="http://www.adobe.com/2006/mxml"
    layout="absolute" creationComplete="init()">
    <mx:Script>
        <![CDATA[
            private function init():void{
                createMainMenu();
            }

            private function createMainMenu():void{
                var mainMenu:NativeMenu = new NativeMenu();
                var minimizeMenu:NativeMenuItem = new NativeMenuItem("Minimize");
                var maximizeMenu:NativeMenuItem = new NativeMenuItem("Maximize");
                var restoreMenu:NativeMenuItem = new NativeMenuItem("Restore");
                var closeMenu:NativeMenuItem = new NativeMenuItem("Close");
                minimizeMenu.addEventListener(Event.SELECT, handleMenuClick);
                maximizeMenu.addEventListener(Event.SELECT, handleMenuClick);
                restoreMenu.addEventListener(Event.SELECT, handleMenuClick);
                closeMenu.addEventListener(Event.SELECT, handleMenuClick);
                mainMenu.addItem(minimizeMenu);
                mainMenu.addItem(maximizeMenu);
                mainMenu.addItem(restoreMenu);
                mainMenu.addItem(closeMenu);
                this.contextMenu=mainMenu;;
            }

            private function handleMenuClick(e:Event):void{
                var menuItem:NativeMenuItem = e.target as NativeMenuItem;
                if(menuItem.label == "Minimize") this.minimize();
                if(menuItem.label == "Maximize") this.maximize();
                if(menuItem.label == "Restore") this.restore();
                if(menuItem.label == "Close") this.close();
            }

        ]]>
    </mx:Script>
</mx:WindowedApplication>
```

One of the cool things about context menus is that, as I previously mentioned, they can be assigned to any object that extends InteractiveObject. This means that we can add specific menus to our content and still have a main context menu assigned to the application. To demonstrate this, add the code from Listing 10-11 to the script block of the Chapter10_Contextmenu.mxml file. You will also need to add a call to createImageMenu() to the init() function and then add <mx:Image id="myImage" source= "@Embed('e128.png')" horizontalCenter="0" verticalCenter="0"/> to the Chapter10_ ContextMenu.mxml file.

The createImageMenu() function will create a new NativeMenu with three NativeMenuItems to either scale or restore the image size. Each NativeMenuItem has an event handler set to call the handleImgClick()

function, which will evaluate which NativeMenuItem was selected and apply the proper scale. The results can be seen in Figure 10-8.

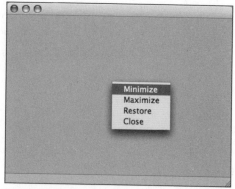

Figure 10-7: The context menu on the root of the application.

Listing 10-11: The functions needed to add a context menu

```
private function createImageMenu():void{
    var imgMenu:NativeMenu = new NativeMenu();
    var scaleBigger:NativeMenuItem = new NativeMenuItem("Scale Bigger");
    var scaleSmaller:NativeMenuItem = new NativeMenuItem("Scale Smaller");
    var restore:NativeMenuItem = new NativeMenuItem("Restore");
    scaleBigger.addEventListener(Event.SELECT, handleImgClick);
    scaleSmaller.addEventListener(Event.SELECT, handleImgClick);
    restore.addEventListener(Event.SELECT, handleImgClick);
    imgMenu.addItem(scaleBigger);
    imgMenu.addItem(scaleSmaller);
    imgMenu.addItem(restore);
    myImage.contextMenu = imgMenu;
}

private function handleImgClick(e:Event):void{
    var menuItem:NativeMenuItem = e.target as NativeMenuItem;
    if(menuItem.label == "Scale Bigger") {
        myImage.scaleX=2;
        myImage.scaleY=2;
    }
    if(menuItem.label == "Scale Smaller") {
        myImage.scaleX=.5;
        myImage.scaleY=.5;
    }
    if(menuItem.label == "Restore") {
        myImage.scaleX=1;
        myImage.scaleY=1;
    }
}
```

Figure 10-8: The context menu being applied to an Image component.

Listing 10-12: The final version of Chapter10_ContextMenu.mxml

```
<?xml version="1.0" encoding="utf-8"?>
<mx:WindowedApplication xmlns:mx="http://www.adobe.com/2006/mxml"
    layout="absolute" creationComplete="init()">
    <mx:Script>
        <![CDATA[
            private function init():void{
                createMainMenu();
                createImageMenu();
            }

            private function createMainMenu():void{
                var mainMenu:NativeMenu = new NativeMenu();
                var minimizeMenu:NativeMenuItem = new NativeMenuItem("Minimize");
                var maximizeMenu:NativeMenuItem = new NativeMenuItem("Maximize");
                var restoreMenu:NativeMenuItem = new NativeMenuItem("Restore");
                var closeMenu:NativeMenuItem = new NativeMenuItem("Close");
                minimizeMenu.addEventListener(Event.SELECT, handleMenuClick);
                maximizeMenu.addEventListener(Event.SELECT, handleMenuClick);
                restoreMenu.addEventListener(Event.SELECT, handleMenuClick);
                closeMenu.addEventListener(Event.SELECT, handleMenuClick);
                mainMenu.addItem(minimizeMenu);
                mainMenu.addItem(maximizeMenu);
                mainMenu.addItem(restoreMenu);
                mainMenu.addItem(closeMenu);
                this.contextMenu=mainMenu;;
            }

            private function handleMenuClick(e:Event):void{
                var menuItem:NativeMenuItem = e.target as NativeMenuItem;
                if(menuItem.label == "Minimize") this.minimize();
                if(menuItem.label == "Maximize") this.maximize();
                if(menuItem.label == "Restore") this.restore();
                if(menuItem.label == "Close") this.close();
            }
```

```
        private function createImageMenu():void{
          var imgMenu:NativeMenu = new NativeMenu();
          var scaleBigger:NativeMenuItem=new NativeMenuItem("Scale Bigger");
          var scaleSmaller:NativeMenuItem=new NativeMenuItem("Scale Smaller");
          var restore:NativeMenuItem = new NativeMenuItem("Restore");
          scaleBigger.addEventListener(Event.SELECT, handleImgClick);
          scaleSmaller.addEventListener(Event.SELECT, handleImgClick);
          restore.addEventListener(Event.SELECT, handleImgClick);
          imgMenu.addItem(scaleBigger);
          imgMenu.addItem(scaleSmaller);
          imgMenu.addItem(restore);
          myImage.contextMenu = imgMenu;
        }

        private function handleImgClick(e:Event):void{
            var menuItem:NativeMenuItem = e.target as NativeMenuItem;
            if(menuItem.label == "Scale Bigger") {
                myImage.scaleX=2;
                myImage.scaleY=2;
            }
            if(menuItem.label == "Scale Smaller") {
                myImage.scaleX=.5;
                myImage.scaleY=.5;
            }
            if(menuItem.label == "Restore") {
                myImage.scaleX=1;
                myImage.scaleY=1;
            }
        }
      ]]>
    </mx:Script>
    <mx:Image id="myImage" source="@Embed('e128.png')"
        horizontalCenter="0" verticalCenter="0"/>
  </mx:WindowedApplication>
```

Summary

This chapter has demonstrated the uses of the dock icons on Mac and the system tray icons on the PC. It also showed how to apply menus to these icons as well as context menus to the components of your AIR applications.

The next chapter covers the SQLite database that is embedded in the AIR runtime. AIR has provided an excellent API for interacting with SQLite, which gives us the ability to store local data within a relational database using familiar SQL syntax. Examples are given on how to create and manipulate data within a SQLite database.

Exercise

Create an application that assigns a different icon (either dock or system tray) when each window is in focus.

The SQLite Database

The release of AIR includes an embedded version of the SQLite database, which in my opinion is the most important feature of AIR. Many of the developers moving to AIR will come from a traditional web development background and will be accustomed to interacting with a database using SQL. The inclusion of SQLite in AIR will allow these developers to use their current SQL skills while interacting with a local offline database specific to their AIR application.

About SQLite

SQLite is a relational database management system contained in a relatively small C programming library. Unlike client-server database management systems, the SQLite engine is not a stand-alone process with which the program communicates. Instead, the SQLite library is linked in and thus becomes an integral part of the program. The program uses SQLite's functionality through simple function calls. This reduces latency in database access because function calls are more efficient than inter-process communication. The entire database (definitions, tables, indices, and the data itself) is stored as a single cross-platform file on a host machine. This simple design is achieved by locking the entire database file at the beginning of a transaction.

Getting Started

Before we can do any examples working with SQLite, we need to create a new SQLite database. The following section will demonstrate how to create such a SQLite database, create a table, insert data, read data, and delete data. For the examples in this chapter, please create a new AIR project named *Chapter11_SQLite*, and copy the contents of Listing 11-1 into *Chapter11_SQLite.mxml*. We will build on this file as we explore the features of SQLite throughout this chapter. At the end of each section, there will be a listing that shows the current version of the Chapter11_SQLite.mxml file.

Creating a SQLite Database

Creating a SQLite database is the same as creating a file. If you remember back in Chapter 8, we used a piece of code like this to create a file:

```
var newFile:File = File.desktopDirectory.resolvePath("MyNewFile.txt");
```

Creating a SQLite database is exactly the same except that the file extension will be .db. Before you can open the database, you will have to create a SQLConnection using the flash.data.SQLConnection class to do so.

To get started, let's take a look at the example in Listing 11-1 to see what is required to create a connection to a SQLite database. The first thing needed is imports of the needed SQL and File classes. Next a SQLConnection variable is set up as a class variable to allow for access by additional functions to come later in this chapter. Looking at the openDatabase function, you will notice that the SQLConnection class is an event-based class. The function begins by creating a new SQLConnection and then sets up an eventListener for handling potential errors. Next, the attempt is made to resolve to the database file using the File class's resolve method. Finally, if the file exists, an eventListener named openHandler is added, and if not, an eventListener named createHandler is added. Remember, that if the file does not exist, it will be created the first time this function runs.

Listing 11-1: The first version of the Chapter11_SQLite.mxml file

```
<?xml version="1.0" encoding="utf-8"?>
<mx:WindowedApplication xmlns:mx="http://www.adobe.com/2006/mxml"
  width="700" height="400">
  <mx:Script>
    <![CDATA[
      import mx.controls.Alert;
      import flash.filesystem.File;
      import flash.data.SQLConnection;
      import flash.events.SQLErrorEvent;
      import flash.events.SQLEvent;

      private var conn:SQLConnection;

      private function openDatabase():void{
        conn = new SQLConnection();
        conn.addEventListener(SQLErrorEvent.ERROR, errorHandler);

        var dbFile:File = File.applicationStorageDirectory.resolvePath("MyDB.db");
          if(dbFile.exists) {
            conn.addEventListener(SQLEvent.OPEN, openHandler);
          } else {
            conn.addEventListener(SQLEvent.OPEN, createHandler);
          }
          conn.openAsync(dbFile);
      }

      private function errorHandler(event:SQLErrorEvent):void {
        var err:String = "Error id:" + event.error.errorID +
          "\nDetails:" + event.error.details;
        Alert.show(err,"Error");
      }
```

```
        private function createHandler(event:SQLEvent):void {
          Alert.show("The database was created successfully", "createHandler");
        }

        private function openHandler(event:SQLEvent):void {
          Alert.show("The database was opened successfully", "openHandler");
        }
      ]]>
    </mx:Script>
    <mx:Button label="Create or Open Database" click="openDatabase()"/>
    <mx:HRule width="100%"/>
</mx:WindowedApplication>
```

On the first run of this application, the MyDB.db will be created on the desktop, and the createHandler will be called. The results can be seen in Figures 11-1 and 11-2.

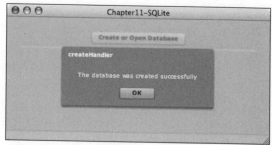

Figure 11-1: The application on its first run.

Figure 11-2: The newly created MyDB.db file within the applicationStorageDirectory.

Once the database has been created, the openHandler will be called on the next run of the application. This is demonstrated in Figure 11-3.

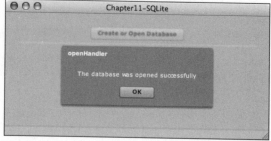

Figure 11-3: openHandler being called when the application runs a second time.

Creating a Table

Now that we have successfully created a new SQLite database, we can move on to creating a table in our new database. The first thing you will need to do is to add a new SQLStatement as a class variable. Right under the declaration of the conn variable, add the following:

```
private var createTableStatement:SQLStatement;
```

Since this new variable is of the type SQLStatement, we will also need to add the following import statement:

```
import flash.data.SQLStatement;
```

Now that we have our createTableStatement variable, we can move on to the actual createTable() function. Add the function contained within Listing 11-2 to the Chapter11_SQLite.mxml file.

Listing 11-2: The createTable() **function**

```
private function createTable():void{
    var sqlText:String = "CREATE TABLE Users(ID INTEGER PRIMARY KEY, " +
                                        "USER_NAME TEXT, PASSWORD TEXT)";
    createTableStatement = new SQLStatement();
    createTableStatement.sqlConnection = conn;
    createTableStatement.addEventListener(SQLEvent.RESULT, createTableResult);
    createTableStatement.addEventListener(SQLErrorEvent.ERROR, errorHandler);
    createTableStatement.text = sqlText;
    createTableStatement.execute();
}
```

Examining this function, you will notice that there is a string named *sqlText* that should be familiar to anyone who has been using SQL. This string will create a table named *Users* with three columns — ID, which is an Integer and also the Primary Key; USER_NAME, which is of type Text; and PASSWORD, which is also of type Text.

Next, an instance of the createTableStatement is created. The createTableStatement has several properties that must be set. The first is the sqlConnection, which is set to the conn variable that was set within the openDatabase() function. The next is the text property, which is set to the sqlText string that was created within the same function. Finally, there are two event listeners added, one to handle the result of the creation of the table and the other to handle any errors that may occur. The result handler named createTableResult means that we need to add an additional function to show the results. For the error handler we simply reuse the same errorHandler() function that was used in the openDatabase() function. Add the createTableResult() method below to the Chapter11_SQLite.mxml file.

```
private function createTableResult(event:SQLEvent):void {
    Alert.show("the table Users was created successfully");
}
```

Finally, simply add the following button to the Chapter11_SQLite.mxml file, and run the application. Be sure to click the "Create or Open Database" button before clicking the "Create Users Table" button to avoid errors, as the table cannot be created until the SQLConnection is opened. The results can be seen in Figures 11-4 and 11-5. Note that Figure 11-5 is of an open source project named *SQLite Database Browser*, which shows the database after it was created. SQLite Database Browser is a free stand-alone application available for both Windows and Mac at `http://sqlitebrowser.sourceforge.net/`.

```
<mx:Button label="Create Users Table" click="createTable()"/>
<mx:HRule width="100%"/>
```

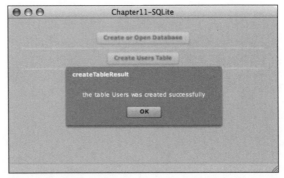

Figure 11-4: Example showing the application after the Users Table was created.

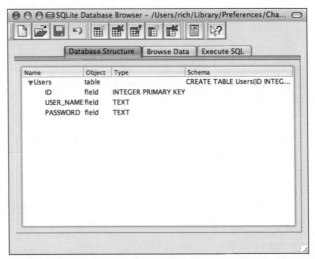

Figure 11-5: Table properties within SQLite Database Browser.

Listing 11-3: Second version of the Chapter11_SQLite.mxml file, which includes the `createTable()` **function**

```
<?xml version="1.0" encoding="utf-8"?>
<mx:WindowedApplication xmlns:mx="http://www.adobe.com/2006/mxml"
  width="700" height="400">
```

(Continued)

Listing 11-3: Second version of the Chapter11_SQLite.mxml file, which includes the `createTable()` **function** *(continued)*

```
<mx:Script>
  <![CDATA[
    import mx.controls.Alert;
    import flash.filesystem.File;
    import flash.data.SQLConnection;
    import flash.events.SQLErrorEvent;
    import flash.events.SQLEvent;
    import flash.data.SQLStatement;

    private var conn:SQLConnection;
    private var createTableStatement:SQLStatement;

    private function openDatabase():void{
      conn = new SQLConnection();
      conn.addEventListener(SQLErrorEvent.ERROR, errorHandler);

      var dbFile:File = File.applicationStorageDirectory.resolvePath("MyDB.db");
        if(dbFile.exists) {
          conn.addEventListener(SQLEvent.OPEN, openHandler);
        } else {
          conn.addEventListener(SQLEvent.OPEN, createHandler);
        }
        conn.openAsync(dbFile);
    }

    private function errorHandler(event:SQLErrorEvent):void {
      var err:String = "Error id:" + event.error.errorID +
          "\nDetails:" + event.error.details;
      Alert.show(err,"Error");
    }

    private function createHandler(event:SQLEvent):void {
      Alert.show("The database was created successfully", "createHandler");
    }

    private function openHandler(event:SQLEvent):void {
      Alert.show("The database was opened successfully", "openHandler");
    }

    private function createTable():void{
      var sqlText:String = "CREATE TABLE Users(ID INTEGER PRIMARY KEY, " +
                                      "USER_NAME TEXT, PASSWORD TEXT)";
      createTableStatement = new SQLStatement();
      createTableStatement.sqlConnection = conn;
      createTableStatement.addEventListener(SQLEvent.RESULT, createTableResult);
      createTableStatement.addEventListener(SQLErrorEvent.ERROR, errorHandler);
      createTableStatement.text = sqlText;
      createTableStatement.execute();
    }
```

```
    private function createTableResult(event:SQLEvent):void {
      Alert.show("the table Users was created successfully");
    }

  ]]>
</mx:Script>
<mx:Button label="Create or Open Database" click="openDatabase()"/>
<mx:HRule width="100%"/>
<mx:Button label="Create Users Table" click="createTable()"/>
<mx:HRule width="100%"/>
</mx:WindowedApplication>
```

Working with Data

Now that we have created a new database and added a new table to the database, we can start to add, retrieve, update, and delete data. The following section demonstrates how to do all of these using the SQLStatement class. Each of these operations is done by creating functions in the same manner as the createTable() function.

Saving Data

Saving data to our new table is a relatively painless process. Before we can work on the SQLStatement to do the data insert, we need to create some TextInput components to hold the data that need to be inserted. Add the block of code from Listing 11-4 to the bottom of the Chapter11_SQLite.mxml file.

Listing 11-4: The MXML code needed for the TextInput components

```
<mx:HBox>
  <mx:Label text="Username:"/>
  <mx:TextInput id="usernameTxt" width="100" text="rich"/>
  <mx:Label text="Password:"/>
  <mx:TextInput id="passwordTxt" displayAsPassword="true" width="100"
                text="password"/>
  <mx:Button label="Insert User" click="insertRecord()"/>
</mx:HBox>
<mx:HRule width="100%"/>
```

Notice, in the <mx:Button> component, the click property calls an insertRecord() function that has yet to be created. Before creating this function, we need to add a SQLStatement to the file named insertStatement. Add this new var to the Chapter11_SQLite.mxml in the same way you did with the createTableStatement var.

```
private var insertStatement:SQLStatement;
```

Now, we can create the new function named insertRecord(), which will actually do the work of inserting the new record into the Users Table. Add the function from Listing 11-5 to the Chapter11_SQLIte.mxml file.

Listing 11-5: The `insertRecord()` **function**

```
private function insertRecord():void{
   var sqlText:String = "INSERT INTO Users(USER_NAME, PASSWORD) " +
                                       "VALUES(:username,:password)";
   insertStatement = new SQLStatement();
   insertStatement.sqlConnection = conn;
   insertStatement.addEventListener(SQLEvent.RESULT, insertResult);
   insertStatement.addEventListener(SQLErrorEvent.ERROR, errorHandler);
   insertStatement.text = sqlText;
   insertStatement.parameters[":username"] = usernameTxt.text;
   insertStatement.parameters[":password"] = passwordTxt.text;
   insertStatement.execute();
}
```

The `insertRecord()` function in Listing 11-5 follows the same format as the `createTable()` function that was previously added. Take a look back at Listing 11-2, and compare it to Listing 11-5. Other than the sqlText string containing an `INSERT SQL` statement, the name of the `SQLStatement`, and the `SQLEvent` `.RESULT` listener pointing to a new function named `insertResult()`, they are identical. Speaking of the `insertResult()` method, we need to add this method as well. Copy the function in Listing 11-6 into the Chapter11_SQLite.mxml file. Notice that this result handler also includes a few lines to clear the values of the TextInput components.

Listing 11-6: The `insertResult()` **function**

```
private function insertResult(event:SQLEvent):void {
   usernameTxt.text = "";
   passwordTxt.text = "";
   Alert.show("the record was inserted successfully", "insertResult");
}
```

Go ahead and run the application, making sure that you first click the button to open the database and then the Create Users Table button. Notice that since you already created the Users Table in the previous section of this chapter, you will see the error handler get fired (see Figure 11-6). Now click the Insert User button to insert the values from the username and password fields into the Users Table. The results can be seen in Figures 11-7 and 11-8. Figure 11-8 shows the view from the SQLite Database Browser of the actual data now existing in the Users Table.

Figure 11-6: Illustration showing the default error handler being called.

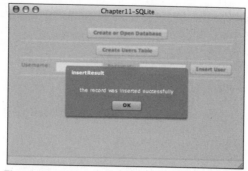

Figure 11-7: The successful insert of the new record.

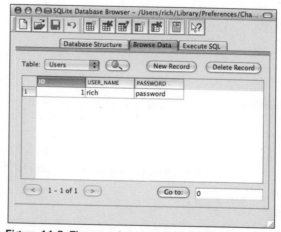

Figure 11-8: The new data in the Users Table.

Listing 11-7: Third version of the Chapter11_SQLite.mxml file, which includes the `insertRecord()` **function**

```
<?xml version="1.0" encoding="utf-8"?>
<mx:WindowedApplication xmlns:mx="http://www.adobe.com/2006/mxml"
 width="700" height="400">

  <mx:Script>
    <![CDATA[
      import mx.controls.Alert;
      import flash.filesystem.File;
      import flash.data.SQLConnection;
      import flash.events.SQLErrorEvent;
      import flash.events.SQLEvent;
      import flash.data.SQLStatement;

      private var conn:SQLConnection;
      private var createTableStatement:SQLStatement;
      private var insertStatement:SQLStatement;
```

(Continued)

```
private function openDatabase():void{
  conn = new SQLConnection();
  conn.addEventListener(SQLErrorEvent.ERROR, errorHandler);

  var dbFile:File = File.applicationStorageDirectory.resolvePath("MyDB.db");
    if(dbFile.exists) {
      conn.addEventListener(SQLEvent.OPEN, openHandler);
    } else {
      conn.addEventListener(SQLEvent.OPEN, createHandler);
    }
    conn.openAsync(dbFile);
}

private function errorHandler(event:SQLErrorEvent):void {
  var err:String = "Error ID:" + event.error.errorID+
      "\nDetails:" + event.error.details;
  Alert.show(err,"Error");
}

private function createHandler(event:SQLEvent):void {
  Alert.show("The database was created successfully", "createHandler");
}

private function openHandler(event:SQLEvent):void {
  Alert.show("The database was opened successfully", "openHandler");
}

private function createTable():void{
  var sqlText:String = "CREATE TABLE Users(ID INTEGER PRIMARY KEY, " +
                                    "USER_NAME TEXT, PASSWORD TEXT)";

  createTableStatement = new SQLStatement();
  createTableStatement.sqlConnection = conn;
  createTableStatement.addEventListener(SQLEvent.RESULT, createTableResult);
  createTableStatement.addEventListener(SQLErrorEvent.ERROR, errorHandler);
  createTableStatement.text = sqlText;
  createTableStatement.execute();
}
private function createTableResult(event:SQLEvent):void {
  Alert.show("the table Users was created successfully");
}

private function insertRecord():void{
  var sqlText:String = "INSERT INTO Users(USER_NAME, PASSWORD) " +
                              "VALUES(:username,:password)";

  insertStatement = new SQLStatement();
  insertStatement.sqlConnection = conn;
  insertStatement.addEventListener(SQLEvent.RESULT, insertResult);
  insertStatement.addEventListener(SQLErrorEvent.ERROR, errorHandler);
  insertStatement.text = sqlText;
  insertStatement.parameters[":username"] = usernameTxt.text;
```

```
        insertStatement.parameters[":password"] = passwordTxt.text;
        insertStatement.execute();
    }

    private function insertResult(event:SQLEvent):void {
        usernameTxt.text = "";
        passwordTxt.text = "";
        Alert.show("the record was inserted successfully", "insertResult");
    }

    ]]>
</mx:Script>
<mx:Button label="Create or Open Database" click="openDatabase()"/>
<mx:HRule width="100%"/>
<mx:Button label="Create Users Table" click="createTable()"/>
<mx:HRule width="100%"/>
<mx:HBox>
  <mx:Label text="Username:"/>
  <mx:TextInput id="usernameTxt" width="100" text="rich"/>
  <mx:Label text="Password:"/>
  <mx:TextInput id="passwordTxt" displayAsPassword="true" width="100"
              text="password"/>
  <mx:Button label="Insert User" click="insertRecord()"/>
</mx:HBox>
<mx:HRule width="100%"/>
</mx:WindowedApplication>
```

Retrieving Data

Now that we have some data in the Users Table, it would be nice if we could retrieve that data. Again, creating the function to get the data is the same as the last two functions for creating the Users Table and inserting data. Add the following variable instance to the Chapter11_SQLite.mxml file.

```
private var selectAllSQL:SQLStatement;
```

We also need an additional import, which will be used as part of the result handler.

```
import flash.data.SQLResult;
```

Now we need to add the function to select all of the users. Please add the selectAllUsers() function from Listing 11-8 into the Chapter11_SQLite.mxml file.

Listing 11-8: The selectAllUsers() **function**

```
private function selectAllUsers():void{
  var sqlText:String = "SELECT * FROM Users";
  selectAllSQL = new SQLStatement();
  selectAllSQL.sqlConnection = conn;
  selectAllSQL.addEventListener(SQLEvent.RESULT, selectAllUsersResult);
  selectAllSQL.addEventListener(SQLErrorEvent.ERROR, errorHandler);
  selectAllSQL.text = sqlText;
  selectAllSQL.execute();
}
```

I hope you've noticed by now that we need to have a result handler. In this case, the result handler function is set as `selectAllUsersResult()`. Add the result handler below.

```
private function selectAllUsersResult(event:SQLEvent):void{
    var result:SQLResult = selectAllSQL.getResult();
    var users:ArrayCollection = new ArrayCollection();
    grid.dataProvider = result.data;
}
```

Also, add import statement for ArrayCollection

```
import mx.collections.ArrayCollection;
```

Now we need to add a `<mx:DataGrid>` to hold the results and another button to call the `selectAllUsers()` function. The dataProvider is being set within the `selectAllUsersResult()` function.

```
<mx:Button click="selectAllUsers()" label="Select All Users"/>
<mx:DataGrid id="grid" width="320" height="100"/>
<mx:HRule width="100%"/>
```

Make sure when you run this code to click the "Create or Open the Database" button and that you have added at least one record. Now hit the "Select All Users" button, and you should see something like Figure 11-9.

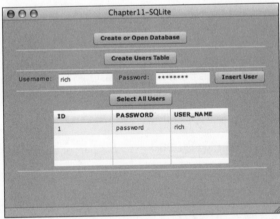

Figure 11-9: The results of the `selectAllUsers()` function.

So now you have selected data and applied the result to a dataProvider of an `<mx:DataGrid>`, but what about individual records?

To select a single user, we will add an additional `SQLStatement` named `selectUserSQL`, a `searchForUser()` function, and a result handler function named `searchForUserResult()`. Add the code from Listing 11-9 to the Chapter11_SQLite.mxml file.

Listing 11-9: The `selectUser` **SQLStatement,** `searchForUser()` **function, and** `searchForUserResult()` **function**

```
private var selectUserSQL:SQLStatement;

private function searchForUser():void{
  var sqlText:String = "SELECT * FROM Users WHERE ID = " + userId.value;
  selectUserSQL = new SQLStatement();
  selectUserSQL.sqlConnection = conn;
  selectUserSQL.addEventListener(SQLEvent.RESULT, searchForUserResult);
  selectUserSQL.addEventListener(SQLErrorEvent.ERROR, errorHandler);
  selectUserSQL.text = sqlText;
  selectUserSQL.execute();
}

private function searchForUserResult(event:SQLEvent):void{
  var result:SQLResult = selectUserSQL.getResult();
  if(result.data.length){
    idTxt.text = result.data[0]["ID"];
    unameTxt.text = result.data[0]["USER_NAME"];
    pwordTxt.text = result.data[0]["PASSWORD"];
  }
}
```

Also, add a Numeric stepper and button to call the `searchForUser()` function and some new TextInput components to hold the result.

Listing 11-10: The components needed to add the search functionality

```
<mx:HBox>
  <mx:NumericStepper id="userId" minimum="1" stepSize="1"  />
  <mx:Button click="searchForUser()" label="Search For User"/>
</mx:HBox>
<mx:Label text="RESULTS"/>
<mx:HBox>
  <mx:Label text="ID:"/>
  <mx:TextInput id="idTxt" width="20" editable="false"/>
  <mx:Label text="Username:"/>
  <mx:TextInput id="unameTxt" width="100"/>
  <mx:Label text="Password:"/>
  <mx:TextInput id="pwordTxt" width="100"/>
</mx:HBox>
<mx:HRule width="100%"/>
```

Run the application, and again be sure to open the database before trying the search for user functionality. If you have been following the steps in this chapter, you should have a user with an ID of 1. Click the "Search for User" button, and you should see something similar to Figure 11-10.

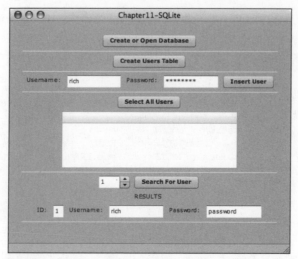

Figure 11-10: The results of the `searchForUser()` function.

Listing 11-11: Fourth version of the Chapter11_SQLite.mxml file, which includes the `selectAllUsers()` **and** `searchForUser()` **functions**

```
<?xml version="1.0" encoding="utf-8"?>
<mx:WindowedApplication xmlns:mx="http://www.adobe.com/2006/mxml"
    width="700" height="400">
  <mx:Script>
    <![CDATA[
      import flash.data.SQLResult;
      import flash.data.SQLStatement;
      import mx.controls.Alert;
      import flash.filesystem.File;
      import flash.data.SQLConnection;
      import flash.events.SQLErrorEvent;
      import flash.events.SQLEvent;

      private var conn:SQLConnection;
      private var createTableStatement:SQLStatement;
      private var insertStatement:SQLStatement;
      private var selectAllSQL:SQLStatement;
      private var selectUserSQL:SQLStatement;

      private function openDatabase():void{
        conn = new SQLConnection();
        conn.addEventListener(SQLErrorEvent.ERROR, errorHandler);

        var dbFile:File = File.applicationStorageDirectory.resolvePath("MyDB.db");
        if(dbFile.exists) {
          conn.addEventListener(SQLEvent.OPEN, openHandler);
        } else {
          conn.addEventListener(SQLEvent.OPEN, createHandler);
        }
```

```
    conn.openAsync(dbFile);
}

private function errorHandler(event:SQLErrorEvent):void {
  var err:String = "Error id:" + event.error.errorID + "\nDetails:" +
                    event.error.details;
  Alert.show(err,"Error");
}

private function createHandler(event:SQLEvent):void {
  Alert.show("The database was created successfully", "createHandler");
}

private function openHandler(event:SQLEvent):void {
  Alert.show("The database was opened successfully", "openHandler");
}

private function createTable():void{
  var sqlText:String = "CREATE TABLE Users(ID INTEGER PRIMARY KEY, " +
                        "USER_NAME TEXT, PASSWORD TEXT)";
  createTableStatement = new SQLStatement();
  createTableStatement.sqlConnection = conn;
  createTableStatement.addEventListener(SQLEvent.RESULT, createTableResult);
  createTableStatement.addEventListener(SQLErrorEvent.ERROR, errorHandler);
  createTableStatement.text = sqlText;
  createTableStatement.execute();
}

private function createTableResult(event:SQLEvent):void {
 Alert.show("the table Users was created successfully", "createTableResult");
}

private function insertRecord():void{
  var sqlText:String = "INSERT INTO Users(USER_NAME, PASSWORD) " +
                          "VALUES(:username,:password)";
  insertStatement = new SQLStatement();
  insertStatement.sqlConnection = conn;
  insertStatement.addEventListener(SQLEvent.RESULT, insertResult);
  insertStatement.addEventListener(SQLErrorEvent.ERROR, errorHandler);
  insertStatement.text = sqlText;
  insertStatement.parameters[":username"] = usernameTxt.text;
  insertStatement.parameters[":password"] = passwordTxt.text;
  insertStatement.execute();
}

private function insertResult(event:SQLEvent):void {
  usernameTxt.text = "";
  passwordTxt.text = "";
  Alert.show("the record was inserted successfully", "insertResult");
}

private function selectAllUsers():void{
  var sqlText:String = "SELECT * FROM Users";
  selectAllSQL = new SQLStatement();
```

(Continued)

183

Listing 11-11: Fourth version of the Chapter11_SQLite.mxml file, which includes the
`selectAllUsers()` **and** `searchForUser()` **functions** *(continued)*

```
            selectAllSQL.sqlConnection = conn;
            selectAllSQL.addEventListener(SQLEvent.RESULT, selectAllUsersResult);
            selectAllSQL.addEventListener(SQLErrorEvent.ERROR, errorHandler);
            selectAllSQL.text = sqlText;
            selectAllSQL.execute();
        }
        private function selectAllUsersResult(event:SQLEvent):void{
            var result:SQLResult = selectAllSQL.getResult();
            grid.dataProvider = result.data;
        }

        private function searchForUser():void{
            var sqlText:String = "SELECT * FROM Users WHERE ID = " + userId.value;
            selectUserSQL = new SQLStatement();
            selectUserSQL.sqlConnection = conn;
            selectUserSQL.addEventListener(SQLEvent.RESULT, searchForUserResult);
            selectUserSQL.addEventListener(SQLErrorEvent.ERROR, errorHandler);
            selectUserSQL.text = sqlText;
            selectUserSQL.execute();
        }

        private function searchForUserResult(event:SQLEvent):void{
            var result:SQLResult = selectUserSQL.getResult();
            if(result.data.length){
                idTxt.text = result.data[0]["ID"];
                unameTxt.text = result.data[0]["USER_NAME"];
                pwordTxt.text = result.data[0]["PASSWORD"];
            }
        }

    ]]>
</mx:Script>
<mx:Button label="Create or Open Database" click="openDatabase()"/>
<mx:HRule width="100%"/>
<mx:Button label="Create Users Table" click="createTable()"/>
<mx:HRule width="100%"/>
<mx:HBox>
  <mx:Label text="Username:"/>
  <mx:TextInput id="usernameTxt" width="100" text="rich"/>
  <mx:Label text="Password:"/>
  <mx:TextInput id="passwordTxt" displayAsPassword="true" width="100"
    text="password"/>
  <mx:Button label="Insert User" click="insertRecord()"/>
</mx:HBox>
    <mx:HRule width="100%"/>
    <mx:Button click="selectAllUsers()" label="Select All Users"/>
    <mx:DataGrid id="grid" width="320" height="100"/>
    <mx:HRule width="100%"/>
<mx:HBox>
    <mx:NumericStepper id="userId" minimum="1" stepSize="1"  />
```

```
    <mx:Button click="searchForUser()" label="Search For User"/>
  </mx:HBox>
  <mx:Label text="RESULTS"/>
  <mx:HBox>
    <mx:Label text="ID:"/>
    <mx:TextInput id="idTxt" width="20" editable="false"/>
    <mx:Label text="Username:"/>
    <mx:TextInput id="unameTxt" width="100"/>
    <mx:Label text="Password:"/>
    <mx:TextInput id="pwordTxt" width="100"/>
  </mx:HBox>
  <mx:HRule width="100%"/>
</mx:WindowedApplication>
```

Updating Data

Adding an update function to the Chapter11_SQLite.mxml file will require minimal changes. All we need to do is add another SQLStatement, update function, and update result handler. Simply add the code from Listing 11-12 to the Chapter11_SQLite.mxml file.

Listing 11-12: The ActionScript needed for update functionality

```
private var updateUserSQL:SQLStatement;

private function updateUser():void{
    var sqlText:String = "UPDATE Users " +
                         "SET USER_NAME = :username, " +
                         "PASSWORD = :password " +
                         "WHERE ID = :id";
    updateUserSQL = new SQLStatement();
    updateUserSQL.sqlConnection = conn;
    updateUserSQL.addEventListener(SQLEvent.RESULT, updateResult);
    updateUserSQL.addEventListener(SQLErrorEvent.ERROR, errorHandler);
    updateUserSQL.text = sqlText;
    updateUserSQL.parameters[":username"] = unameTxt.text;
    updateUserSQL.parameters[":password"] = pwordTxt.text;
    updateUserSQL.parameters[":id"] = Number(idTxt.text);
    updateUserSQL.execute();
}

private function updateResult(event:SQLEvent):void{
    idTxt.text = "";
    unameTxt.text = "";
    pwordTxt.text = "";
    selectAllUsers();
    Alert.show("the record was updated successfully", "updateResult");
}
```

If you take a quick look at the updateUser() function, you will notice that it is a standard SQL update statement with the TextInput component's text properties used for the new values and the idTxt's text property cast as a Number for the where clause. The updateResult() function simply resets the text properties to "empty string," calls selectAllUsers() to repopulate the DataGrid, and throws an Alert.

Now, we need to add a button that will call the updateUser() function. Add the following right under the <mx:TextInput> component with the ID pwordTxt.

```
<mx:Button click="updateUser()" label="Update User"/>
```

You should now be able to run the application. Start by opening the database connection by clicking on the "Create or Open Database" button, and then click the "Select All Users" button. You should now see at least one user; if not, add one using the "Insert User" button, and refresh by clicking "Select All Users" again. Use the "Search for User" button to load in one of the users by ID. Edit the username or password, and click the "Update User" button. You should see something like Figure 11-11.

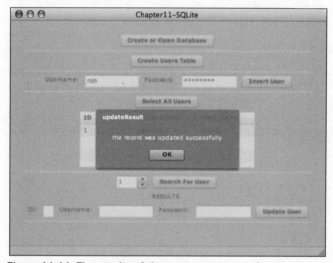

Figure 11-11: The results of the updateUser() function.

Listing 11-13: The fifth version of the Chapter11_SQLite.mxml file, which includes the updateUser() function

```xml
<?xml version="1.0" encoding="utf-8"?>
<mx:WindowedApplication xmlns:mx="http://www.adobe.com/2006/mxml"
    width="700" height="400">
  <mx:Script>
    <![CDATA[
      import flash.data.SQLResult;
      import flash.data.SQLStatement;
      import mx.controls.Alert;
      import flash.filesystem.File;
      import flash.data.SQLConnection;
      import flash.events.SQLErrorEvent;
      import flash.events.SQLEvent;

      private var conn:SQLConnection;
```

```
private var createTableStatement:SQLStatement;
private var insertStatement:SQLStatement;
private var selectAllSQL:SQLStatement;
private var selectUserSQL:SQLStatement;
private var updateUserSQL:SQLStatement;

private function openDatabase():void{
  conn = new SQLConnection();
  conn.addEventListener(SQLErrorEvent.ERROR, errorHandler);

  var dbFile:File = File.applicationStorageDirectory.resolvePath("MyDB.db");
  if(dbFile.exists) {
    conn.addEventListener(SQLEvent.OPEN, openHandler);
  } else {
    conn.addEventListener(SQLEvent.OPEN, createHandler);
  }
  conn.openAsync(dbFile);
}

private function errorHandler(event:SQLErrorEvent):void {
  var err:String = "Error id:" + event.error.errorID + "\nDetails:" +
                    event.error.details;
  Alert.show(err,"Error");
}

private function createHandler(event:SQLEvent):void {
  Alert.show("The database was created successfully", "createHandler");
}

private function openHandler(event:SQLEvent):void {
  Alert.show("The database was opened successfully", "openHandler");
}

private function createTable():void{
  var sqlText:String = "CREATE TABLE Users(ID INTEGER PRIMARY KEY, " +
                        "USER_NAME TEXT, PASSWORD TEXT)";
  createTableStatement = new SQLStatement();
  createTableStatement.sqlConnection = conn;
  createTableStatement.addEventListener(SQLEvent.RESULT, createTableResult);
  createTableStatement.addEventListener(SQLErrorEvent.ERROR, errorHandler);
  createTableStatement.text = sqlText;
  createTableStatement.execute();
}

private function createTableResult(event:SQLEvent):void {
  Alert.show("the table Users was created successfully", "createTableResult");
}

private function insertRecord():void{
  var sqlText:String = "INSERT INTO Users(USER_NAME, PASSWORD) " +
                        "VALUES(:username,:password)";
  insertStatement = new SQLStatement();
  insertStatement.sqlConnection = conn;
```

(Continued)

```
    insertStatement.addEventListener(SQLEvent.RESULT, insertResult);
    insertStatement.addEventListener(SQLErrorEvent.ERROR, errorHandler);
    insertStatement.text = sqlText;
    insertStatement.parameters[":username"] = usernameTxt.text;
    insertStatement.parameters[":password"] = passwordTxt.text;
    insertStatement.execute();
}

private function insertResult(event:SQLEvent):void {
    usernameTxt.text = "";
    passwordTxt.text = "";
    Alert.show("the record was inserted successfully", "insertResult");
}

private function selectAllUsers():void{
    var sqlText:String = "SELECT * FROM Users";
    selectAllSQL = new SQLStatement();
    selectAllSQL.sqlConnection = conn;
    selectAllSQL.addEventListener(SQLEvent.RESULT, selectAllUsersResult);
    selectAllSQL.addEventListener(SQLErrorEvent.ERROR, errorHandler);
    selectAllSQL.text = sqlText;
    selectAllSQL.execute();
}
private function selectAllUsersResult(event:SQLEvent):void{
    var result:SQLResult = selectAllSQL.getResult();
    grid.dataProvider = result.data;
}

private function searchForUser():void{
    var sqlText:String = "SELECT * FROM Users WHERE ID = " + userId.value;
    selectUserSQL = new SQLStatement();
    selectUserSQL.sqlConnection = conn;
    selectUserSQL.addEventListener(SQLEvent.RESULT, searchForUserResult);
    selectUserSQL.addEventListener(SQLErrorEvent.ERROR, errorHandler);
    selectUserSQL.text = sqlText;
    selectUserSQL.execute();
}
private function searchForUserResult(event:SQLEvent):void{
    var result:SQLResult = selectUserSQL.getResult();
    if(result.data.length){
        idTxt.text = result.data[0]["ID"];
        unameTxt.text = result.data[0]["USER_NAME"];
        pwordTxt.text = result.data[0]["PASSWORD"];
    }
}

private function updateUser():void{
    var sqlText:String = "UPDATE Users " +
```

```
                              "SET USER_NAME = :username, " +
                              "PASSWORD = :password " +
                              "WHERE ID = :id";
        updateUserSQL = new SQLStatement();
        updateUserSQL.sqlConnection = conn;
        updateUserSQL.addEventListener(SQLEvent.RESULT, updateResult);
        updateUserSQL.addEventListener(SQLErrorEvent.ERROR, errorHandler);
        updateUserSQL.text = sqlText;
        updateUserSQL.parameters[":username"] = unameTxt.text;
        updateUserSQL.parameters[":password"] = pwordTxt.text;
        updateUserSQL.parameters[":id"] = Number(idTxt.text);
        updateUserSQL.execute();
    }

    private function updateResult(event:SQLEvent):void{
        idTxt.text = "";
        unameTxt.text = "";
        pwordTxt.text = "";
        selectAllUsers();
        Alert.show("the record was updated successfully", "updateResult");
    }

  ]]>
</mx:Script>
<mx:Button label="Create or Open Database" click="openDatabase()"/>
<mx:HRule width="100%"/>
<mx:Button label="Create Users Table" click="createTable()"/>
<mx:HRule width="100%"/>
<mx:HBox>
  <mx:Label text="Username:"/>
  <mx:TextInput id="usernameTxt" width="100" text="rich"/>
  <mx:Label text="Password:"/>
  <mx:TextInput id="passwordTxt" displayAsPassword="true" width="100"
    text="password"/>
  <mx:Button label="Insert User" click="insertRecord()"/>
  </mx:HBox>
    <mx:HRule width="100%"/>
    <mx:Button click="selectAllUsers()" label="Select All Users"/>
    <mx:DataGrid id="grid" width="320" height="100"/>
    <mx:HRule width="100%"/>
  <mx:HBox>
    <mx:NumericStepper id="userId" minimum="1" stepSize="1"  />
    <mx:Button click="searchForUser()" label="Search For User"/>
  </mx:HBox>
  <mx:Label text="RESULTS"/>
  <mx:HBox>
    <mx:Label text="ID:"/>
    <mx:TextInput id="idTxt" width="20" editable="false"/>
    <mx:Label text="Username:"/>
    <mx:TextInput id="unameTxt" width="100"/>
    <mx:Label text="Password:"/>
    <mx:TextInput id="pwordTxt" width="100"/>
```

(Continued)

Listing 11-13: The fifth version of the Chapter11_SQLite.mxml file, which includes the `updateUser()` **function** *(continued)*

```
        <mx:Button click="updateUser()" label="Update User"/>
    </mx:HBox>
    <mx:HRule width="100%"/>
</mx:WindowedApplication>
```

Deleting Data

The last SQL functionality this chapter will cover is the code needed to delete data from the SQLite database. Again, there will be a single property and two functions that will be added. Add the contents of Listing 11-14 to the Chapter11_SQLite.mxml file.

Listing 11-14: The ActionScript needed for delete functionality

```
private var deleteUserSQL:SQLStatement;

private function deleteUser():void{
   var sqlText:String = "DELETE FROM Users " +
                        "WHERE ID = :id";
   deleteUserSQL = new SQLStatement();
   deleteUserSQL.sqlConnection = conn;
   deleteUserSQL.addEventListener(SQLEvent.RESULT, deleteResult);
   deleteUserSQL.addEventListener(SQLErrorEvent.ERROR, errorHandler);
   deleteUserSQL.text = sqlText;
   deleteUserSQL.parameters[":id"] = Number(idTxt.text);
   deleteUserSQL.execute();
}

private function deleteResult(event:SQLEvent):void{
   idTxt.text = "";
   unameTxt.text = "";
   pwordTxt.text = "";
   selectAllUsers();
   Alert.show("the record was deleted successfully", "deleteResult");
}
```

The `deleteUser()` function follows the same format as the `searchForUser()` and `updateUser()` functions. The result handler resets the TextInput components to empty string values and then calls `selectAllUsers()` to repopulate the data grid.

Next, you will need to add a button to call the `deleteUser()` function. Add the button below to the Chapter11_SQLite.mxml file directly under the Update User button.

```
<mx:Button click="deleteUser()" label="Delete User"/>
```

Run the application, making sure to open the database connection by clicking the "Create or Open Database" button, and then click the "Select All Users" button. Now load a user by clicking the "Search for User" button. Click the "Delete User" button, and the user record that you loaded will be deleted. The results can be seen in Figure 11-12.

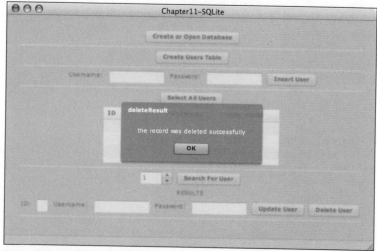

Figure 11-12: The result of the deleteUser() function.

Listing 11-15: The sixth and last version of the Chapter11_SQLite.mxml file, which includes the deleteUser() function

```
<?xml version="1.0" encoding="utf-8"?>
<mx:WindowedApplication xmlns:mx="http://www.adobe.com/2006/mxml"
    width="700" height="400">
  <mx:Script>
    <![CDATA[
      import flash.data.SQLResult;
      import flash.data.SQLStatement;
      import mx.controls.Alert;
      import flash.filesystem.File;
      import flash.data.SQLConnection;
      import flash.events.SQLErrorEvent;
      import flash.events.SQLEvent;

      private var conn:SQLConnection;
      private var createTableStatement:SQLStatement;
      private var insertStatement:SQLStatement;
      private var selectAllSQL:SQLStatement;
      private var selectUserSQL:SQLStatement;
      private var updateUserSQL:SQLStatement;
      private var deleteUserSQL:SQLStatement;

      private function openDatabase():void{
        conn = new SQLConnection();
        conn.addEventListener(SQLErrorEvent.ERROR, errorHandler);

        var dbFile:File = File.applicationStorageDirectory.resolvePath("MyDB.db");
        if(dbFile.exists) {
          conn.addEventListener(SQLEvent.OPEN, openHandler);
```

(Continued)

Listing 11-15: The sixth and last version of the Chapter11_SQLite.mxml file, which includes the deleteUser() **function** *(continued)*

```
        } else {
          conn.addEventListener(SQLEvent.OPEN, createHandler);
        }
        conn.openAsync(dbFile);
    }

    private function errorHandler(event:SQLErrorEvent):void {
        var err:String = "Error id:" + event.error.errorID + "\nDetails:" +
                         event.error.details;
        Alert.show(err,"Error");
    }

    private function createHandler(event:SQLEvent):void {
        Alert.show("The database was created successfully", "createHandler");
    }

    private function openHandler(event:SQLEvent):void {
        Alert.show("The database was opened successfully", "openHandler");
    }

    private function createTable():void{
        var sqlText:String = "CREATE TABLE Users(ID INTEGER PRIMARY KEY, " +
                             "USER_NAME TEXT, PASSWORD TEXT)";
        createTableStatement = new SQLStatement();
        createTableStatement.sqlConnection = conn;
        createTableStatement.addEventListener(SQLEvent.RESULT, createTableResult);
        createTableStatement.addEventListener(SQLErrorEvent.ERROR, errorHandler);
        createTableStatement.text = sqlText;
        createTableStatement.execute();
    }

    private function createTableResult(event:SQLEvent):void {
        Alert.show("the table Users was created successfully", "createTableResult");
    }

    private function insertRecord():void{
        var sqlText:String = "INSERT INTO Users(USER_NAME, PASSWORD) " +
                             "VALUES(:username,:password)";
        insertStatement = new SQLStatement();
        insertStatement.sqlConnection = conn;
        insertStatement.addEventListener(SQLEvent.RESULT, insertResult);
        insertStatement.addEventListener(SQLErrorEvent.ERROR, errorHandler);
        insertStatement.text = sqlText;
        insertStatement.parameters[":username"] = usernameTxt.text;
        insertStatement.parameters[":password"] = passwordTxt.text;
        insertStatement.execute();
    }

    private function insertResult(event:SQLEvent):void {
        usernameTxt.text = "";
```

```
    passwordTxt.text = "";
    Alert.show("the record was inserted successfully", "insertResult");
}

private function selectAllUsers():void{
  var sqlText:String = "SELECT * FROM Users";
  selectAllSQL = new SQLStatement();
  selectAllSQL.sqlConnection = conn;
  selectAllSQL.addEventListener(SQLEvent.RESULT, selectAllUsersResult);
  selectAllSQL.addEventListener(SQLErrorEvent.ERROR, errorHandler);
  selectAllSQL.text = sqlText;
  selectAllSQL.execute();
}
private function selectAllUsersResult(event:SQLEvent):void{
  var result:SQLResult = selectAllSQL.getResult();
  grid.dataProvider = result.data;
}

private function searchForUser():void{
  var sqlText:String = "SELECT * FROM Users WHERE ID = " + userId.value;
  selectUserSQL = new SQLStatement();
  selectUserSQL.sqlConnection = conn;
  selectUserSQL.addEventListener(SQLEvent.RESULT, searchForUserResult);
  selectUserSQL.addEventListener(SQLErrorEvent.ERROR, errorHandler);
  selectUserSQL.text = sqlText;
  selectUserSQL.execute();
}

private function searchForUserResult(event:SQLEvent):void{
  var result:SQLResult = selectUserSQL.getResult();
  if(result.data.length){
      idTxt.text = result.data[0]["ID"];
      unameTxt.text = result.data[0]["USER_NAME"];
      pwordTxt.text = result.data[0]["PASSWORD"];
  }
}

private function updateUser():void{
  var sqlText:String = "UPDATE Users " +
                       "SET USER_NAME = :username, " +
                       "PASSWORD = :password " +
                       "WHERE ID = :id";
  updateUserSQL = new SQLStatement();
  updateUserSQL.sqlConnection = conn;
  updateUserSQL.addEventListener(SQLEvent.RESULT, updateResult);
  updateUserSQL.addEventListener(SQLErrorEvent.ERROR, errorHandler);
  updateUserSQL.text = sqlText;
  updateUserSQL.parameters[":username"] = unameTxt.text;
  updateUserSQL.parameters[":password"] = pwordTxt.text;
  updateUserSQL.parameters[":id"] = Number(idTxt.text);
  updateUserSQL.execute();
}
```

(Continued)

Listing 11-15: The sixth and last version of the Chapter11_SQLite.mxml file, which includes the deleteUser() **function** *(continued)*

```
      private function updateResult(event:SQLEvent):void{
         idTxt.text = "";
         unameTxt.text = "";
         pwordTxt.text = "";
         selectAllUsers();
         Alert.show("the record was updated successfully", "updateResult");
      }

      private function deleteUser():void{
         var sqlText:String = "DELETE FROM Users " +
                              "WHERE ID = :id";
         deleteUserSQL = new SQLStatement();
         deleteUserSQL.sqlConnection = conn;
         deleteUserSQL.addEventListener(SQLEvent.RESULT, deleteResult);
         deleteUserSQL.addEventListener(SQLErrorEvent.ERROR, errorHandler);
         deleteUserSQL.text = sqlText;
         deleteUserSQL.parameters[":id"] = Number(idTxt.text);
         deleteUserSQL.execute();
      }

      private function deleteResult(event:SQLEvent):void{
         idTxt.text = "";
         unameTxt.text = "";
         pwordTxt.text = "";
         selectAllUsers();
         Alert.show("the record was deleted successfully", "deleteResult");
      }
   ]]>
</mx:Script>
<mx:Button label="Create or Open Database" click="openDatabase()"/>
<mx:HRule width="100%"/>
<mx:Button label="Create Users Table" click="createTable()"/>
<mx:HRule width="100%"/>
<mx:HBox>
  <mx:Label text="Username:"/>
  <mx:TextInput id="usernameTxt" width="100" text="rich"/>
  <mx:Label text="Password:"/>
  <mx:TextInput id="passwordTxt" displayAsPassword="true" width="100"
    text="password"/>
  <mx:Button label="Insert User" click="insertRecord()"/>
  </mx:HBox>
    <mx:HRule width="100%"/>
    <mx:Button click="selectAllUsers()" label="Select All Users"/>
    <mx:DataGrid id="grid" width="320" height="100"/>
    <mx:HRule width="100%"/>
  <mx:HBox>
  <mx:NumericStepper id="userId" minimum="1" stepSize="1"  />
  <mx:Button click="searchForUser()" label="Search For User"/>
  </mx:HBox>
  <mx:Label text="RESULTS"/>
```

```
<mx:HBox>
  <mx:Label text="ID:"/>
  <mx:TextInput id="idTxt" width="20" editable="false"/>
  <mx:Label text="Username:"/>
  <mx:TextInput id="unameTxt" width="100"/>
  <mx:Label text="Password:"/>
  <mx:TextInput id="pwordTxt" width="100"/>
  <mx:Button click="updateUser()" label="Update User"/>
  <mx:Button click="deleteUser()" label="Delete User"/>
</mx:HBox>
<mx:HRule width="100%"/>
</mx:WindowedApplication>
```

Summary

This chapter has demonstrated all of the major functionality of AIR to interact with a SQLite embedded database. There were examples that showed how to create a database, create a table, add data, select data, update data, and delete data.

In the next chapter, I will discuss the ability of AIR to interact with the operating system. Features including drag and drop from the file system to AIR and from AIR to the file system will be demonstrated. Also, there will be a section showing how to read and write from the operating system's clipboard.

Exercise

Create an application that reads in XML files and converts them into a local database table.

See Chapter 8 for information on how to read in files and Chapter 7 for information on how to parse XML.

Communication between AIR and the Operating System

Communicating between the AIR application and the operating system is very useful when creating an elegant user experience. The ability of the application to read and write to the user's clipboard or accept a file that has been dragged into it creates a very user-friendly experience. This chapter will focus on drag-and-drop support as well as clipboard access. Finally, it will cover the use of native menus and how they are utilized within an AIR application.

Drag-and-Drop Support

Those of you who have come to AIR from a Flex background understand how to drag objects between native Flex components. The ease of doing this was always one of the killer features of Flex applications. However, owing to Flash player sandbox restrictions, it was never possible to drag a file from the user's file system into a Flash application. This is now possible with AIR. The quick overview of this is that you will have the ability to drag any file type into the AIR application, and it is then up to the application to determine whether or not to accept the file and how to handle that file.

DragIn

Let's start off by creating an application that allows for a file to be dragged in from the file system to the AIR application. Create a new AIR project named *Chapter12_DragIn*. You should now have a new file named Chapter12_DragIn.mxml. The completed code from this sample will be seen in Listing 12-5.

The first thing we'll need to add to this file is some import statements for the necessary classes to handle drag and drop. The `mx.controls.Image` class is needed to show the image within the AIR application, and the `mx.controls.Alert` class will show when an unmapped extension appears. Although the `flash.filesystem.File` class is not needed when working from the root window of an AIR project, it is best practice to import it. Copy the script block from Listing 12-1 into the Chapter12_DragIn.mxml file.

Listing 12-1: The necessary import statements

```
<mx:Script>
  <![CDATA[
    import mx.controls.Alert;
    import mx.controls.Image;
    import flash.filesystem.File;
  ]]>
</mx:Script>
```

Next, we'll add an `init()` function to set up the necessary listeners that will handle the drag-in and drop events. This function will create two listeners. The first listens for a `NativeDragEvent.NATIVE_DRAG_ENTER` event and sets the handler as `onDragIn`, and the second listens for `NativeDragEvent.NATIVE_DRAG_DROP` and sets its handler function as `onDrop`. Add the code from Listing 12-2 to the script block, and then also add `creationComplete="init()"` to the `<mx:WindowedApplication>`.

Listing 12-2: The `init` function, which creates listeners

```
private function init():void{
  this.addEventListener(NativeDragEvent.NATIVE_DRAG_ENTER,onDragIn);
  this.addEventListener(NativeDragEvent.NATIVE_DRAG_DROP,onDrop);
}
```

Now that our listeners are set up, we need to create the two handler functions. Take a look at Listing 12-3, and let's examine the handler functions. The first is `onDragIn()`, which in our case means that we will be accepting all file types. The second is the `onDrop()` function, which will handle the file once it is dropped. This particular example will handle only files that are images. The `onDrop()` function then creates an Array of the drop files by grabbing them using the `getData()` function of the `event.clipboard object` and sets them to an Array named *dropfiles*. It passes the `ClipboardFormats.FILE_LIST_FORMAT` property into the `getData()` method to retrieve the contents of the clipboard. It then loops through the Array of dropfiles, casting each to a `flash.filesystem.File`, and then checks the extension of the file. If the extension matches one of the case statements, the `addImage()` function is called with the file's `nativePath` being passed in. If the extension does not exist in the case statement, an Alert is thrown to the user. Add the code from Listing 12-3 to the Chapter12_DragIn.mxml file.

Listing 12-3: The handler functions

```
private function onDragIn(event:NativeDragEvent):void{
  NativeDragManager.acceptDragDrop(this);
}

private function onDrop(event:NativeDragEvent):void{
var dropfiles:Array =
event.clipboard.getData(ClipboardFormats.FILE_LIST_FORMAT) as Array;
for each (var file:File in dropfiles){
    switch (file.extension.toLowerCase()){
      case "png" :
```

```
         addImage(file.nativePath);
          break;
       case "jpg" :
         addImage(file.nativePath);
          break;
      case "jpeg" :
        addImage(file.nativePath);
         break;
      case "gif" :
        addImage(file.nativePath);
         break;
      default:
        Alert.show("Unmapped Extension");
    }
  }
}
```

Finally, the last need of this sample is to include the `addImage()` function. This function simply creates a new `mx.controls.Image object`, sets its source, and, finally, adds it as a child to the application. Add the code from Listing 12-4 to the Chapter12_DragIn.mxml file.

Listing 12-4: The `addImage()` function

```
private function addImage(nativePath:String):void{
  var i:Image = new Image();
    if(Capabilities.os.search("Mac") >= 0){
      i.source = "file://" + nativePath;
    } else {
      i.source = nativePath;
    }
  this.addChild(i);
}
```

After adding the final function from Listing 12-4, try running the application. You should now be able to drag a file over the application and see an indicator appear. This is demonstrated in Figure 12-1. After releasing the file, if it is an image that is in the case statement, it will drop onto the application and be added as a child, or the application will throw an Alert saying that it could not handle the file type. This is demonstrated in Figures 12-2 and 12-3. The results that are shown in Figure 12-3 occurred when attempting to drag in a PDF file. Finally, try dragging multiple images into the application, and you should see something similar to Figure 12-4.

Figure 12-1: The image being dragged into the application.

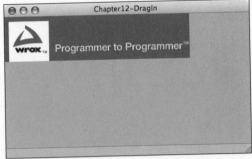

Figure 12-2: The image after it has been dropped and added as a child.

Figure 12-3: An unmapped extension being dropped into the application.

Figure 12-4: Multiple files being dragged into the application.

Listing 12-5: The completed code for Chapter12_DragIn.mxml

```
<?xml version="1.0" encoding="utf-8"?>
<mx:WindowedApplication xmlns:mx="http://www.adobe.com/2006/mxml" layout="vertical"
  creationComplete="init()">
```

```
<mx:Script>
  <![CDATA[
    import mx.controls.Alert;
    import mx.controls.Image;
    import flash.filesystem.File;

    private function init():void{
      this.addEventListener(NativeDragEvent.NATIVE_DRAG_ENTER,onDragIn);
      this.addEventListener(NativeDragEvent.NATIVE_DRAG_DROP,onDrop);
    }

    private function onDragIn(event:NativeDragEvent):void{
      NativeDragManager.acceptDragDrop(this);
    }

    private function onDrop(event:NativeDragEvent):void{
      var dropfiles:Array =
event.clipboard.getData(ClipboardFormats.FILE_LIST_FORMAT) as Array;
      for each (var file:File in dropfiles){
        switch (file.extension.toLowerCase()){
          case "png" :
            addImage(file.nativePath);
            break;
          case "jpg" :
            addImage(file.nativePath);
            break;
          case "jpeg" :
            addImage(file.nativePath);
            break;
          case "gif" :
            addImage(file.nativePath);
            break;
          default:
            Alert.show("Unmapped Extension");
          }
        }
      }

    private function addImage(nativePath:String):void{
      var i:Image = new Image();
      if(Capabilities.os.search("Mac") >= 0){
        i.source = "file://" + nativePath;
      } else {
        i.source = nativePath;
      }
      this.addChild(i);
    }

  ]]>
</mx:Script>

</mx:WindowedApplication>
```

DragOut

Now that you know how to create an application that allows files to be dragged in, the next drag event to look at is the ability to drag a file out of an AIR application to the user's file system. Let's start by creating a new AIR project named *Chapter12_DragOut*. You should now have a file named *Chapter12_DragOut.mxml*. Note that the completed version of Chapter12_DragOut.mxml will be shown in Listing 12-9.

The first thing we'll need to add is an import statement for the `flash.filesystem.File class`. Copy the script block from Listing 12-6 into the Chapter12_DragOut.mxml file.

Listing 12-6: The necessary import statements

```
<mx:Script>
  <![CDATA[
    import flash.filesystem.File;
  ]]>
</mx:Script>
```

Next, you will need to copy an image into your project folder and add an `<mx:Image>` component to the Chapter12_DragOut.mxml file. Add the code from Listing 12-7 to the Chapter12_DragOut.mxml file. Note that this sample assumes that you have an image named *wrox_logo.gif* in the root of your Chapter12_DragOut application.

Listing 12-7: The `<mx:Image>` tag

```
<mx:Image id="image" source="wrox_logo.gif" mouseDown="onMouseDown(event)"/>
```

Examining the contents of Listing 12-7, you will notice that there is a method named onMouseDown() attached to the mouseDown event. Listing 12-8 includes the onMouseDown() function as well as another function named createTransferableData().

Listing 12-8: The `onMouseDown()` and `createTransferableData()` functions

```
private function onMouseDown(event:MouseEvent):void{
    var bitmap:Bitmap = Bitmap(event.target.content);
    var bitmapFile:File = new File(event.target.content.loaderInfo.url);
    var transferObject:Clipboard = createTransferableData(bitmap,bitmapFile);
    NativeDragManager.doDrag(this,transferObject,bitmap.bitmapData,
                             new Point(-mouseX,- mouseY));
}

private function createTransferableData(image:Bitmap, sourceFile:File):Clipboard{
    var transfer:Clipboard = new Clipboard();
    transfer.setData(ClipboardFormats.BITMAP_FORMAT,image.bitmapData,false);
    transfer.setData(ClipboardFormats.BITMAP_FORMAT,image.bitmapData,false);
    transfer.setData(ClipboardFormats.FILE_LIST_FORMAT,new Array(sourceFile),false);
    return transfer;
}
```

OK, before you run the application, let's take a look as the functions in Listing 12-8. The onMouseDown() function creates a new Bitmap object from the content of the event target, which is the <mx:Image> component with the ID of *image*. Next, it creates a new File object using the loaderInfo URL from the <mx:Image> component. Next, it creates a Clipboard object using the createTransferableData() function and passes in the Bitmap and File object data. The createTransferableData() function creates the Clipboard object from the image data and returns it. Finally, the onMouseDown() function tells the DragManager to do a drag by calling the doDrag() method.

Now, run the application and you should be able to drag the image out of the AIR application and into the file system of the host computer. See Figure 12-5.

Figure 12-5: Example showing the image being dragged out of the AIR application.

Listing 12-9: The completed version of Chapter12_DragOut.mxml

```
<?xml version="1.0" encoding="utf-8"?>
<mx:WindowedApplication xmlns:mx="http://www.adobe.com/2006/mxml"
        layout="absolute">
  <mx:Script>
  <![CDATA[
  import flash.filesystem.File;

    private function onMouseDown(event:MouseEvent):void{
      var bitmap:Bitmap = Bitmap(event.target.content);
      var bitmapFile:File = new File(event.target.content.loaderInfo.url);
      var transferObject:Clipboard = createTransferableData(bitmap,bitmapFile);
      NativeDragManager.doDrag(this,transferObject,bitmap.bitmapData,
                        new Point(-mouseX,- mouseY));
  }

    private function createTransferableData(image:Bitmap, sourceFile:File):Clipboard{
      var transfer:Clipboard = new Clipboard();
      transfer.setData(ClipboardFormats.BITMAP_FORMAT,image.bitmapData,false);
      transfer.setData(ClipboardFormats.BITMAP_FORMAT,image.bitmapData,false);
      transfer.setData(ClipboardFormats.FILE_LIST_FORMAT,new Array(sourceFile),
                  false);
```

(Continued)

Listing 12-9: The completed version of Chapter12_DragOut.mxml *(continued)*

```
        return transfer;
    }


        ]]>
    </mx:Script>

    <mx:Image id="image" source="wrox_logo.gif"
            mouseDown="onMouseDown(event)"/>
</mx:WindowedApplication>
```

Copy and Paste

Although Flex 2 allowed the ability to read the clipboard, it was limited to text only, and there was no way to write to the clipboard. AIR has removed these restrictions and given full access to read and write all types of data to and from the system clipboard. This section demonstrates how to copy and paste image files in and out of an AIR application.

Paste

The first half of this application will address the ability to paste data into an AIR application. This involves the use of the Clipboard class to access the clipboard and read in the file. Start off by creating a new AIR application named *Chapter12_Paste*. This will create a new file named *Chapter12_Paste.mxml*, which we will build on throughout this section. Listing 12-14 will show the completed version of this application.

We'll start off by bringing in the necessary import statements. This application will require the flash .filesystem.File. We will also be using the mx.controls.Alert and mx.controls.Image classes. Copy the contents of Listing 12-10 into the Chapter12_Paste.mxml file.

Listing 12-10: The necessary import statements

```
<mx:Script>
  <![CDATA[
    import mx.controls.Alert;
    import mx.controls.Image;
    import flash.filesystem.File;
]]>
</mx:Script>
```

Next we'll add in a simple button to simulate the paste action. Add the Button component in Listing 12-11 to the Chapter12_Paste.mxml file. To accomplish this using Ctrl-v on Windows or Cmd-v on Mac, you can use the Flex KeyboardEvent class (see the Exercise at the end of this chapter).

Listing 12-11: The Button component

```
<mx:Button click="paste()" label="Paste"/>
```

The button we just added is what triggers the paste by calling the paste() function. The paste() function shown in Listing 12-12 first calls on the getData() function of the Clipboard.generalClipboard class to access the clipboard contents. The getData() function accepts the ClipboardFormats .FILE_LIST_FORMATS property to determine the data to read from the clipboard. The result of the getData() function is cast to a new Array named *clipboardFiles*. The clipboardFiles array is looped over, and each file is pulled out and examined. In our example, we are specifically looking for files that have an extension of type image. If an image is found in the switch statement, the addImage() function is called and passed the file's nativePath property.

Listing 12-12: The paste() **function**

```
private function paste():void{
        var clipboardfiles:Array =
Clipboard.generalClipboard.getData(ClipboardFormats.FILE_LIST_FORMAT) as Array;
    for each (var file:File in clipboardfiles){
      switch (file.extension.toLowerCase()){
        case "png" :
              addImage(file.nativePath);
              break;
        case "jpg" :
              addImage(file.nativePath);
              break;
        case "jpeg" :
              addImage(file.nativePath);
              break;
        case "gif" :
              addImage(file.nativePath);
              break;
        default:
              Alert.show("Unmapped Extension");
      }
    }
  }
```

Next, we need to add the addImage() function, and it's identical to the one that was used previously in the drag-in example. It simply adds a new Image object to the application by creating the Image using the nativePath that was passed in and using addChild() to include it in the application. Copy the contents of Listing 12-13 into the Chapter12_Paste.mxml file.

Listing 12-13: The addImage() **function**

```
private function addImage(nativePath:String):void{
  var i:Image = new Image();
    if(Capabilities.os.search("Mac") >= 0){
      i.source = "file://" + nativePath;
    } else {
      i.source = nativePath;
    }
    this.addChild(i);
}
```

That's it — go ahead and run the application. You should be able to copy an image file from anywhere in your file system and then hit the Paste button and see something like Figure 12-6.

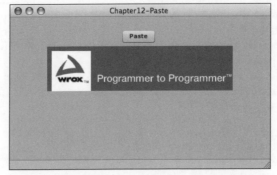

Figure 12-6: A file being pasted into the application.

Now, try copying a few images, and you should see something like Figure 12-7.

Figure 12-7: Multiple images being pasted into the application.

Listing 12-14: The completed version of Chapter12_Paste.mxml

```
<?xml version="1.0" encoding="utf-8"?>
<mx:WindowedApplication xmlns:mx="http://www.adobe.com/2006/mxml"
  layout="vertical"
    creationComplete="init()">
  <mx:Script>
    <![CDATA[
      import mx.controls.Alert;
      import mx.controls.Image;
      import flash.filesystem.File;

private function paste():void{
```

```
            var clipboardfiles:Array =
    Clipboard.generalClipboard.getData(ClipboardFormats.FILE_LIST_FORMAT) as Array;
        for each (var file:File in clipboardfiles){
          switch (file.extension.toLowerCase()){
            case "png" :
                 addImage(file.nativePath);
                 break;
            case "jpg" :
                 addImage(file.nativePath);
                 break;
            case "jpeg" :
                 addImage(file.nativePath);
                 break;
            case "gif" :
                 addImage(file.nativePath);
                 break;
            default:
                 Alert.show("Unmapped Extension");
          }
        }
    }


        private function addImage(nativePath:String):void{
          var i:Image = new Image();
          if(Capabilities.os.search("Mac") >= 0){
            i.source = "file://" + nativePath;
          } else {
            i.source = nativePath;
          }
          this.addChild(i);
        }

    ]]>
  </mx:Script>
  <mx:Button click="paste()" label="Paste"/>
</mx:WindowedApplication>
```

Copy

To copy a file from AIR to the file system, we'll need a few more classes than in previous examples in this chapter. To start, we'll need flash.filesystem.FileMode, flash.filesystem.FileStream, flash.filesystem.File, and mx.graphics.codec.JPEGEncoder to create the copy of the image file to place onto the clipboard, and also the mx.controls.Alert class to let us know that the file is now on the clipboard. The completed version of the Chapter12_Copy.mxml file can be seen in Listing 12-18.

Let's get started by creating a new application called Chapter12_Copy. This will create a new main file named Chapter12_Copy.mxml.

Add the script block from Listing 12-15 to the Chapter12_Copy.mxml file.

Listing 12-15: The necessary import statements

```
<mx:Script>
  <![CDATA[
    import mx.controls.Alert;
    import flash.filesystem.FileMode;
    import flash.filesystem.FileStream;
    import flash.filesystem.File;
    import mx.graphics.codec.JPEGEncoder;
  ]]>
</mx:Script>
```

Next, you'll need to add a few <mx:Image> components to hold the images that will be copied out of the application. Add a few images to the root of your application, and then create two <mx:Image> components where the source of the images is embedded into the component. Each <mx:Image> component will call the copyToClipboard() function on click. Your code should look similar to Listing 12-16.

Listing 12-16: An example of two Image components

```
<mx:Image source="@Embed('wrox_logo.gif')" click="copyToClipboard(event)"/>
<mx:Image source="@Embed('ApolloApp_128.png')" click="copyToClipboard(event)"/>
```

Now, we simply need to add the copyToClipboard() function. Before adding it to the application, let's examine the contents of the copyToClipboard() function. After casting the event target to a type of Image, a tempFile is created using the image name plus the jpg extension. We will be using the JPEGEncoder later in this function, which is why the tempFile has the jpg extension. Next, we grab the BitmapData from the image, and using the JPEGEncoder, we encode it to a ByteArray. Then using the FileStream class, the ByteArray is written to the tempFile. Now, we can call the setData() function of the Clipboard .generalClipboard class and pass in the format type, which will be ClipboardFormats.FILE_LIST_FORMAT as well as the tempFile. That is it. The image is now on the system clipboard and can be pasted to the file system. If you examine the section of the setData() function where the tempFile is added, you'll see that it is added as a single item in an Array. You can also add multiple items to this Array and thus have multiple items added to the clipboard. Now, add the contents of Listing 12-17 to the Chapter12_Copy.mxml file.

Listing 12-17: The copyToClipboard() function

```
private function copyToClipboard(event:MouseEvent):void {
    var i:Image = event.target as Image;
    var tempFile:File = File.createTempDirectory().resolvePath(i.name + ".jpg");
    var bd:BitmapData = new BitmapData(i.width, i.height);
    bd.draw(i);
    var encoder:JPEGEncoder = new JPEGEncoder();
    var ba:ByteArray = encoder.encode(bd);
    var fs:FileStream = new FileStream();
    fs.open(tempFile, FileMode.WRITE);
    fs.writeBytes(ba);
    fs.close();
Clipboard.generalClipboard.setData(ClipboardFormats.FILE_LIST_FORMAT,
                             [tempFile],false);
    Alert.show("Image has been copied to clipboard", "Success");
}
```

Now go ahead and run the application, and click on one of the image files; you should see something similar to Figure 12-8. Try pasting to the file system, and you should see a new jpg file added.

Figure 12-8: An image being copied to the clipboard.

Listing 12-18: The completed version of Chapter12_Copy.mxml

```
<?xml version="1.0" encoding="utf-8"?>
<mx:WindowedApplication xmlns:mx="http://www.adobe.com/2006/mxml"
    layout="vertical">

    <mx:Script>
      <![CDATA[
        import mx.controls.Alert;
        import flash.filesystem.FileMode;
        import flash.filesystem.FileStream;
        import flash.filesystem.File;
        import mx.graphics.codec.JPEGEncoder;

    private function copyToClipboard(event:MouseEvent):void {
        var i:Image = event.target as Image;
        var tempFile:File = File.createTempDirectory().resolvePath(i.name + ".jpg");
        var bd:BitmapData = new BitmapData(i.width, i.height);
        bd.draw(i);
        var encoder:JPEGEncoder = new JPEGEncoder();
        var ba:ByteArray = encoder.encode(bd);
        var fs:FileStream = new FileStream();
        fs.open(tempFile, FileMode.WRITE);
        fs.writeBytes(ba);
        fs.close();
    Clipboard.generalClipboard.setData(ClipboardFormats.FILE_LIST_FORMAT,
                            [tempFile],false);
        Alert.show("Image has been copied to clipboard", "Success");
    }

      ]]>
    </mx:Script>
```

(Continued)

Listing 12-18: The completed version of Chapter12_Copy.mxml *(continued)*

```
    <mx:Image source="@Embed('wrox_logo.gif')" click="copyToClipboard(event)"/>
    <mx:Image source="@Embed('ApolloApp_128.png')" click="copyToClipboard(event)"/>

  </mx:WindowedApplication>
```

Native Menus

AIR has the ability to integrate into the operating system's menu system through the use of its Native Menu API. The `NativeMenu` object consists of one or many `NativeMenuItems` and can include dividers and keyboard shortcuts.

Basic NativeMenu

To demonstrate this, let's start by creating a new AIR application named *Chapter12_NativeMenu*, which will create the main application file of Chapter12_NativeMenu.mxml. Listing 12-25 will show the completed version of Chapter12_NativeMenu.mxml. Please note that this example will only work on the Mac OS X operating system, as Windows does not support native menus on the root application window. For information on how to add native menus to `NativeWindows`, please refer to Chapter 9.

Since `NativeMenu` and `NativeMenuItem` are members of the `flash.display` package, there are no imports needed to add `NativeMenus`. However, we will use the `Alert` class, so please add the script block from Listing 12-19 into the Chapter12_NativeMenu.mxml file.

Listing 12-19: The needed import statement

```
<mx:Script>
  <![CDATA[
    import mx.controls.Alert;
  ]]>
</mx:Script>
```

Now let's add a simple `NativeMenu` to the application. First add `creationComplete="init()"` to the `<mx:WindowedApplication>` root tag. The code in Listing 12-20 will create a simple menu on creationComplete of the application. It first creates a `NativeMenu` object named *nativeMenu* and then a `NativeMenuItem` object named *menuItem* with the label "My Menu". It then sets the nativeMenu to the submenu property of the menuItem object. Finally, it adds the new menuItem to the `NativeApplication` `.nativeApplication.menu` class. Add the `init()` function to the Chapter12_NativeMenu.mxml file. The result in shown in Figure 12-9.

Listing 12-20: A simple `NativeMenu`

```
private function init():void{
  var nativeMenu:NativeMenu = new NativeMenu();
  var menuItem:NativeMenuItem = new NativeMenuItem("My Menu");
```

```
        menuItem.submenu = nativeMenu;
        NativeApplication.nativeApplication.menu.addItem(menuItem);
    }
```

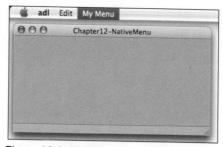

Figure 12-9: The new `NativeMenu`.

Native Menu with Submenus

Next we'll add submenus to the new native menu. To do this, we'll create three additional `NativeMenuItems` that will be called *SubMenuA*, *SubMenuB*, and *SubMenuC*. Listing 12-21 contains the updated version of the `init()` function. Examining this function, you will see that there are three new MenuItems created and each is added to the nativeMenu object by using the `addItem()` method. Update the `init()` function in the Chapter12_NativeMenu.mxml file to the code in Listing 12-21.

The results of this new version can be seen in Figure 12-10.

Listing 12-21: The second version of the `init()` **function**

```
private function init():void{
    var nativeMenu:NativeMenu = new NativeMenu();
    var menuItem:NativeMenuItem = new NativeMenuItem("My Menu");
    var subMenuA:NativeMenuItem = new NativeMenuItem("Sub Menu A");
    var subMenuB:NativeMenuItem = new NativeMenuItem("Sub Menu B");
    var subMenuC:NativeMenuItem = new NativeMenuItem("Sub Menu C");
    nativeMenu.addItem(subMenuA);
    nativeMenu.addItem(subMenuB);
    nativeMenu.addItem(subMenuC);
    menuItem.submenu = nativeMenu;
    NativeApplication.nativeApplication.menu.addItem(menuItem);
}
```

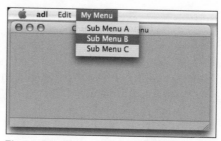

Figure 12-10: Example showing the menu with three submenus.

Native Menu with Dividers

To add some separation between submenus, AIR has the ability to add dividers. Adding a divider is easy; you simply need to add another empty `NativeMenuItem` and then set the second argument to True. An example of a divider menu looks like this: `nativeMenu.addItem(new NativeMenuItem("",true));`.

We will also add an additional menu ("Sub Menu D") below the new divider. Update your `init()` function in the Chapter12_NativeMenu.mxml file to look like Listing 12-22. Figure 12-11 shows the results of the third version of the `init()` function.

Listing 12-22: Third version of `init()` function shows the addition of a divider and subMenuD

```
private function init():void{
  var nativeMenu:NativeMenu = new NativeMenu();
  var menuItem:NativeMenuItem = new NativeMenuItem("My Menu");
  var subMenuA:NativeMenuItem = new NativeMenuItem("Sub Menu A");
  var subMenuB:NativeMenuItem = new NativeMenuItem("Sub Menu B");
  var subMenuC:NativeMenuItem = new NativeMenuItem("Sub Menu C");
  var subMenuD:NativeMenuItem = new NativeMenuItem("Sub Menu D");
  nativeMenu.addItem(subMenuA);
  nativeMenu.addItem(subMenuB);
  nativeMenu.addItem(subMenuC);
  nativeMenu.addItem(new NativeMenuItem("",true));
  nativeMenu.addItem(subMenuD);
  menuItem.submenu = nativeMenu;
  NativeApplication.nativeApplication.menu.addItem(menuItem);
}
```

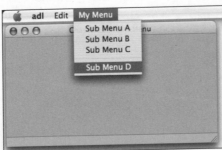

Figure 12-11: The new menu with the addition of a divider.

Menu Select Handler

OK, so we have a nice menu now, but when a menu item is selected, nothing happens. To resolve this, we need to add event listeners to listen for menu selections. To add an event listener, you simply need to apply an event listener for each menu item. An example of an event listener looks like this:

```
subMenuA.addEventListener(Event.SELECT,handleMenuClick);
```

The listener is added to the menu item; it is set to listen for Event.SELECT and calls the handleMenuClick() function when it is selected. The code in Listing 12-23 includes event listeners for each of the submenus. Update the init() function in the Chapter12_NativeMenu.mxml file to the code in Listing 12-23. Also add the handleMenuClick() function to the Chapter12_NativeMenu.mxml file. The results of this, showing the event listener being called, can be seen in Figure 12-12.

Listing 12-23: The fourth version of init() function with event listeners and the handleMenuClick() **function**

```
private function init():void{
    var nativeMenu:NativeMenu = new NativeMenu();
    var menuItem:NativeMenuItem = new NativeMenuItem("My Menu");
    var subMenuA:NativeMenuItem = new NativeMenuItem("Sub Menu A");
    var subMenuB:NativeMenuItem = new NativeMenuItem("Sub Menu B");
    var subMenuC:NativeMenuItem = new NativeMenuItem("Sub Menu C");
    var subMenuD:NativeMenuItem = new NativeMenuItem("Sub Menu D");

    subMenuA.addEventListener(Event.SELECT,handleMenuClick);
    subMenuB.addEventListener(Event.SELECT,handleMenuClick);
    subMenuC.addEventListener(Event.SELECT,handleMenuClick);
    subMenuD.addEventListener(Event.SELECT,handleMenuClick);

    nativeMenu.addItem(subMenuA);
    nativeMenu.addItem(subMenuB);
    nativeMenu.addItem(subMenuC);
    nativeMenu.addItem(new NativeMenuItem("",true));
    nativeMenu.addItem(subMenuD);
    menuItem.submenu = nativeMenu;
    NativeApplication.nativeApplication.menu.addItem(menuItem);
}

private function handleMenuClick(e:Event):void {
    var menuItem:NativeMenuItem = e.target as NativeMenuItem;
    Alert.show(menuItem.label + " has been selected");
}
```

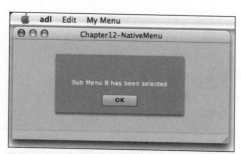

Figure 12-12: Example showing the Alert after being triggered by the event listener.

Keyboard Activated Menu

AIR NativeMenus also allow the ability to set a keyboard shortcut to any menu item. This can be very useful, as it will allow the developer to offer quick access to the custom menu system that has been created for the application. To add a keyboard shortcut, you simply set the keyEquivalent property of the menu item to a letter. Here is an example of adding a keyboard shortcut: subMenuC.keyEquivalent = "C";. Listing 12-24 shows the updated version of the init() function, which now includes a keyboard shortcut for the subMenuC menu item. Update the init() function of Chapter12_NativeMenu.mxml to the contents of Listing 12-24. The results of this can be seen in Figure 12-13.

Listing 12-24: The fifth version of the init() **function including a keyEquivalent**

```
private function init():void{
    var nativeMenu:NativeMenu = new NativeMenu();
    var menuItem:NativeMenuItem = new NativeMenuItem("My Menu");
    var subMenuA:NativeMenuItem = new NativeMenuItem("Sub Menu A");
    var subMenuB:NativeMenuItem = new NativeMenuItem("Sub Menu B");
    var subMenuC:NativeMenuItem = new NativeMenuItem("Sub Menu C");
    var subMenuD:NativeMenuItem = new NativeMenuItem("Sub Menu D");

    subMenuA.addEventListener(Event.SELECT,handleMenuClick);
    subMenuB.addEventListener(Event.SELECT,handleMenuClick);
    subMenuC.addEventListener(Event.SELECT,handleMenuClick);
    subMenuD.addEventListener(Event.SELECT,handleMenuClick);

    subMenuC.keyEquivalent = "C";

    nativeMenu.addItem(subMenuA);
    nativeMenu.addItem(subMenuB);
    nativeMenu.addItem(subMenuC);
    nativeMenu.addItem(new NativeMenuItem("",true));
    nativeMenu.addItem(subMenuD);

    menuItem.submenu = nativeMenu;
    NativeApplication.nativeApplication.menu.addItem(menuItem);
}
```

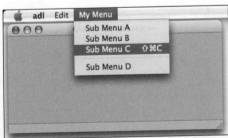

Figure 12-13: The keyboard shortcut assigned to Sub Menu C.

Listing 12-25: The completed version of Chapter12_NativeMenu.mxml

```xml
<?xml version="1.0" encoding="utf-8"?>
<mx:WindowedApplication xmlns:mx="http://www.adobe.com/2006/mxml" layout="absolute"
  creationComplete="init()">
  <mx:Script>
    <![CDATA[
      import mx.controls.Alert;

      private function init():void{
        var nativeMenu:NativeMenu = new NativeMenu();
        var menuItem:NativeMenuItem = new NativeMenuItem("My Menu");
        var subMenuA:NativeMenuItem = new NativeMenuItem("Sub Menu A");
        var subMenuB:NativeMenuItem = new NativeMenuItem("Sub Menu B");
        var subMenuC:NativeMenuItem = new NativeMenuItem("Sub Menu C");
        var subMenuD:NativeMenuItem = new NativeMenuItem("Sub Menu D");

        subMenuA.addEventListener(Event.SELECT,handleMenuClick);
        subMenuB.addEventListener(Event.SELECT,handleMenuClick);
        subMenuC.addEventListener(Event.SELECT,handleMenuClick);
        subMenuD.addEventListener(Event.SELECT,handleMenuClick);

        subMenuC.keyEquivalent = "C";

        nativeMenu.addItem(subMenuA);
        nativeMenu.addItem(subMenuB);
        nativeMenu.addItem(subMenuC);
        nativeMenu.addItem(new NativeMenuItem("",true));
        nativeMenu.addItem(subMenuD);

        menuItem.submenu = nativeMenu;
        NativeApplication.nativeApplication.menu.addItem(menuItem);
      }

      private function handleMenuClick(e:Event):void {
        var menuItem:NativeMenuItem = e.target as NativeMenuItem;
        Alert.show(menuItem.label + " has been selected");
      }

    ]]>
  </mx:Script>
</mx:WindowedApplication>
```

Summary

This chapter has demonstrated three different ways in which AIR can interact with the host operating system. I first demonstrated how to drag files into and out of AIR applications. Next, we examined how to interact with the system clipboard. Then I demonstrated how to read the contents of the clipboard and also how to write to the clipboard. Finally, we examined AIR's NativeMenu API and demonstrated how to create menus, submenus, dividers, and keyboard shortcuts.

In the next chapter, we'll examine how AIR can determine when there is an Internet connection present. The chapter will also demonstrate my methodology for creating AIR applications that can check for newer versions and update themselves when needed.

Exercise

Using the Flex 3 KeyboardEvent class, add support to the Chapter12_Paste example for Ctrl-v keyboard shortcut for pasting an image into the application.

Application Status

There will certainly be times when you will want to know if the client who is running your AIR application has a connection to the Internet. This information can be very useful for applications that need to be occasionally connected to synchronize data, check for updates, and the like. This chapter will demonstrate how to test for Internet connections and also how to create an application that can check for updates and update itself when necessary.

Checking for an Internet Connection

AIR has made it very easy to test for Internet connections using the `Event.NETWORK_CHANGE` event, which is an event broadcast by the main `Shell` class.

To demonstrate how to test for network connections, create a new AIR project named *Chapter13_ConnStatus*. You should now have an empty file named *Chapter13_ConnStatus.mxml*. Set the title to Connection Status and the width to 400. Your file should now look like Listing 13-1.

Listing 13-1: The beginning of the Chapter13_ConnStatus.mxml file

```
<?xml version="1.0" encoding="utf-8"?>
<mx:WindowedApplication xmlns:mx="http://www.adobe.com/2006/mxml"
  layout="absolute"
  title="Connection Status" width="400">

</mx:WindowedApplication>
```

The next thing we're going to need to add to the Chapter13_ConnStatus.mxml file is a block of import statements to bring in the `URLMonitor`, `URLRequest`, and `StatusEvent` classes. Create a new `<mx:Script>` block in this file, and add the contents of Listing 13-2.

Listing 13-2: The new Script block with import statements

```
<mx:Script>
  <![CDATA[
```

(Continued)

Listing 13-2: The new Script block with import statements *(continued)*

```
        import flash.events.StatusEvent;

        import flash.net.URLRequest;
        import air.net.URLMonitor;
        ]]>
    </mx:Script>
```

Now we need to add a variable to hold the current connection status, which is set to False by default. We also need to create a variable of type URLMonitor, which needs to be a class variable so that the events can be announced. Add the following right below the import statements:

```
    [Bindable]
    private var isConnected:Boolean = false;
    private var urlMonitor:URLMonitor;
```

The isConnected variable will be updated every time the connection status changes. To start the URLMonitor, which will notify us of connection status changes, we will include this functionality within the init() function, which will be called on applicationComplete. The init() function shown in Listing 13-3 will first create a new URLRequest with the method set to HEAD. The reason we use HEAD is that we don't care about retrieving any content; we simply wish to know if the request can be done successfully. HEAD will return the least amount of data and thus will be the fastest way to get a response. Although in this case Google is being used as the test URL in the URLRequest's URL variable passed into the constructor, it can be any URL as long as you know that it's one that is available. An instance of the URLMonitor class is created, and the URLRequest variable is passed in. Next, an event listener is added to listen for status changes and call the statusChanged() function when a change does occur. Finally, the start() method is called on the URLMonitor to begin listening for status changes. Add the contents of Listing 13-3 to Chapter13_ConnStatus.mxml.

Listing 13-3: The `init()` function that starts the `URLMonitor`

```
    private function init():void{
        var urlRequest:URLRequest = new URLRequest('http://www.google.com')
        urlRequest.method = "HEAD";
        urlMonitor = new URLMonitor(urlRequest);
        urlMonitor.addEventListener(StatusEvent.STATUS, statusChanged);
        urlMonitor.start();
    }
```

Now, we need to define the event listeners to handle the StatusEvent_ being broadcast by the URLMonitor. Listing 13-4 contains the function named statusChanged(), which is needed to handle the change in status and set the isConnected variable. Add the function from Listing 13-4 to the Chapter13_ConnStatus .mxml file.

Listing 13-4: Event listener for handling events broadcast by the `URLMonitor`

```
    private function statusChanged(event:StatusEvent):void{
      isConnected = urlMonitor.available;
    }
```

All that's needed now is to add a few visual components so that we can see the current connection status. Listing 13-5 contains <mx:Label> and <mx:Text> components, which are bound to the isConnected variable and will show either True or False. Add the components from Listing 13-5 to the Chapter13_ConnStatus .mxml file.

Listing 13-5: The visual components for the Chapter13_ConnStatus.mxml file

```
<mx:Label text="Connected: " x="141" y="70"/>
<mx:Text text="{isConnected}" x="222" y="70"/>
```

After you have the components from Listing 13-5 in your file, you will need to add the call to the init() function within the applicationComplete property of the WindowedApplication tag. Listing 13-6 shows the final version of the Chapter 13_ConnStatus.mxml file. You should now be able to run the application and see something like what is shown in Figure 13-1, assuming that you have an Internet connection that can reach google.com. If you unplug your connection, the status should change automatically. This is represented in Figure 13-2.

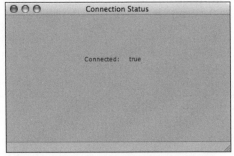

Figure 13-1: The Chapter13_ConnStatus application when a connection exists.

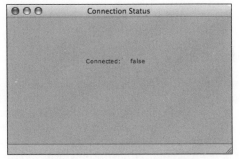

Figure 13-2: The Chapter13_ConnStatus application after disabling the connection.

219

Listing 13-6: The final version of Chapter13_ConnStatus.mxml

```xml
<?xml version="1.0" encoding="utf-8"?>
<mx:WindowedApplication xmlns:mx="http://www.adobe.com/2006/mxml"
    layout="absolute"
    applicationComplete="init()"
    title="Connection Status" width="400">
    <mx:Script>
<![CDATA[
import air.net.URLMonitor;
import flash.net.URLRequest;
import flash.events.StatusEvent;

[Bindable]
private var isConnected:Boolean = false;

private var urlMonitor:URLMonitor;

private function init():void{
    var urlRequest:URLRequest = new URLRequest('http://www.google.com')
    urlRequest.method = "HEAD";
    urlMonitor = new URLMonitor(urlRequest);
    urlMonitor.addEventListener(StatusEvent.STATUS, statusChanged);
    urlMonitor.start();
}

private function statusChanged(event:StatusEvent):void {
    isConnected = urlMonitor.available;
}

]]>
</mx:Script>
<mx:Label text="Connected: " x="141" y="70"/>
<mx:Text text="{isConnected}" x="222" y="70"/>

</mx:WindowedApplication>
```

About the <Updater> Class

The Updater class is an extremely important class to AIR developers, as it allows the AIR application to update itself. Why is this so important? Those who come from Web development have the ability to push out a change to one single location and ensure that the next time someone visits your web site the new version of the application will be the one the user sees. However, with a desktop application, there can be a disconnect between the most recent code and the application that is actually running on the client's machine. As the developer of the AIR application, the only way you can handle this is to build your application so that it checks for updates automatically and either alerts the user that there is an update available or forces the user to download the update before using the application again. As you will see, the download and install of the new version of the application is completely seamless.

Methodology for Application Updates

Using the Updater class to install a new version of the application is well defined and will be demonstrated below in this chapter. The methodology for determining whether or not an update is required is a personal decision. The following method is one that I came up with and use in my AIR applications. To demonstrate this method, create a new AIR application named *Chapter13_SelfUpdating*. This example shows how the update functionality works. I have also released a public UpdateManager class that encapsulates much of the code from this example. It can be downloaded for free at http://blog.everythingflex.com/2007/10/01/air-update-manager/.

To determine whether or not an application is up to date, there are two things you need to know:

❑ What is the version of the currently installed AIR application?

❑ What is the most current version available?

Determine the Current Version

Let's start with the first item. To determine what the current version of the installed application is, we will parse out the version property from the NativeApplication.nativeApplication.applicationDescriptor information. This information is the XML information that is part of every AIR application within the application's XML descriptor file. So let's get started with our Chapter13_SelfUpdater application.

Open the Chapter13_SelfUpdating-app.xml file and set the version property of the <application> tag to 1.0. For more information on the AIR configuration file, please refer to Chapter 6.

Now, create an <mx:Script> block and add a private variable named appXML of type XML to hold the contents of the NativeApplication.nativeApplication.applicationDescriptor, a variable named ns of type NameSpace, and currentVersion of type String to Chapter13_SelfUpdater.mxml. Listing 13-7 shows the current version of the Chapter13_SelfUpdater.mxml file.

Listing 13-7: The first version of the Chapter13_SelfUpdater.mxml file

```
<?xml version="1.0" encoding="utf-8"?>
<mx:WindowedApplication xmlns:mx="http://www.adobe.com/2006/mxml"
    layout="absolute">

  <mx:Script>
    <![CDATA[
    private var appXML:XML =
NativeApplication.nativeApplication.applicationDescriptor;
    private var ns : Namespace = appXML.namespace();

    [Bindable]
    private var currentVersion : String = appXML.ns::version;
    ]]>
  </mx:Script>
</mx:WindowedApplication>
```

Now, add a Label component to display the `currentVersion` value to the main `<mx:WindowedApplication>` file. This can be seen in Listing 13-8.

Listing 13-8: A Label component, which will display the `currentVersion`

```
<mx:Label text="Current Version {currentVersion}" fontWeight="bold"  x="0" y="36"
textAlign="center" width="100%"/>
```

Now, run the application and you should see something like Figure 13-3.

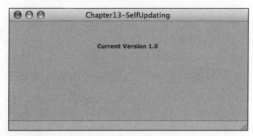

Figure 13-3: Chapter13_SelfUpdater running as an installed application.

Determine Newest Version Available

Now that we know the current version, we need something to compare it to the most recent version. To do this, we'll use an `<mx:HTTPService>` to read an XML document on a remote server.

Listing 13-9 is an example of the version.xml file. You will need to adjust the properties to your own information. Copy the version.xml file to your server. You can use `localhost` if you do not have a public server.

Listing 13-9: An example of the version.xml file

```
<?xml version="1.0" encoding="ISO-8859-1"?>
<currentVersion version="1.1"
        downloadLocation="http://www.yourserver.com/NewAirFile.air"
        forceUpdate="false"/>
```

Loading this file into your AIR application and parsing the information is pretty simple. Edit the URL, and then copy the contents of Listing 13-10 into the Chapter13_SelfUpdater.mxml file.

Listing 13-10: The `<mx:HTTPService>` tag

```
<mx:HTTPService
    id="versionTest"
    url="http://www.yourdomain.com/version.xml"
    useProxy="false" method="GET" resultFormat="xml"
    result="testVersion(event)"/>
```

Notice that the <mx:HTTPService> tag in Listing 13-10 has a testVersion()method defined as the result handler. This method will parse the results of the service and compare them to the currentVersion variable that was defined above in this chapter. Listing 13-11 shows how this will look.

Listing 13-11: The testVersion() **function**

```
private function testVersion(event:ResultEvent):void{
  version = XML(event.result);
  if((currentVersion != version.@version) && version.@forceUpdate == true){
    getUpdate();
  }else if(currentVersion != version.@version){
    Alert.show("There is an update available, would you like to get it now?",
"Choose Yes or No", 3, this, alertClickHandler);
  } else {
    Alert.show("There are no new updates available", "Notice");
  }
}
```

Let's examine Listing 13-11. First, you will notice that the event.result is cast as XML and set to a variable named version that we have not added yet. Next, you will see that it has three possible actions:

❑   If the versions are different and forceUpdate is set to True, it will do an automatic update without asking the user.

❑   If the versions are different and forceUpdate is set to False, it will ask users if they wish to update.

❑   If the most current version is installed, it simply alerts the user of this. This would not be shown in a production environment unless you had a user-triggered button checking for updates. In this case, the test for updates is occurring upon launch of the application.

Updating the Application

To actually update the application, we're going to need some additional import statements, variables, and ActionScript to get all the possible options working properly.

Please add the import statements and variables from Listing 13-12 to the top of your <mx:Script> block in the Chapter13_SelfUpdating.mxml file.

Listing 13-12: Additional import statements and variables needed for Chapter13_SelfUpdater.mxml

```
import flash.filesystem.FileMode;
import flash.filesystem.FileStream;
import flash.filesystem.File;
import mx.events.CloseEvent;
import mx.rpc.events.ResultEvent;
import mx.controls.Alert;
```

(Continued)

Listing 13-12: Additional import statements and variables needed for Chapter13_SelfUpdater.mxml *(continued)*

```
private var version:XML;
private var urlStream:URLStream = new URLStream();
private var fileData:ByteArray = new ByteArray();
```

Now we simply need to add the functions in Listing 13-13. These functions handle the remaining functionality needed for the application to be self-updating. Go ahead and add these functions to the Chapter13_SelfUpdating.mxml file, and we'll discuss how the whole process flows.

Listing 13-13: The last set of functions needed to complete the Chapter13_SelfUpdating.mxml file

```
private function alertClickHandler(event:CloseEvent):void {
  if (event.detail==Alert.YES){
    getUpdate();
  }
}

private function getUpdate():void{;
  var urlReq:URLRequest = new URLRequest(version.@downloadLocation);
      urlStream.addEventListener(Event.COMPLETE, loaded);
      urlStream.load(urlReq);
}

private function loaded(event:Event):void {
  urlStream.readBytes(fileData, 0, urlStream.bytesAvailable);
  writeAirFile();
}

private function writeAirFile():void {
  var file:File = File.applicationStorageDirectory.resolvePath("Update.air");
  var fileStream:FileStream = new FileStream();
      fileStream.addEventListener(Event.CLOSE, fileClosed);
      fileStream.openAsync(file, FileMode.WRITE);
      fileStream.writeBytes(fileData, 0, fileData.length);
      fileStream.close();
}

private function fileClosed(event:Event):void {
  var updater:Updater = new Updater();
  var airFile:File = File.applicationStorageDirectory.resolvePath("Update.air");
  updater.update(airFile,version.@version);
}
```

Now, we will add a `checkForUpdate()` function that will trigger the `<mx:HTTPService>` to check the remote server and start the process. We also need to call this function within the `applicationComplete` property of the `<WindowedApplication/>` tag. Add the contents of Listing 13-14 to the Chapter13_SelfUpdating.mxml file. Then add `applicationComplete="checkForUpdate()"` to the main `<WindowedApplication/>` tag.

Listing 13-14: The `checkForUpdate()` **function**

```
private function checkForUpdate():void {
    versionTest.send();
}
```

Here is the full flow of the update process:

1. The application loads, which triggers the applicationComplete event.

2. The applicationComplete event calls the `checkForUpdate()` function.

3. The `checkForUpdate()` function calls the `versionTest.send()` method.

4. `versionTest.send()` triggers the `<mx:HTTPService>` to load the remote version.xml file.

5. `<mx:HTTPService>` calls the `testVersion()` function.

6. The `testVersion()` function sets the result to an XML variable named version.

7. `testVersion()` checks to see if the remote version file matches what was set in the `currentVersion` property;

8. If `currentVersion` is different from the remote version and `forceUpdate` is True, `getUpdate()` is called.

9. If `currentVersion` is different from the remote version and `forceUpdate` is False, an Alert is shown informing the user that an update is available — if they choose to update, `getUpdate()` is called.

10. `getUpdate()` creates a `URLRequest` passing in the new AIR package's URL.

11. `getUpdate()` loads the `URLRequest` using `URLStream`.

12. When the `URLStream` is completed, the `loaded()` function is called.

13. `loaded()` reads in the data using `URLStream` and calls the `writeAirFile()` function.

14. `writeAirFile()` uses the `File` class to resolve to a location for the new AIR package.

15. `writeAirFile()` uses `FileStream` to write the new AIR package to disk.

16. Upon completion of the `FileStream` write, the `fileClosed()` function is called.

17. `fileClosed()` creates an instance of the `Updater` class.

18. The `Updater` updates the application by calling `updater.update()` and passing in the new AIR package and version.

19. The application reloads itself automatically.

To try this yourself, be sure to package the application to an AIR package and install the application before running it. If you run it in test mode, it will not work properly. If you have trouble, compare your Chapter13_SelfUpdating.mxml file to the completed version shown in Listing 13-15. The results of running this application can be seen in Figure 13-4.

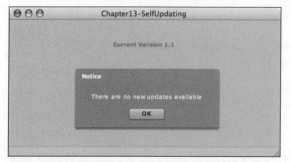

Figure 13-4: The application after it has been updated.

Listing 13-15: The completed version of Chapter13_SelfUpdating.mxml

```xml
<?xml version="1.0" encoding="utf-8"?>
<mx:WindowedApplication xmlns:mx="http://www.adobe.com/2006/mxml"
    layout="absolute" applicationComplete="checkForUpdate()">

    <mx:Script>
      <![CDATA[
      import flash.filesystem.FileMode;
      import flash.filesystem.FileStream;
      import flash.filesystem.File;
      import mx.events.CloseEvent;
      import mx.rpc.events.ResultEvent;
      import mx.controls.Alert;

        private var appXML:XML =
NativeApplication.nativeApplication.applicationDescriptor;
        private var ns : Namespace = appXML.namespace();

        [Bindable]
        private var currentVersion : String = appXML.ns::version;

        private var version:XML;
        private var urlStream:URLStream = new URLStream();
        private var fileData:ByteArray = new ByteArray();

        private function checkForUpdate():void {
            versionTest.send();
        }

        private function testVersion(event:ResultEvent):void{
            version = XML(event.result);
            if((currentVersion != version.@version) && version.@forceUpdate == true){
                getUpdate();
            }else if(currentVersion != version.@version){
                Alert.show("There is an update available," +
                        "would you like to get it now?",
                        "Choose Yes or No", 3, this, alertClickHandler);
            } else {
```

```
                    Alert.show("There are no new updates available", "Notice");
            }
        }

        private function alertClickHandler(event:CloseEvent):void {
            if (event.detail==Alert.YES){
                getUpdate();
            }
        }

        private function getUpdate():void{;
            var urlReq:URLRequest = new URLRequest(version.@downloadLocation);
            urlStream.addEventListener(Event.COMPLETE, loaded);
            urlStream.load(urlReq);
        }

        private function loaded(event:Event):void {
            urlStream.readBytes(fileData, 0, urlStream.bytesAvailable);
            writeAirFile();
        }

        private function writeAirFile():void {
            var file:File =
File.applicationStorageDirectory.resolvePath("Update.air");
            var fileStream:FileStream = new FileStream();
            fileStream.addEventListener(Event.CLOSE, fileClosed);
            fileStream.openAsync(file, FileMode.WRITE);
            fileStream.writeBytes(fileData, 0, fileData.length);
            fileStream.close();
        }

        private function fileClosed(event:Event):void {
            var updater:Updater = new Updater();
            var airFile:File =
File.applicationStorageDirectory.resolvePath("Update.air");
            updater.update(airFile,version.@version);
        }

    ]]>
    </mx:Script>

    <mx:HTTPService
        id="versionTest"
        url="http://www.yourdomain.com/version.xml"
        useProxy="false"
        method="GET" resultFormat="xml" result="testVersion(event)"/>

    <mx:Label text="Current Version {currentVersion}" fontWeight="bold"
        horizontalCenter="0" y="36" textAlign="center" width="100%"/>
    <mx:Button horizontalCenter="0" y="71"
        label="Check for Update" click="checkForUpdate()"/>

</mx:WindowedApplication>
```

Putting It All Together

This chapter has shown how to test for an Internet connection and also how to automatically update the application. Now let's put the two together. Create a new AIR application named *Chapter13_Combined*. Copy the contents of the Chapter13_SelfUpdating.mxml to the new Chapter13_Combined.mxml file.

Now we'll update the contents of the Chapter13_Combined.mxml file by adding in the functions needed to check for a connection before attempting the update.

Start by adding the import statements and variable definition from Listing 13-16 to the Chapter13_Combined.mxml file.

Listing 13-16: The import statements and variable necessary to add connection status to Chapter13_Combined.mxml

```
import air.net.URLMonitor;
import flash.net.URLRequest;
import flash.events.StatusEvent;

private var urlMonitor:URLMonitor;
```

Next, add the init() function from Listing 13-17 to the Chapter13_Combined.mxml file. We will change the applicationComplete to call this method first when the application loads a little below in this section.

Listing 13-17: The init() function

```
private function init():void{
    var urlRequest:URLRequest = new URLRequest('http://www.google.com')
    urlRequest.method = "HEAD";
    urlMonitor = new URLMonitor(urlRequest);
    urlMonitor.addEventListener(StatusEvent.STATUS, statusChanged);
    urlMonitor.start();
}
```

Now add the statusChanged() function from Listing 13-18 to handle the StatusEvent from the init() function. This function has also changed from the one originally used in the Chapter13_ConnStatus.mxml file. This function simply makes a call to the checkForUpdate() function.

Listing 13-18: The event handler for the StatusEvent

```
private function statusChanged(event:StatusEvent):void {
    checkForUpdate();
}
```

To prevent checking for updates when there is no Internet connection, we will update the checkForUpdate() function to test to see if a connection exists. Replace the current checkForUpdate() function within the Chapter13_Combined.mxml file with the contents from Listing 13-19.

Listing 13-19: The updated checkForUpdate() function

```
private function checkForUpdate():void {
    if(urlMonitor.available)versionTest.send();
}
```

The last thing that you need to do before packaging, installing, and running the application is to change the applicationComplete property in the <mx:WindowedApplication> tag to call init() instead of checkForUpdate(). The checkForUpdate() function will be called only when the status changes and the application is connected.

You should now be able to run the Chapter13_Combined application. Listing 13-20 shows the full source code for Chapter13_Combined.mxml.

Listing 13-20: The full completed source code for Chapter13_Combined.mxml

```
<?xml version="1.0" encoding="utf-8"?>
<mx:WindowedApplication xmlns:mx="http://www.adobe.com/2006/mxml"
    layout="absolute" applicationComplete="init()">

  <mx:Script>
  <![CDATA[
    import flash.filesystem.FileMode;
    import flash.filesystem.FileStream;
    import flash.filesystem.File;
    import mx.events.CloseEvent;
    import mx.rpc.events.ResultEvent;
    import mx.controls.Alert;

    import air.net.URLMonitor;
    import flash.net.URLRequest;
    import flash.events.StatusEvent;

    private var appXML:XML =
NativeApplication.nativeApplication.applicationDescriptor;
    private var ns : Namespace = appXML.namespace();

    [Bindable]
    private var currentVersion : String = appXML.ns::version;

    private var version:XML;
    private var urlStream:URLStream = new URLStream();
    private var fileData:ByteArray = new ByteArray();

    private var urlMonitor:URLMonitor;

    private function init():void{
        var urlRequest:URLRequest = new URLRequest('http://www.google.com')
        urlRequest.method = "HEAD";
        urlMonitor = new URLMonitor(urlRequest);
        urlMonitor.addEventListener(StatusEvent.STATUS, statusChanged);
        urlMonitor.start();
    }
```

(Continued)

Listing 13-20: The full completed source code for Chapter13_Combined.mxml *(continued)*

```
    private function statusChanged(event:StatusEvent):void {
        checkForUpdate();
    }

    private function checkForUpdate():void {
        if(urlMonitor.available)versionTest.send();
    }

    private function testVersion(event:ResultEvent):void{
        version = XML(event.result);
        if((currentVersion != version.@version) && version.@forceUpdate == true){
            getUpdate();
        }else if(currentVersion != version.@version){
            Alert.show("There is an update available, " +
                        "would you like to get it now?",
                        "Choose Yes or No", 3, this, alertClickHandler);
        } else {
            Alert.show("There are no new updates available", "Notice");
        }
    }

    private function alertClickHandler(event:CloseEvent):void {
        if (event.detail==Alert.YES){
            getUpdate();
        }
    }

    private function getUpdate():void{;
        var urlReq:URLRequest = new URLRequest(version.@downloadLocation);
        urlStream.addEventListener(Event.COMPLETE, loaded);
        urlStream.load(urlReq);
    }

    private function loaded(event:Event):void {
        urlStream.readBytes(fileData, 0, urlStream.bytesAvailable);
        writeAirFile();
    }

    private function writeAirFile():void {
        var file:File =
        File.applicationStorageDirectory.resolvePath("Update.air");
        var fileStream:FileStream = new FileStream();
        fileStream.addEventListener(Event.CLOSE, fileClosed);
        fileStream.openAsync(file, FileMode.WRITE);
        fileStream.writeBytes(fileData, 0, fileData.length);
        fileStream.close();
    }

    private function fileClosed(event:Event):void {
        var updater:Updater = new Updater();
        var airFile:File =
        File.applicationStorageDirectory.resolvePath("Update.air");
```

```
        updater.update(airFile,version.@version);
    }

    ]]>
    </mx:Script>

    <mx:HTTPService
        id="versionTest"
        url="http://www.yourdomain.com/version.xml"
        useProxy="false" method="GET" resultFormat="xml"
        result="testVersion(event)"/>

    <mx:Label text="Current Version {currentVersion}" fontWeight="bold"
        horizontalCenter="0" y="36" textAlign="center" width="100%"/>
    <mx:Button horizontalCenter="0" y="71" label="Check for Update"
        click="checkForUpdate()"/>

</mx:WindowedApplication>
```

Summary

This chapter has demonstrated how to determine if there is a current connection to the Internet from an AIR application and how to set up the AIR application to trigger events whenever a change in network status occurs. Next, the ability to have an application update itself was demonstrated, utilizing the Updater class. Finally, the two concepts were combined to create an application that first checks for an Internet connection and then checks to see if there is a new version of the application available for download.

The next chapter will take a look at the new FileSystem components available exclusively to AIR applications. This set of components makes viewing the local file system within an AIR application a very easy thing to do.

Exercises

1. Start out with a simple HelloWorld application and add the functionality to test for an Internet connection.

2. Next, add functionality to make your HelloWorld application a self-updating application.

   You may use the ConnectionManager *and* UpdateManager *classes that I have provided at* http://blog.everythingflex.com.

Part IV
The AIR Components

The File System Components

As we have already seen in Chapter 8, AIR has full access to the operating system's file system. AIR has provided five components that have been specifically created to help make navigating the file system easier. This chapter will demonstrate how to use each of these components. This chapter covers each of the following components: FileSystemComboBox, FileSystemDataGrid, FileSystemList, FileSystemTree, and FileSystemHistoryButton. Each component will be added to a single application sample and will be tied together when appropriate. The full source code for the Chapter14_Comps .mxml file is shown in Listing 14-7.

To get started, create a new AIR project within Flex Builder 3 named *Chapter14_Comps*. This will create our application file with the name *Chapter14_Comps.mxml* as shown in Listing 14-1.

Listing 14-1: The newly created Chapter4_Comps.mxml file

```
<?xml version="1.0" encoding="utf-8"?>
<mx:WindowedApplication xmlns:mx="http://www.adobe.com/2006/mxml"
    layout="absolute" width="650" height="550">

</mx:WindowedApplication>
```

FileSystemDataGrid

The FileSystemDataGrid control displays file information in a data-grid format. The file information displayed can include the file name, creation date, modification date, type, and size. Using this component is very simple — you can either choose to provide a directory property, which will display as the starting directory, or simply leave this property off and the FileSystemDataGrid will use the root of the file system as the starting point. To demonstrate this, add the contents of Listing 14-2 to the Chapter14_Comps.mxml file. The results of this can be seen in Figure 14-1. Double-click on the root directory within the FileSystemDataGrid and you will see that you can easily drill into the file system. The results of this are demonstrated in Figure 14-2.

Listing 14-2: The FileSystemDataGrid component

```
<mx:FileSystemDataGrid id="fsdg"
        horizontalCenter="0" y="10" width="600" height="250"/>
```

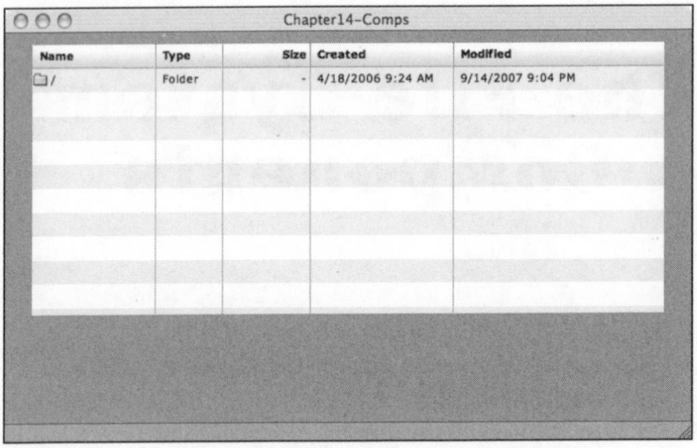

Figure 14-1: The FileSystemComboBox.

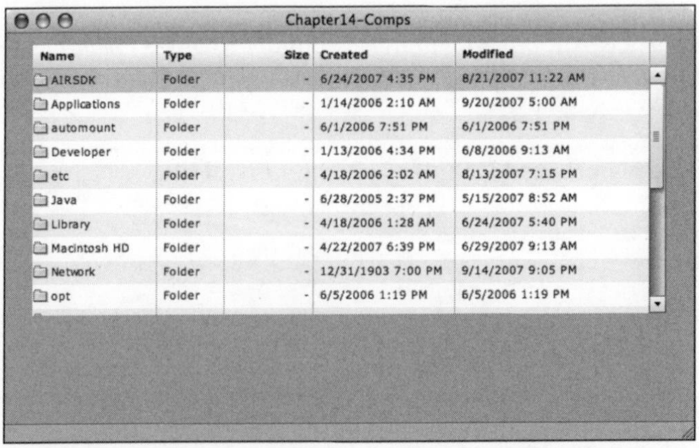

Figure 14-2: The FileSystemDataGrid after double-clicking on the root folder shown in Figure 14-1.

If you continue to navigate the file system by double-clicking on folders, you will quickly notice that there is no way to get back up the directory structure. Fortunately, AIR has provided a control specifically for this use called the *FileSystemHistoryButton*.

FileSystemHistoryButton

The FileSystemHistoryButton component is actually more than a simple button — it is a combination of two buttons and a dropdown menu. The control will broadcast a simple click event when the main part of the button is clicked or itemClick when the dropdown menu is clicked. This component, used in conjunction with the FileSystemDataGrid, allows for easy navigation either back through the history or forward through the history of the target control. In our example, we will add two FileSystemHistoryButtons. The first will be used to navigate back through the history of the FileSystemDataGrid, and the second will be used to navigate forward through the history of the FileSystemDataGrid. Add the contents of Listing 14-3 to the Chapter14_Comps.mxml file.

If you examine the code from Listing 14-3, you will notice that each uses a property of the FileSystemDataGrid as its dataProvider. The Back button uses the backHistory Array of the FileSystemDataGrid to populate the dataProvider. This is then displayed in the dropdown menu of the FileSystemHistoryButton. The Forward button uses the forwardHistory Array to populate its dropdown menu. You will also notice that each component has a click and itemClick handler defined. The click handler calls either the `navigateBack()` or the `navigateForward()` method on the FileSystemDataGrid to update the grids data. The itemClick handler also calls the `navigateBack()` or the `navigateForward()`, but this time provides the index of the FileSystemHistoryButton, which allows you to move back for forward multiple directories. Figure 14.3 shows the FileSystemHistoryButtons with the dropdown menu opened on the Forward button.

Listing 14-3: The FileSystemHistoryButton components

```
<mx:FileSystemHistoryButton dataProvider="{fsdg.backHistory}"
  click="fsdg.navigateBack()"
  itemClick="fsdg.navigateBack(event.index)"
  label="Back" x="252" y="268"/>

<mx:FileSystemHistoryButton dataProvider="{fsdg.forwardHistory}"
  click="fsdg.navigateForward()"
  itemClick="fsdg.navigateForward(event.index)"
  label="Forward" x="318" y="268"/>
```

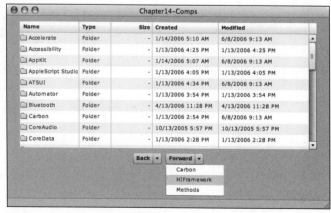

Figure 14-3: The FileSystemHistoryButton components

The FileSystemDataGrid also has some useful properties for editing the displayed data.

The enumerationMode allows you to set the order of the display or filter the display to show folders and files, or only folders, or only files, and also which shows on top. This property accepts a FileSystemEnumerationMode object and has static properties to set the mode. You can also set the component to show the file extensions, icons, or hidden files by setting the showIcons, showExtensions, or showHidden properties to True. You can also control the file types that you wish to show within the FileSystemDataGrid by setting the Extension property. This property accepts an array of extension types.

Simply updating the FileSystemDataGrid to the code shown in Listing 14-4 will look like Figure 14-4. Don't forget to add the import statement as well.

Listing 14-4: Updated version of FileSystemDataGrid with additional properties

```
<mx:Script>
  <![CDATA[
    import mx.controls.FileSystemEnumerationMode;
  ]]>
</mx:Script>
<mx:FileSystemDataGrid id="fsdg"
    horizontalCenter="0" y="10" width="600" height="250"
    enumerationMode="{FileSystemEnumerationMode.FILES_FIRST}"
    showExtensions="false"/>
```

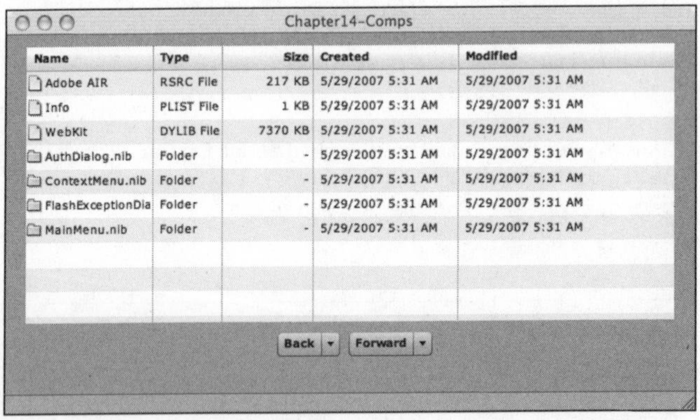

Name	Type	Size	Created	Modified
Adobe AIR	RSRC File	217 KB	5/29/2007 5:31 AM	5/29/2007 5:31 AM
Info	PLIST File	1 KB	5/29/2007 5:31 AM	5/29/2007 5:31 AM
WebKit	DYLIB File	7370 KB	5/29/2007 5:31 AM	5/29/2007 5:31 AM
AuthDialog.nib	Folder	-	5/29/2007 5:31 AM	5/29/2007 5:31 AM
ContextMenu.nib	Folder	-	5/29/2007 5:31 AM	5/29/2007 5:31 AM
FlashExceptionDia	Folder	-	5/29/2007 5:31 AM	5/29/2007 5:31 AM
MainMenu.nib	Folder	-	5/29/2007 5:31 AM	5/29/2007 5:31 AM

Figure 14-4: The FileSystemDataGrid with file extensions hidden and sorted with files on top.

FileSystemList

The FileSystemList is very similar to the FileSystemDataGrid and shares many of the same properties. To add a FileSystemList, simply include <mx:FileSystemList id="fsl" x="24" y="299"/> within the Chapter14_Comps.mxmml file. Since this example did not include a directory property, this will create a FileSystemList that starts at the root directory of your system's hard drive. See Figure 14-5.

To use this component, you will simply double-click on any directories in the current view to navigate into the directory tree. Thus you can navigate into the file system, but it is currently a one-way street. In the FileSystemDataGrid example, we used FileSystemHistoryButton to navigate back and forward through the history of the FileSystemDataGrid control.

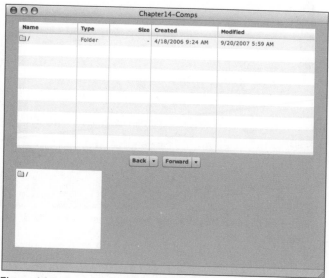

Figure 14-5: Example showing the addition of a FileSystemList component.

In this example, we will use simple buttons to add back, forward, down, and up navigation to the FileSystemList. The Back and Forward buttons will use the navigateBack() and navigateForward() methods as we have seen previously; however, the Down and Up buttons will use the navigateDown() and navigateUp() methods. So what is the difference? Well, navigateBack() will go back though the history of clicks that occurred when navigating the FileSystemList, which may or may not go up the directory tree. The navigateUp() method will simply move the controls contents up a single directory. The navigateDown() method will drill into the directory currently selected within the FileSystemList.

FileSystemList shares many of the properties that we mentioned in the section on the FileSystemDataGrid. In that case, we demonstrated the enumerationMode and showExtensions properties. This time, let's take a look at the Extensions property. Update the contents of Chapter14_Comps.mxml to include the updated FileSystemList component, and add the buttons shown in Listing 14-5. The result will be that as you navigate through your file system, only image files with a jpg or gif extension will be visible. This can be seen in Figure 14-6.

Listing 14-5: The updated FileSystemList and navigation buttons

```
<mx:FileSystemList id="fsl" x="24" y="299" extensions="['.jpg','.gif']"/>

<mx:Button click="fsl.navigateBack()" label="Back" x="27" y="461" width="75"/>
<mx:Button click="fsl.navigateForward()" label="Forward" x="110" y="461"/>
<mx:Button click="fsl.navigateDown()" label="Down" x="27" y="491" width="75"/>
<mx:Button click="fsl.navigateUp()" label="Up" x="110" y="491" width="73"/>
```

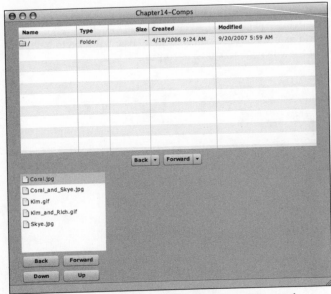

Figure 14-6: The FileSystemList with extensions filter and navigation buttons.

FileSystemTree

FileSystemTree is again very similar to FileSystemDataGrid and FileSystemList except that it will show the directory structure in a tree layout. Add a FileSystemTree to the Chapter14_Comps.mxml file by including `<mx:FileSystemTree id="fst" x="204" y="299" height="214"/>`. The results will look like Figure 14-7.

The FileSystemTree has many of the same properties as the FileSystemDataGrid and FileSystemList including enumeration, showHidden, and so on. For this example, we will show how to read the data associated with the folder or file that is selected. Update the FileSystemList to include a change handler by adding `change="showFileDetails()"`. Next add a TextArea component by including `<mx:TextArea id="log" x="384" y="298" width="240" height="109"/>` in the Chapter14_Comps.mxml file. Finally, add the `showFileDetails()` method and import statement for the `File` class to the script block as defined in Listing 14-6. If we look into the `showFileDetails()` method, you will see that the tree node is cast as a `File` object, at which point all of the File object's properties are available. The `name`, `size`, and `nativePath` are added to the text property of the TextArea component. The results of these additions are shown in Figure 14-8.

Listing 14-6: The import statement and showFileDetails **method**

```
import flash.filesystem.File;

public function showFileDetails():void {
    var file:File = fst.selectedItem as File;
    log.text += "name: " + file.name  + " size: " + file.size + "\n";
    log.text += "          nativepath: " + file.nativePath + "\n";
}
```

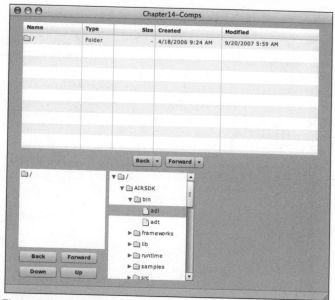

Figure 14-7: Example showing the newly added FileSystemTree component.

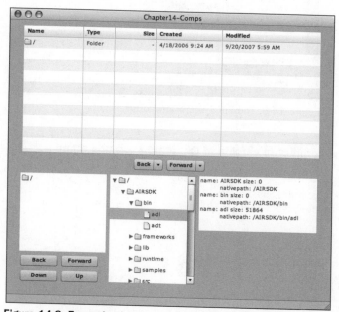

Figure 14-8: Example showing the properties of the selected node of the FileSystemTree.

FileSystemComboBox

The FileSystemComboBox is the last of the file system components. It accepts the same directory property as the other file system components that we have previously covered. It will always allow you to see the full path from the file set as the directory property back up to the root of the file system. To demonstrate this, add `<mx:FileSystemComboBox id="fscb" x="384" y="419" width="240"/>` to the Chapter14_Comps.mxml file. Next add `fscb.directory = file;` to the end of the `showFileDetails()` method. This will set the directory property of the FileSystemComboBox to the selected folder of the FileSystemTree. The results can be seen in Figure 14-9.

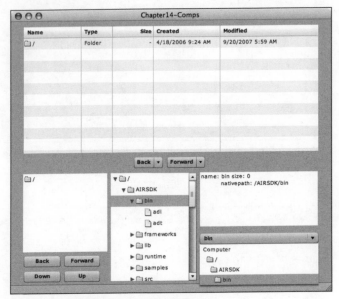

Figure 14-9: The FileSystemComboBox.

Listing 14-7: The completed version of Chapter14_Comps.mxml

```
<?xml version="1.0" encoding="utf-8"?>
<mx:WindowedApplication xmlns:mx="http://www.adobe.com/2006/mxml"
    layout="absolute" width="650" height="550">

    <mx:Script>
        <![CDATA[
            import mx.controls.FileSystemEnumerationMode;
            import flash.filesystem.File;

            public function showFileDetails():void {
                var file:File = fst.selectedItem as File;
                log.text += "name: " + file.name  + " size: " + file.size + "\n";
                log.text += "          nativepath: " + file.nativePath + "\n";
                fscb.directory = file;
            }
```

```
        ]]>
    </mx:Script>

    <mx:FileSystemDataGrid id="fsdg"
        horizontalCenter="0" y="10" width="600" height="250"
        enumerationMode="{FileSystemEnumerationMode.FILES_FIRST}"
        showExtensions="false"/>

    <mx:FileSystemHistoryButton dataProvider="{fsdg.backHistory}"
        click="fsdg.navigateBack()"
        itemClick="fsdg.navigateBack(event.index)"
        label="Back" x="252" y="268"/>

    <mx:FileSystemHistoryButton dataProvider="{fsdg.forwardHistory}"
        click="fsdg.navigateForward()"
        itemClick="fsdg.navigateForward(event.index)"
        label="Forward" x="318" y="268"/>

    <mx:FileSystemList id="fsl" x="24" y="299" extensions="['.jpg','.gif']"/>

    <mx:Button click="fsl.navigateBack()" label="Back" x="27" y="461" width="75"/>
    <mx:Button click="fsl.navigateForward()" label="Forward" x="110" y="461" width="75"/>
    <mx:Button click="fsl.navigateDown()" label="Down" x="27" y="491" width="75"/>
    <mx:Button click="fsl.navigateUp()" label="Up" x="110" y="491" width="73"/>

    <mx:FileSystemTree id="fst" x="204" y="299" change="showFileDetails()"
        height="214"/>
    <mx:TextArea id="log" x="384" y="298" width="240" height="109"/>

    <mx:FileSystemComboBox id="fscb"  x="384" y="419" width="240"/>
</mx:WindowedApplication>
```

Summary

This chapter introduced and demonstrated some uses for the file system components that are part of AIR. The FileSystemComboBox, FileSystemDataGrid, FileSystemList, FileSystemTree, and FileSystemHistoryButton were all added to our sample AIR project named *Chapter14_Comps*. Several components were linked together, and some of the more useful properties were demonstrated.

Exercise

Create a sample application that will read the folder or file properties from the selected rows of the FileSystemDataGrid and the FileSystemList components.

The HTML Component

The HTML component is one of the coolest new components within AIR. Built on top of the Safari WebKit, the HTML component will display full HTML content within your AIR applications. This includes support for JavaScript, Flash, and PDF content. HTML content can either be packaged within an AIR application or loaded from a local path, or can be any accessible content loaded through a public or private URL. You can alternatively supply an HTML string as the source of the HTML component, allowing you to create content at runtime without saving it to a file.

About the Safari WebKit

WebKit is an open source web browser engine that is hosted at `http://webkit.org`. *WebKit* is also the name of the Mac OS X system framework version of the engine that's used by Safari, Dashboard, Mail, and many other OS X applications. Recently the Safari browser, which uses the WebKit engine, was tested as the fastest browser in the world. Having WebKit as the engine for AIR's HTML parsing ensures a fast and consistent experience for any HTML content being used within your AIR applications.

Using the HTML Component

Unlike the Flex 2 TextArea component that allowed a limited subset of HTML tags, the *AIR HTML component* will display any compliant HTML content that runs in any modern browser. The HTML component can accept a basic HTML text string or can point to a local or external URL.

Basic HTML

To demonstrate how to load basic HTML, please create a new AIR project named *Chapter15_HTML_Basic*, which will create a new file named *Chapter15_HTML_Basic.mxml*. Listing 15-1 shows an example that includes a variable named `htmlString` that is some basic HTML code. It is set as [Bindable] and bound to the `htmlText` property of the HTML component. To test this, add the contents of Listing 15-1 to the Chapter15_HTML_Basic.mxml file, and then run the application. The results can be seen in Figure 15-1.

Listing 15-1: An example of an HTML component with a basic HTML string

```
<?xml version="1.0" encoding="utf-8"?>
<mx:WindowedApplication xmlns:mx="http://www.adobe.com/2006/mxml"
    layout="absolute">
    <mx:Script>
        <![CDATA[
        [Bindable]
        private var htmlString:String = '<html>' +
            '<body>' +
            '<p align="center"><font size="2" id="f1">' +
            'This is a paragraph with font size of 2 and aligned center.' +
            '</font></p>' +
            '<p><font size="5" id="f2"><i>' +
            'This is paragraph with a font size of 5 and italics.' +
            '</i></font></p>' +
            '</body>' +
            '</html>'
        ]]>
        </mx:Script>
    <mx:HTML id="html" htmlText="{htmlString}" width="200" height="200"
        horizontalCenter="0" verticalCenter="0"/>
</mx:WindowedApplication>
```

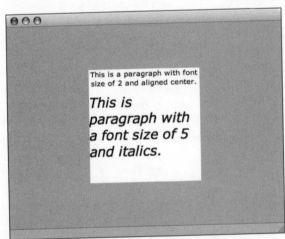

Figure 15-1: A basic HTML string set to the `htmlText` property of an HTML component.

Using the Location Property

The HTML component can also load its contents based on the URL entered within its location property. To use the location property, simply provide a full http:// or file path within the location property. Create a new AIR project named *Chapter15_HTML* within Flex Builder 3. This will also create a new file named *Chapter15_HTML.mxml*. Now simply add a new HTML component to the file, and set the location property to http://blog.everythingflex.com so that your code now looks like Listing 15-2. Running this code will result in something similar to Figure 15-2.

Listing 15-2: The HTML component with a location set

```
<?xml version="1.0" encoding="utf-8"?>
<mx:WindowedApplication xmlns:mx="http://www.adobe.com/2006/mxml"
    layout="absolute">

    <mx:HTML width="100%" height="100%"
        location="http://blog.everythingflex.com"/>
</mx:WindowedApplication>
```

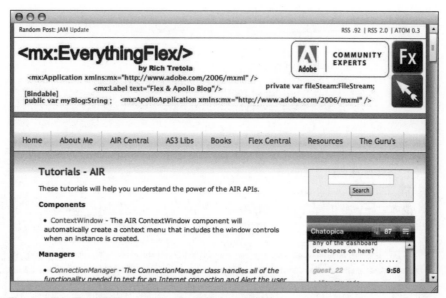

Figure 15-2: The HTML component with a location set.

Navigating History

Now that you have seen how to use the location property of the HTML component, it would be useful if we could give users the option to move forward or backward throughout their browser history. Fortunately, the HTML component makes this pretty simple. In this section, we will build a basic Web browser with current location as well as forward and back history controls. To get started, create a new AIR project named *Chapter15_Browser*, which will also create a new file named *Chapter15_Browser.mxml*. Next, add the contents of Listing 15-3 to the Chapter15_Browser.mxml file.

Listing 15-3 is the base of the browser example with additional functionality to be added within this section. There is a TextInput component that has its text property bound to the location property of the HTML component property. The TextInput component allows the user to type in a URL and then click [Enter], which calls the goToURL() function. The goToURL() function sets the HTML component's location property to the text value of the TextInput component. The Go! button will also call the goToURL() function when clicked. Running the application will result in something similar to Figure 15-3.

Listing 15-3: The base of the browser example

```
<?xml version="1.0" encoding="utf-8"?>
<mx:WindowedApplication xmlns:mx="http://www.adobe.com/2006/mxml"
    layout="absolute" width="800" height="600">

    <mx:Script>
        <![CDATA[
        private function goToURL():void {
            html.location=loc.text;
        }
        ]]>
    </mx:Script>
    <mx:TextInput text="{html.location}" width="500" x="10"
        id="loc" enter="goToURL()" y="3"/>
    <mx:Button click="goToURL()" label="Go!" x="511" y="3"/>
    <mx:HTML width="100%" height="100%" id="html"
        location="http://blog.everythingflex.com" y="30"/>
</mx:WindowedApplication>
```

Figure 15-3: The results of Listing 15-3

historyBack()

The `historyBack()` method does exactly what you would think it should do, and that is to navigate back through the history that has been created with each URL loaded into the HTML component. To demonstrate this, add `<mx:Button click="html.historyBack()" label="Back" x="559" y="3"/>` to the Chapter15_Browser.mxml file.

historyForward()

The `historyForward()` method also does exactly what you would think it should do — it navigates forward through the history that has been created with each URL loaded into the HTML component. To demonstrate this, add `<mx:Button click="html.historyForward()" label="Forward" x="617" y="3"/>` to the Chapter15_Browser.mxml file.

historyGo()

The `historyGo()` method allows you to navigate forward by passing in a positive number or backward by passing in a negative number. Passing a zero will reload the current page. To test this, try changing the calls to `historyBack()` and `historyForward()` to `historyGo(-1)` and `historyGo(1)`.

HTMLHistoryItem

The history of the HTML component is stored as HTMLHistoryItems. The HTMLHistoryItem contains properties like `title`, which contains the title of the page; `url`, which contains the URL of the page; and `isPost`, which shows whether the page contains POST data.

To demonstrate the properties of an HTMLHistoryItem, we will add a TextArea component and a Button to dump out the HTMLHistoryItems. Add the contents of Listing 15-4 to the Chapter15_Browser.mxml file. You will also need to change the `y` property of the HTML component to 163 to make room for the TextArea. Finally, you will need to add a function to create the contents of the history log TextArea. Add the contents of Listing 15-5 to the script block of the Chapter15_Browser.mxml file. If you examine the `showHistoryItems()` function from Listing 15-5, you'll see that it first sets the contents of the TextArea component to empty. Next, there is a For loop that loops from 0 to the `historyLength` of the HTML component. This property returns the current length of the history items. Within the loop, a new HTMLHistoryItem object is created by using the `getHistoryAt()` method to return an HTMLHistoryItem from the HTML component. Finally, it adds the `title` and `url` properties to the `text` property of the historyLog TextArea component.

If you have gone through all of the steps of this section, the Chapter15_Browser.mxml file should now look like Listing 15-6. The results can be seen in Figure 15-4.

Listing 15-4: Components needed to show history log

```
<mx:Button click="showHistoryItems()" x="694" label="Show History" y="3"/>
<mx:TextArea id="historyLog" width="100%" height="125" y="30" x="0"/>
```

Listing 15-5: The function needed to show the contents of the HTML component history

```
private function showHistoryItems():void{
    historyLog.text = "";
    for(var i:int=0; i<html.historyLength; i++){
        var histItem:HTMLHistoryItem = html.getHistoryAt(i);
        historyLog.text += histItem.title + " : " + histItem.url + "\n";
    }
}
```

Listing 15-6: The Chapter15_Browser.mxml file

```
<?xml version="1.0" encoding="utf-8"?>
<mx:WindowedApplication xmlns:mx="http://www.adobe.com/2006/mxml"
    layout="absolute" width="800" height="600">

    <mx:Script>
        <![CDATA[
        [Bindable]
        private var startLocation:String = "http://blog.everythingflex.com";

        private function goToURL():void{
            html.location=loc.text;
        }
        private function showHistoryItems():void{
            historyLog.text = "";
            for(var i:int=0; i<html.historyLength; i++){
                var histItem:HTMLHistoryItem = html.getHistoryAt(i);
                historyLog.text += histItem.title + " : " + histItem.url + "\n";
            }
        }
        ]]>
    </mx:Script>
    <mx:TextInput text="{html.location}" width="500" x="10"
        id="loc" enter="goToURL()" y="3"/>
    <mx:Button click="goToURL()" label="Go!" x="511" y="3"/>
    <mx:Button click="html.historyGo(-1)" label="Back" x="559" y="3"/>
    <mx:Button click="html.historyGo(1)" x="617" label="Forward" y="3"/>
    <mx:Button click="showHistoryItems()" x="694" label="Show History" y="3"/>
    <mx:TextArea id="historyLog" width="100%" height="125" y="30" x="0"/>
    <mx:HTML  width="100%" height="435" id="html"
        location="{startLocation}" y="163" x="0"/>
</mx:WindowedApplication>
```

HTML Document Object Model

The contents of the *HTML Document Object Model (DOM)* are fully accessible. By accessing the `docu-ment` property of the HTML component's htmlLoader, you will have full access to all of the DOM's properties and methods. This section will demonstrate a few ways to access parts of the DOM. For more information on the properties and methods available, you may reference the WebKit DOM reference at `developer.apple.com/documentation/AppleApplications/Reference/WebKitDOMRef/index.html`.

To demonstrate a few of the DOM properties and methods, create a new AIR project named Chapter15_DOM, which will create a new file named *Chapter15_DOM.mxml*. Within this file, please add the contents of Listing 15-7. Listing 15-7 currently has only an HTML component with its location set to `www.google.com`. The results can be seen in Figure 15-5. We will add to this file in the following sections on accessing the DOM.

Figure 15-4: The HTML component's HTMLHistoryItems.

Listing 15-7: The base of the Chapter15_DOM.mxml file

```
<?xml version="1.0" encoding="utf-8"?>
<mx:WindowedApplication xmlns:mx="http://www.adobe.com/2006/mxml"
    layout="absolute" width="850" height="700">
    <mx:HTML id="html" location="http://www.google.com" width="800" height="509"
        horizontalCenter="0" y="120"/>
</mx:WindowedApplication>
```

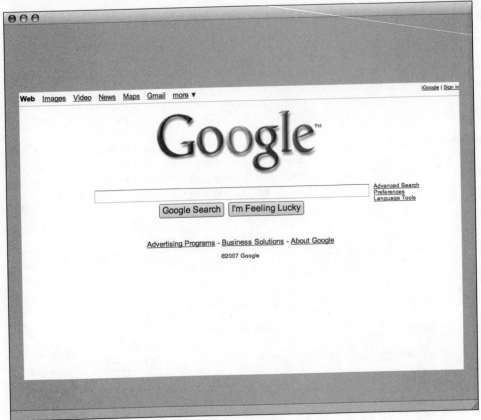

Figure 15-5: The base of the Chapter15_DOM.mxml file.

innerHTML

The innerHTML is a DOM property that will return all of the contents that occur within the <html> </html> tags in a web page. To demonstrate this, we will need to add a TextArea and Button component as well as a function to parse out the HTML. Add the contents of Listings 15-8 and 15-9 to the Chapter15_DOM.mxml file. When examining the showHTML() function within Listing 15-9, you will notice that it creates a String variable named str and sets its contents to html.htmlLoader.window.document .documentElement.innerHTML. At this point, its contents are only what was contained within the <html> </html> tags of the Google homepage. The next line simply adds these tags back into the str variable. Finally, the text property of the TextArea component is set to the str variable that shows the HTML code. The results of this can be seen in Figure 15-6.

Listing 15-8: The components needed to show the HTML

```
<mx:Button click="showHTML()" label="Show HTML" x="321.5" y="5"/>
<mx:TextArea horizontalCenter="0" y="30" width="800" height="68" id="htmlLog"/>
```

Listing 15-9: The function needed to show the HTML

```
<mx:Script>
    <![CDATA[
    private function showHTML():void{
        var str:String=html.htmlLoader.window.document.documentElement.innerHTML;
        str = '<html>' + str + '</html>';
        htmlLog.text = str;
    }
    ]]>
</mx:Script>
```

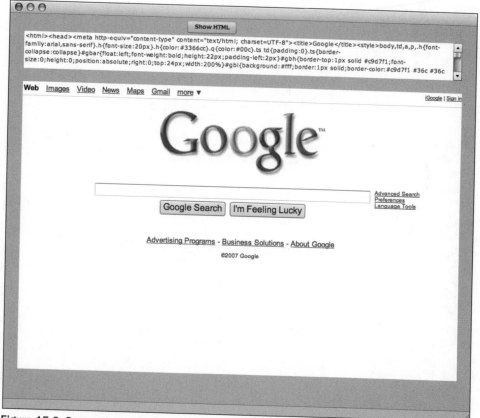

Figure 15-6: Screenshot showing the HTML being parsed out of the Google homepage.

getElementsByTagName()

We can also get the elements of the DOM by tag name. In other words, we can parse out all of the <p> paragraph tags or the <a> link tags. To demonstrate this, we will parse out the Google logo and replace it with another image. We will need to add another button to trigger the image switch and a function to do the work. Add `<mx:Button click="changeImage()" x="417.5" label="Change Image" y="5"/>` to the Chapter15_DOM.mxml file and also the function from Listing 15-10. The `changeImage()` function uses the `getElementsByTagName()` function to get all of the `<img>` tags within the DOM and sets them to an images object of type Object. It then loops through the images object and sets the `src`, `alt`, `title`, `width`, and `height` properties of the image to new values. Figure 15-7 shows the results after clicking the Change Image button.

Listing 15-10: The `changeImage()` function

```
private function changeImage():void{
    var images:Object =
html.htmlLoader.window.document.documentElement.getElementsByTagName("img");
    if(images != null)
        for(var i:Number=0; i < images.length; i++) {
            images[i].src = "http://www.everythingflex.com/assets/images/logo.jpg";
            images[i].alt = "EverythingFlex";
            images[i].title = "EverythingFlex";
            images[i].width=334;
            images[i].height=61;
        }
}
```

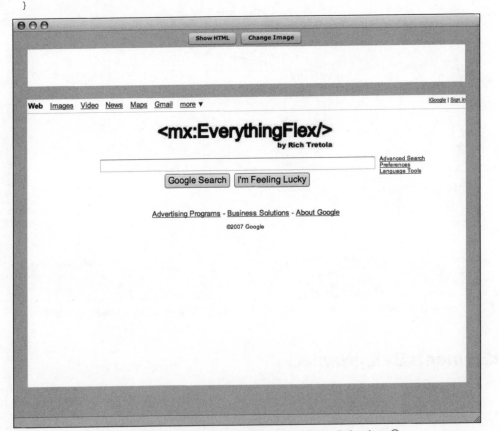

Figure 15-7: The Google logo has been replaced by something a little nicer ☺.

getElementById()

Similar to the use of `getElementsByTagName()`, `getElementById()` allows you to find specific elements within the DOM. For instance, if you have an `<img>` with an ID of "myImage," you would access that `<img>` and its properties by using `html.htmlLoader.window.document.getElementById("myImage")`. To demonstrate this, open the Chapter15_HTML_Basic.mxml file that was previously Listing 15-1 and add `<mx:Button click="changeFonts()" label="Change Fonts" horizontalCenter="0" y="10"/>` to the file. Next add the `changeFonts()` function from Listing 15-11 to the script block of the Chapter15_HTML_Basic.mxml file. Notice that the `changeFonts()` function accesses the `<font>` tags by ID. Once the `<font>` tag is accessed, the font sizes are reversed from the way they were in the original htmlString. The results can be seen in Figure 15-8. To see the difference, compare it to the original shown in Figure 15-1.

Listing 15-11: The use of the `getElementById()` **function**

```
private function changeFonts():void{
    html.htmlLoader.window.document.getElementById("f1").size = 5;
    html.htmlLoader.window.document.getElementById("f2").size = 2;
}
```

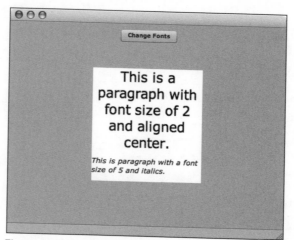

Figure 15-8: Font sizes are shown after updating with the `getElementById()` function.

PDF Support

The HTML component will support the display of Adobe PDF only if the installed version is Acrobat Reader 8.1 or later. You can test for this by using the static `pdfCapability` property of the HTML class. The easiest way to confirm that a user can load PDF files into the HTML component is to test `HTML.pdfCapability` against the `STATUS_OK` static property of the `HTMLPDFCapability` class. Listing 15-12 shows a simple function that will check to see if the user has the correct version of Adobe Reader. If Reader is found, a sample PDF is loaded; if not, the user is shown the Adobe Reader download page. The results can be seen in Figures 15-9 and 15-10.

Listing 15-12: The use of the `pdfCapability` **property**

```
<?xml version="1.0" encoding="utf-8"?>
<mx:WindowedApplication xmlns:mx="http://www.adobe.com/2006/mxml" layout="absolute"
    creationComplete="testPDFCapability()" width="825" height="625">
    <mx:Script>
        <![CDATA[
        private function testPDFCapability():void{
            if(HTML.pdfCapability== HTMLPDFCapability.STATUS_OK){
                html.location="http://www.everythingflex.com/assets/pdfs/sample.pdf";
            }else{
                html.location="http://www.adobe.com/products/acrobat/readstep2.html";
            }
        }
        ]]>
    </mx:Script>
    <mx:HTML id="html" width="800" height="600"/>
</mx:WindowedApplication>
```

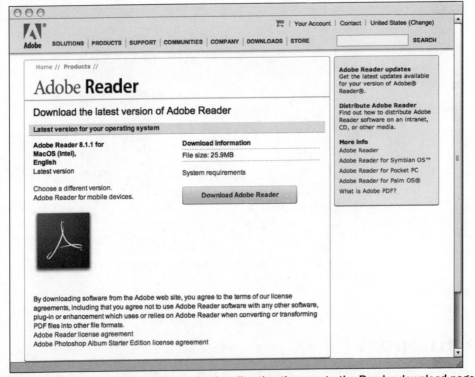

Figure 15-9: The Chapter15_PDF application directing the user to the Reader download page when HTML.pdfCapability fails.

Figure 15-10: A sample PDF being loaded into the HTML component.

Summary

This chapter showed some of the capabilities of the HTML component including how to access the HTML Document Object Modl as well as the ability to display PDF content. The HTML component is a very powerful component, and I highly recommend that you explore the additional features of this component.

Exercise

Create an application that shows all of the images that a web page contains in a separate window.

You will need to parse out the images using `getElementsByTagName()`. *Also, see Chapter 9 for information on the Windowing API.*

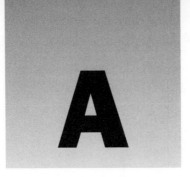

Taking a Flex App to the Desktop

The introduction of the Adobe Integrated Runtime opens many doors to those who have been developing in technologies such as Adobe Flex, Adobe Flash, HTML, and JavaScript to create desktop applications using a technology they are familiar with. This appendix focuses on taking an Adobe Flex application and deploying it on the desktop as well. The new AIR application will add some features specific to AIR but will also continue to share parts of the original Flex application.

The Original Flex Application

First let's examine the existing Flex application. This application is a very simple mash-up using the Yahoo Weather API (`AstraWebAPIs.swc`) to populate local weather conditions. On first run, the application switches to the Preferences view (`Edit.mxml`), where the local zip code is collected as well as the automatic refresh rate. These values are stored in a shared object for persistence between visits. The Results.mxml view displays the Yahoo weather details and also links to the full forecast by utilizing `URLRequest` class. Finally, the `Flip effect` class within Alex Uhlmann's distortion effect (`DistortionEffects.swc`) classes handles the transition between the `Results.mxml` and `Edit.mxml` views. Figures A-1 and A-2 show the Results and Preferences views, respectively.

Figure A-1: The original Flex application Results view.

**Figure A-2: The Preferences
view of the original
Flex application.**

Convert It to AIR

If you haven't already done so, please download the original Weather Flex project from the Wrox down-load site, and import it into Flex Builder 3.

Now create a new project within Flex Builder 3 named *WeatherAIR*. Make sure you choose "Desktop Application" for the "Application Type." Click Next, and then leave the "Output Folder" as bin-debug and click Next again. Now click "Add Folder," and add the src folder from the WeatherFlex project as a source folder and click Finish. Finally, copy the `DistortionEffects.swc` file and `AstraWebAPIs.swc` from the libs folder of the WeatherFlex project to the libs folder of the WeatherAIR project. Your project should now look like the image shown in Figure A-3.

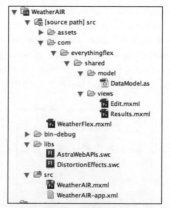

**Figure A-3: The Navigation view
of the new AIR project.**

Now simply copy the contents of the WeatherFlex.mxml file into the WeatherAIR.mxml `file`. Next change the base tag from `<mx:Application>` to `<mx:WindowedApplication>`. You should now be able to test the AIR application. After running the new application, you should see something similar to Figure A-4.

Figure A-4: The newly created AIR application.

Checking for a Connection

When this was a Flex Web-based application, there was never a concern about whether or not there was an Internet connection at the time the application was loaded. With an AIR application, we can't be assured that an Internet connection exists.

It's up to us to put the code in place to check for an Internet connection and alert the user of potential problems. Therefore, we need to add code to check for a connection by pinging against a well-known domain. So let's get started. The first thing you will need to do is to create a new folder path under src of `com/everythingflex/air/managers`. Make sure you are working in the src folder of the WeatherAIR project and not the [source path] src folder, which is the shared source. Within this new package, create a new ActionScript class named `ConnectionManager.as` and enter the contents of Listing A-1 into this new file.

Listing A-1: The `ConnectionManager` **class**

```
package com.everythingflex.air.managers
{
    import air.net.URLMonitor;
    import flash.events.StatusEvent;
    import flash.net.URLRequest;
    import mx.controls.Alert;

    public class ConnectionManager
{
```

(Continued)

Listing A-1: The `ConnectionManager` **class** *(continued)*

```
private var eventObj:StatusEvent;
private var urlMonitor:URLMonitor;
// if true, show the Alert window
private var showMessage:Boolean;
// message to display when connection fails and showMessage is true
private var message:String;
// URL to test for a connection
[Bindable]
public var connectionURL:String;
[Bindable]
public var isConnected:Boolean = false;

public function ConnectionManager(showMessage:Boolean=true,
    connectionURL:String="http://www.google.com",
    message:String="This application requires\nan Internet connection"):void{

    this.showMessage = showMessage;
    this.connectionURL = connectionURL;
    this.message = message;
        startMonitor();
}

// start the URLMonitor and test against the connectionURL
public function startMonitor():void{
    var urlRequest:URLRequest = new URLRequest(connectionURL)
    urlRequest.method = "HEAD";
    urlMonitor = new URLMonitor(urlRequest);
    urlMonitor.addEventListener(StatusEvent.STATUS, statusChanged);
    urlMonitor.start();
}

// handle changes in the connection status and dispatches StatusEvent
public function statusChanged(event:StatusEvent):void{
    this.isConnected = urlMonitor.available;
    if(!this.isConnected && this.showMessage){
        Alert.show(this.message, "Connection Failure");
    }
    eventObj = new StatusEvent(StatusEvent.STATUS);
    dispatchEvent(eventObj);
    }
    }
}
```

Now complete the following updates to the WeatherAIR.mxml file.

Add the import statement and var shown below into the WeatherAIR.mxml file; this will be our instance of the `ConnectionManager` that will be used to test the connection.

```
import com.everythingflex.air.managers.ConnectionManager;
private var cm:ConnectionManager = new ConnectionManager();
```

Add the event listener shown below to the WeatherAIR.mxml `init()` function. This will listen for changes to the `isConnected` property of the `ConnectionManager`.

```
cm.addEventListener(StatusEvent.STATUS, connectionStatusChanged);
```

Add the function below to the WeatherAIR.mxml file. This function will handle the connection status changes. If there is a connection, it will call `getWeather()`.

```
public function connectionStatusChanged(event:StatusEvent):void{
    if(event.target.isConnected){
        this.getWeather();
    }
}
```

To make sure a connection exists before trying to call out to Yahoo, update the WeatherAIR.mxml `getWeather()` function to check for connection.

```
public function getWeather():void{
    if(cm.isConnected){
        model.weather = null;
        weatherService.getWeather(model.zip, "f");
    }
}
```

After completing these changes, test the application. You can test to see if it is working properly by disconnecting and reconnecting your Internet connection. The image in Figure A-5 represents a failed test for an Internet connection.

Figure A-5: The `ConnectionManager` alerting the user to a failed connection.

Use HTML Control and Windowing API

When this was a Flex Web-based application, the only option available to show Yahoo's Full Forecast for the selected city was to use the `URLRequest` class to navigate to a new web page. Now that it is an AIR application, we can use the HTML control to load the same URL into our application rather than relying on a Web browser.

This step will also use the Window component to easily create a new application window that is independent from the root application window. This is important because, since it is independent, it can be any size we want. This allows us to display the full browser window when displaying Yahoo's full forecast link.

The first thing you will need to do is to create a views folder under `com.everythingflex.air` and then create a new MXML component named `Details.mxml` of type `Window` within this folder. This will be a new application window and will contain an HTML component, which is bound to the weather link that is returned from the Yahoo weather service. Enter the contents of Listing A-2 into this new component.

Listing A-2: The Details.mxml Window component

```xml
<?xml version="1.0" encoding="utf-8"?>
<mx:Window xmlns:mx="http://www.adobe.com/2006/mxml"
           layout="absolute" width="800" height="600">

    <mx:Script>
        <![CDATA[
        import com.everythingflex.shared.model.DataModel;
        [Bindable]
        private var model:DataModel = DataModel.getInstance();
        ]]>
    </mx:Script>

    <mx:HTML location="{model.weather.link}" width="100%" height="100%"/>

</mx:Window>
```

Next, update the `showFullForecast()` method within the WeatherAIR.mxml file to create a new window rather than opening a browser window with a `URLRequest`. The method should be updated so that it looks like the `showFullForecats()` method below.

```
public function showFullForecast():void{
    var details:Details = new Details();
        details.open();
}
```

You will also need to add an import statement to import the Details component into the WeatherAIR .mxml file.

```
import com.everythingflex.air.views.Details;
```

Test the application again and click on the Full Forecast button. You should now see a new AIR window open and Yahoo's weather details page open, looking similar to Figure A-6.

Figure A-6: The Details.mxml Window.

Integrate SQLite

Since AIR has the ability to easily integrate with SQLite, we can use a database to store some of the data that are retrieved from the weather service. These data will be utilized in a later portion of this Appendix. To handle all of the interactions with the SQLite database, we will use a `DataManager` class. Create a new ActionScript class named `DataManager.as` within the `com.everythingflex.air.managers` package, and enter the contents of Listing A-3.

Listing A-3: The `DataManager` **class**

```
package com.everythingflex.air.managers
{
    import flash.data.SQLConnection;
    import flash.filesystem.File;
    import flash.events.SQLErrorEvent;
    import flash.events.SQLEvent;
    import flash.data.SQLStatement;
    import flash.filesystem.FileStream;
    import flash.filesystem.FileMode;
    import flash.data.SQLResult;
    import mx.collections.ArrayCollection;
    import com.everythingflex.shared.model.DataModel;

    public class DataManager {

        private var conn:SQLConnection;
        private var createTableStatement:SQLStatement;
        private var insertStatement:SQLStatement;
        private var selectHistorySQL:SQLStatement;

        // open or create the database
        public function openDatabase():void{
            conn = new SQLConnection();
```

(Continued)

265

Listing A-3: The `DataManager` **class** *(continued)*

```
            conn.addEventListener(SQLErrorEvent.ERROR, errorHandler);
            var dbFile:File =
File.applicationStorageDirectory.resolvePath("WeatherAIR.db");
            if(dbFile.exists) {
                conn.addEventListener(SQLEvent.OPEN, openHandler);
            } else {
                conn.addEventListener(SQLEvent.OPEN, createHandler);
            }
            conn.openAsync(dbFile);
        }

    // handle and log errors
    private function errorHandler(event:SQLErrorEvent):void {
        var err:String = "Error Id:" + event.error.errorID + "\nDetails:" +
event.error.details;

    // handle a new database being created
    private function createHandler(event:SQLEvent):void {
        trace("The database was created successfully");
        createTable();
    }

    // handle the database being opened
    private function openHandler(event:SQLEvent):void {
        trace("The database was opened successfully");
    }

// create the table if it doesn't yet exist
    private function createTable():void{
        var sqlText:String = "CREATE TABLE CALLS(ID INTEGER PRIMARY KEY, " +
        "DATETIMESTAMP TEXT, TEMPERATURE TEXT, PRESSURE TEXT, ZIPCODE TEXT, "+
        "WEATHERDATETIMESTAMP TEXT)";
        createTableStatement = new SQLStatement();
        createTableStatement.sqlConnection = conn;
        createTableStatement.addEventListener(SQLEvent.RESULT,
                                            createTableResult);
        createTableStatement.addEventListener(SQLErrorEvent.ERROR,
                                            errorHandler);
        createTableStatement.text = sqlText;
        createTableStatement.execute();
    }

    // handle the create table result
    private function createTableResult(event:SQLEvent):void {
        trace("The table CALLS was created successfully");
    }

    // insert a record into the table
    public function insertRecord(dateTime:Date,temperature:Number,
                                pressure:Number,zipCode:String):void{
```

```
        var sqlText:String = "INSERT INTO CALLS(DATETIMESTAMP, TEMPERATURE,"+
            "PRESSURE, ZIPCODE, WEATHERDATETIMESTAMP) " +
            "VALUES(:dateTimeStamp,:temperature,:pressure,:zipCode,:dateTime)";
        insertStatement = new SQLStatement();
        insertStatement.sqlConnection = conn;
        insertStatement.addEventListener(SQLEvent.RESULT, insertResult);
        insertStatement.addEventListener(SQLErrorEvent.ERROR, errorHandler);
        insertStatement.text = sqlText;
        insertStatement.parameters[":dateTimeStamp"] = new Date().toString();
        insertStatement.parameters[":temperature"] = temperature;
        insertStatement.parameters[":pressure"] = pressure;
        insertStatement.parameters[":zipCode"] = zipCode;
        insertStatement.parameters[":dateTime"] = dateTime.toString();
        insertStatement.execute();
    }

    // handle a successful insert
    private function insertResult(event:SQLEvent):void {
        trace("The record was inserted successfully");
    }


    }
}
```

To use this new class, perform the following steps.

Add an instance of this new class to WeatherAIR.mxml:

```
import com.everythingflex.air.managers.DataManager;
private var dm:DataManager = new DataManager();
```

To open or create the new database, add `dm.openDatabase();` to the `WeatherAIR.mxml init()` method.

To record each call to the Yahoo weather service, add the following to the `weatherResultWeatherHadler()` method in the WeatherAIR.mxml file.

```
dm.insertRecord(model.weather.date,
                model.weather.current.temperature,
                model.weather.current.atmosphere.pressure,
                model.zip);
```

To see this in action, open up the Finder on Mac or Explorer on Windows, and navigate to where the database was created. This will be under `/Users/username/Library/Preferences/WeatherAIR` on Mac or `C:\Documents and Settings\username\Application Data\WeatherAIR\Local Store` on Windows. Now run the application, and you will see the WeatherAIR.db file get created.

Figure A-7 shows the WeatherAIR.db file that was created with the `DataManager`. It was opened with the SQLite Database Browser.

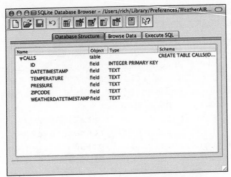

Figure A-7: The newly created database within the SQLite Database Browser.

Logging with the File API

The ability to log errors is common to desktop applications and can be very helpful when offering support for your applications. Since the `File` and `FileStream` classes give us the ability to write to the local file system, we can use these classes to log any application errors. In this example, we will set the application to log any SQL errors that occur when using the `DataManager` class. You can create additional log files for errors occurring when there are other types of exceptions thrown.

To accomplish this, we will simply need to update the `DataManager.as` class with the following steps.

Add the following import statements to the `DataManager.as` class needed for writing to the file system.

```
import flash.filesystem.File;
import flash.filesystem.FileStream;
import flash.filesystem.FileMode;
```

Instantiate the new log file by adding a class variable to the `DataManager.as` class.

```
private var sqlLog:File =
File.applicationStorageDirectory.resolvePath("SQLErrorLog.log");
```

Finally, add the following to the `errorHandler()` function that is called on any error within the DataManager class. Note that the file is open with FileMode.APPEND as the mode argument. This allows us to append to the file without losing previous log information.

```
var fileStream:FileStream = new FileStream();
    fileStream.open(sqlLog, FileMode.APPEND);
    fileStream.writeUTFBytes(new Date() + ': ' + err+'\n\n');
    fileStream.close();
```

Running the application will not show this new error logging in action unless there is a SQL error thrown. You can temporarily change one of the field names within the SQL of the DataManagers `insertRecord()` method. This will then throw an error and log it to the SQLErrorLog.log file, which will reside in the same directory as the WeatherAIR.db SQLite database.

Figure A-8 shows the SQLErrorLog.log file that was created when I was testing the application and forcing it to throw errors by changing the name of the ZIPCODE field in the insertStatement.

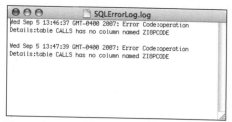

Figure A-8: The SQLErrorLog.log file after intentionally creating an error.

DockIcon and SystemTray

AIR allows us to customize the dock icon on Mac and the system tray icon on Windows at runtime. This means that even when our application is not in focus, we still have the ability to alert users of important information about our application. We also have the ability to make the dock icon bounce to get the user's attention and force the user to move focus to our application. The following code will create a custom dock icon by using the image returned from the Yahoo weather service and layering the current temperature on top. The icon will be recreated each time a new image is loaded by listening for an update event of the img object within the Results view.

To implement the DockIcon and SystemTray icons, please perform the following steps. Add an import statement to the WeatherAIR.mxml file:

```
import mx.events.FlexEvent;
```

Set up an event listener within the init() function of WeatherAIR.mxml by adding the line below to the init() function.

```
resultsView.img.addEventListener(FlexEvent.UPDATE_COMPLETE,setDockIcon);
```

Next add the setDockIcon() method to the WeatherAIR.mxml file. This method will be called each time the weather image changes. It creates a new BitmapData object by reading the bytes of the `<mx:Image>` object holding the weather image and the `<mx:Text>` object holding the current temperature. This new BitmapaData object is then passed into the NativeApplication.nativeApplication.icon.bitmaps array.

```
private function setDockIcon(event:FlexEvent):void{
    var weatherImage:BitmapData=new BitmapData(resultsView.img.width,
                                               resultsView.img.height);
        weatherImage.draw(resultsView.img);
        weatherImage.draw(resultsView.temp);
    NativeApplication.nativeApplication.icon.bitmaps = [weatherImage];
}
```

Test the application, and, depending on your operating system, you will either see the dock icon on your Mac get updated or the system tray icon on Windows get updated.

To make the dock icon bounce whenever the weather is updated (Mac only), add the following to the `weatherResultEventHandler()` function of the WeatherAIR.mxml file:

```
if(NativeApplication.supportsDockIcon){
    var dock:DockIcon = NativeApplication.nativeApplication.icon as DockIcon;
    dock.bounce(NotificationType.CRITICAL);
}
```

Note that setting the NotificationType to CRITICAL will force interaction with the icon before it stops bouncing. Leaving the `dock.bounce()` method empty will trigger the icon to bounce only once. Make sure the application is minimized to trigger the bounce; if the user is currently using the application, it will not bounce.

Figures A-9 and A-10 show the system tray on WindowsXP and the dock on Mac OSX, respectively.

Figure A-9: The system tray icon within the WindowsXP operating system.

Figure A-10: The dock icon within Mac OS X operating system.

Add a Native Menu

The `NativeMenu` class gives us the ability to integrate to the menu system that is native to the operating system. This creates an interface that is more in line with what users expect from a desktop application running in their computers' environment. We also have the ability to add keyboard shortcuts to access these menu items. To add a `NativeMenu`, you will first need to build up the `NativeMenu` and `NativeMenuItems` before adding them to the shell using the `addItem()` method of the `NativeApplication.nativeApplication.menu` object. Add the following code to the `init()` method of the WeatherAIR.mxml file. The code in Listing A-4 will create a menu named *Navigation* with two submenus, Preferences and Full Forecast. It also adds keyboard shortcuts for selecting the menu items. Finally, it adds an event listener listening for the SELECT event and calling the `handleMenuClick()` function. Copy the code from Listing A-4 to the `init()` method within the WeatherAIR.mxml file.

Listing A-4: Code to build up `NativeMenu`

```
var nativeMenu:NativeMenu = new NativeMenu();
var menuItem:NativeMenuItem = new NativeMenuItem("Navigation");
var prefMenu:NativeMenuItem = new NativeMenuItem("Preferences");
var forecastMenu:NativeMenuItem = new NativeMenuItem("Full Forecast");

prefMenu.addEventListener(Event.SELECT,handleMenuClick);
prefMenu.keyEquivalent = "P";

forecastMenu.addEventListener(Event.SELECT,handleMenuClick);
forecastMenu.keyEquivalent = "F";

nativeMenu.addItem(prefMenu);
nativeMenu.addItem(forecastMenu);
nativeMenu.addItem(new NativeMenuItem("",true));

menuItem.submenu = nativeMenu;
NativeApplication.nativeApplication.menu.addItem(menuItem);
```

Next, add the `handleMenuClick()` function to the WeatherAIR.mxml file.

```
private function handleMenuClick(e:Event):void {
    var menuItem:NativeMenuItem = e.target as NativeMenuItem;
    if(menuItem.label == "Preferences")flipToEdit();
    if(menuItem.label == "Full Forecast")showFullForecast();
}
```

Test the application, and you should now see a menu within the top menu bar on Mac as pictured in Figure A-11.

Figure A-11: The `NativeMenu`.

Add a ContextMenu

Since the `NativeMenu` we previously added will only show on Mac OS X, we need to accommodate our Windows users. Fortunately, it's very simple to add the same `NativeMenu` to the application as a `ContextMenu` (right mouse click). To do this, simply add `this.contextMenu = nativeMenu;` right below the creation of the `NativeMenu` within the `init()` function. The results can be seen in Figure A-12.

Figure A-12: The `ContextMenu` **(right mouse click).**

Make It Self-Updating

Another issue that was a non-issue when this was a Flex Web-based application is version control. Back then, if we wanted to push out a new version, we would simply upload the changes to the server, and on the next visit the user would get the new version. With an AIR application, our users are not visiting our server on each run of the application, so we could easily lose control over our application. The solution to this is to program a self-updating scheme. It is very important that you implement this on the first version you release or you will wind up with applications that are orphans with no chance of being updated unless the user actively requests the update. Note that this solution is one that I created and is not an official Adobe method for doing application updates.

Please follow these steps to add self-updating to the WeatherAIR application.

Create a new ActionScript class named `UpdateManager` within the `com.everthingflex.air.man-agers` package, and enter the contents of Listing A-5 into this new class.

Listing A-5: The `UpdateManager` **class**

```
package com.everythingflex.air.managers
{
    import flash.desktop.NativeApplication;
    import flash.desktop.Updater;
```

```
import flash.events.Event;
import flash.filesystem.File;
import flash.filesystem.FileMode;
import flash.filesystem.FileStream;
import flash.net.URLRequest;
import flash.net.URLStream;
import flash.utils.ByteArray;

import mx.controls.Alert;
import mx.events.CloseEvent;
import mx.rpc.events.FaultEvent;
import mx.rpc.events.ResultEvent;
import mx.rpc.http.HTTPService;

public class UpdateManager
{
    // URL of the remote version.xml file
    private var versionURL:String;
    // load in the applicationDescriptor
    private var appXML:XML =
NativeApplication.nativeApplication.applicationDescriptor;
    private var ns : Namespace = appXML.namespace();
    // set the currentVersion information
    private var currentVersion:String = appXML.ns::version;
    // holder for remote version.xml XML data
    private var version:XML;
    private var urlStream:URLStream = new URLStream();
    private var fileData:ByteArray = new ByteArray();

    // the constructor requires the versionURL
    public function UpdateManager(versionURL:String,
                                autoCheck:Boolean=true):void{
        this.versionURL = versionURL;
        if(autoCheck)loadRemoteFile();
    }

    // load the remote version.xml file
    private function loadRemoteFile():void{
        var http:HTTPService = new HTTPService();
        http.url = this.versionURL;
        http.useProxy=false;
        http.method = "GET";
        http.resultFormat="xml";
        http.send();
        http.addEventListener(ResultEvent.RESULT,testVersion);
        http.addEventListener(FaultEvent.FAULT,versionLoadFailure);
    }

    /*
    test the currentVersion against the remote version file and
    either alert the user of
    an update available or force the update, if no update available,
    alert user
    */
```

(Continued)

Listing A-5: The `UpdateManager` **class** *(continued)*

```
public function checkForUpdate():Boolean{
    if(version == null){
        this.loadRemoteFile();
        return true;
    }
    if((currentVersion != version.@version)&&version.@forceUpdate == true){
        getUpdate();
    }else if(currentVersion != version.@version){
        Alert.show("There is an update available,\nwould you like to " +
                    "get it now? \n\nDetails:\n" + version.@message,
                "Choose Yes or No", 3, null, alertClickHandler);
    }else{
        Alert.show("There are no new updates available", "NOTICE");
    }
    return true;
}

/*
test the currentVersion against the remote version file and
either alert the user of
an update available or force the update
*/
private function testVersion(event:ResultEvent):void{
    version = XML(event.result);
    if((currentVersion != version.@version)&&version.@forceUpdate == true){
        getUpdate();
    }else if(currentVersion != version.@version){
        Alert.show("There is an update available,\nwould you like to " +
                    "get it now? \n\nDetails:\n" + version.@message,
                "Choose Yes or No", 3, null, alertClickHandler);

    }
}

/*
Load of the version.xml file failed
*/
private function versionLoadFailure(event:FaultEvent):void{
    Alert.show("Failed to load version.xml file from "+
    this.versionURL,"ERROR");
}

// handle the Alert window decission
private function alertClickHandler(event:CloseEvent):void {
    if (event.detail==Alert.YES){
        getUpdate();
    }
}

// get the new version from the remote server
private function getUpdate():void{
    var urlReq:URLRequest = new URLRequest(version.@downloadLocation);
    urlStream.addEventListener(Event.COMPLETE, loaded);
```

```
        urlStream.load(urlReq);
    }


    // read in the new AIR package
    private function loaded(event:Event):void {
        urlStream.readBytes(fileData, 0, urlStream.bytesAvailable);
        writeAirFile();
    }


    /*
    write the newly downloaded AIR package to the
    application storage directory
    */
    private function writeAirFile():void {
        var file:File = File.applicationStorageDirectory.resolvePath("Update.air");
        var fileStream:FileStream = new FileStream();
        fileStream.addEventListener(Event.CLOSE, fileClosed);
        fileStream.openAsync(file, FileMode.WRITE);
        fileStream.writeBytes(fileData, 0, fileData.length);
        fileStream.close();
    }


    // after the write is complete, call the update method on the Updater class
    private function fileClosed(event:Event):void {
        var updater:Updater = new Updater();
        var airFile:File =
File.applicationStorageDirectory.resolvePath("Update.air");
        updater.update(airFile,version.@version);
    }


    }
}
```

To use this new class, please perform the following steps.

Add an instance of this new class to WeatherAIR.mxml by adding an import statement and class variable as shown below. The constructor of the UpdateManager requires that the URL to the version .xml file be passed in. There is a second optional argument of type Boolean that tells the UpdateManager whether to automatically check for an update. It defaults to True; however, in this case, we have set this to False.

```
import com.everythingflex.air.managers.UpdateManager;

private var um:UpdateManager = new
UpdateManager("http://www.everythingflex.com/AIR/WeatherAIR/version.xml", false);
```

The UpdateManager will attempt to read the remote file named *version.xml*. Listing A-6 shows a sample of what the version.xml should look like. Notice that the version property is what will be compared to the version stored in the application.xml of the installed application. The download location is where the new version is stored and will be downloaded. If the forceUpdate property if set to True, the application will automatically update without ever prompting the user. Finally, if forceUpdate is False, the message will display within the Alert window when an update is available. Listing A-6 shows an example of the version.xml file that you would keep on your server.

Since we set the `UpdateManager` not to automatically check for updates, we will need to add some code to do this work. Add `um.checkForUpdate();` within the `if` block of the `connectionStatusChanged()` function within the `WeatherAIR.mxml`. This will trigger the application to check for an update only when there is an Internet connection present. The results can be seen in Figure A-13, which shows the Alert the user will see when an update is available and the `forceUpdate` is False.

Listing A-6: A sample version.xml file

```xml
<?xml version="1.0" encoding="ISO-8859-1"?>
<currentVersion version="1.41"
        downloadLocation="http://www.yourdomain.com/WeatherAIR.air"
        forceUpdate="false"
        message="Added all sorts of cool things!"/>
```

Figure A-13: An Alert indicating that a new version is available.

Add History Window

The last step in this Appendix is to utilize the data stored in the SQLite database. To use the data, we will create a simple history window showing the last 10 results of the weather service for the zip code that is currently being used. We will also need to add some methods to the `DataManager` class to retrieve the history data. The data will be returned as a `SQLResult` object and then cast as an ArrayCollection and set into the DataModel's `historyData` property, which is bound to a DataGrid in the History.mxml Window component. Here are the steps needed to add the history window.

Add a new SQLStatement to the `DataManager` class.

```
private var selectHistorySQL:SQLStatement;
```

Add import statements to the `DataManager` class.

```
import flash.data.SQLResult;
import com.everythingflex.shared.model.DataModel;
import mx.collections.ArrayCollection;
```

Create an instance of the DataModel within the `DataManager` class to hold the results of the `selectHistorySQL` statement:

```
private var model:DataModel = DataModel.getInstance();
```

Next, add the `getHistory()` function to the `DataManager` class.

```
public function getHistory(zipCode:String):void{
    var sqlText:String = "SELECT MAX(TEMPERATURE) AS HIGH, " +
                         "ZIPCODE, WEATHERDATETIMESTAMP " +
                         "FROM CALLS " +
                         "WHERE ZIPCODE = :zipCode " +
                         "GROUP BY WEATHERDATETIMESTAMP " +
                         "ORDER BY ID DESC " +
                         "LIMIT 10 ";
    selectHistorySQL = new SQLStatement();
    selectHistorySQL.sqlConnection = conn;
    selectHistorySQL.addEventListener(SQLEvent.RESULT,getHistoryResult);
    selectHistorySQL.addEventListener(SQLErrorEvent.ERROR,errorHandler);
    selectHistorySQL.text = sqlText;
    selectHistorySQL.parameters["zipCode"] = zipCode;
    selectHistorySQL.execute();
}
```

Now add a result handler to the `DataManager` class for the `getHistory()` function.

```
private function getHistoryResult(event:SQLEvent):void {
    var result:SQLResult = selectHistorySQL.getResult();
    model.historyData = new ArrayCollection(result.data);
}
```

Create a new MXML component within the `com.everythingflex.air.views` package of type Window named History.mxml, and enter the code in Listing A-7.

Listing A-7: The History.mxml Window component

```
<?xml version="1.0" encoding="utf-8"?>
<mx:Window xmlns:mx="http://www.adobe.com/2006/mxml"
    layout="absolute" width="400" height="300"
    title="Last {model.historyData.length} results for {model.zip}">

    <mx:Script>
        <![CDATA[
            import com.everythingflex.shared.model.DataModel;
            [Bindable]
            private var model:DataModel = DataModel.getInstance();
        ]]>
    </mx:Script>

    <mx:DataGrid dataProvider="{model.historyData}"
        width="100%" height="100%">
        <mx:columns>
            <mx:DataGridColumn dataField="WEATHERDATETIMESTAMP"
                headerText="Date/Time"/>
```

(Continued)

Listing A-7: The History.mxml Window component *(continued)*

```
                <mx:DataGridColumn dataField="HIGH"
                    headerText="Temperature" width="100"/>
            </mx:columns>
        </mx:DataGrid>

    </mx:Window>
```

Next, add the `showHistory()` function below to the WeatherAIR.mxml file.

```
public function showHistory():void{
    dm.getHistory(so.data.zip);
    var history:History = new History();
    history.open();
}
```

You will also need to import the History component into the WeatherAIR.mxml file.

```
import com.everythingflex.air.views.History;
```

You can now add this new window to the `NativeMenu` by updating the `init()` function within the WeatherAIR.mxml file. Replace the section of the `init()` function that added the `NativeMenus` with the code in Listing A-8.

Listing A-8: The updated code for creating `NativeMenus`

```
var nativeMenu:NativeMenu = new NativeMenu();
var menuItem:NativeMenuItem = new NativeMenuItem("Navigation");
var prefMenu:NativeMenuItem = new NativeMenuItem("Preferences");
var forecastMenu:NativeMenuItem = new NativeMenuItem("Full Forecast");
var historyMenu:NativeMenuItem = new NativeMenuItem("History");

prefMenu.addEventListener(Event.SELECT,handleMenuClick);
prefMenu.keyEquivalent = "P";
forecastMenu.addEventListener(Event.SELECT,handleMenuClick);
forecastMenu.keyEquivalent = "F";
historyMenu.addEventListener(Event.SELECT,handleMenuClick);
historyMenu.keyEquivalent = "H";

nativeMenu.addItem(prefMenu);
nativeMenu.addItem(forecastMenu);
nativeMenu.addItem(historyMenu);
nativeMenu.addItem(new NativeMenuItem("",true));
menuItem.submenu = nativeMenu;
NativeApplication.nativeApplication.menu.addItem(menuItem);
```

You will also then need to add the call to `showHistory()` within the `handleMenuClick()` function of the WeatherAIR.mxml file.

```
if(menuItem.label == "History")showHistory();
```

Finally, add the `historyData` property to the shared `com.everythingflex.shared.model.DataModel` class to hold the results of the selectHistorySQL statement. Since this is an ArrayCollection, you will also need to add an import statement.

```
import mx.collections.ArrayCollection;
public var historyData:ArrayCollection;
```

You can now run the application and use the `NativeMenu` to open the new History window. Figure A-14 shows the History window.

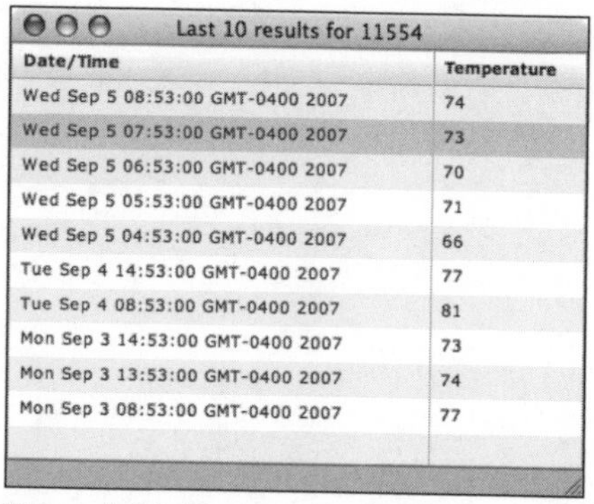

Last 10 results for 11554

Date/Time	Temperature
Wed Sep 5 08:53:00 GMT-0400 2007	74
Wed Sep 5 07:53:00 GMT-0400 2007	73
Wed Sep 5 06:53:00 GMT-0400 2007	70
Wed Sep 5 05:53:00 GMT-0400 2007	71
Wed Sep 5 04:53:00 GMT-0400 2007	66
Tue Sep 4 14:53:00 GMT-0400 2007	77
Tue Sep 4 08:53:00 GMT-0400 2007	81
Mon Sep 3 14:53:00 GMT-0400 2007	73
Mon Sep 3 13:53:00 GMT-0400 2007	74
Mon Sep 3 08:53:00 GMT-0400 2007	77

Figure A-14: The newly added History window.

Where to Go from Here

Many other new features are unique to AIR and are not part of Flex 3. You can experiment and expand this application even further by utilizing AIR transparency and custom chrome, drag and drop between the application and the operating system, creating additional log files for other types of application errors, or adding a Notification window to draw windows users' attention to the application when it is in the background. Feel free to add, update, or change this sample application, but please send me links to what you have created.

Solutions for Exercises

Most of the example solutions here are not the only way to accomplish the goal of the exercises, thus don't be concerned if your solution is different from mine. As long as it compiles and accomplishes the goals, you should be satisfied with your solution.

Chapter 1 Exercise

This simple exercise asked you to create a new application and add some components. To create this sample, I simply created a new application within Flex Builder 3, switched to Design view, and added some components. Listing B-1 shows what I came up with. Figure B-1 shows the results.

Listing B-1: The solution for the Chapter 1 Exercise

```
<?xml version="1.0" encoding="utf-8"?>
<mx:WindowedApplication xmlns:mx="http://www.adobe.com/2006/mxml"
    layout="absolute">
    <!--
    Create a new AIR application within Flex Builder,
    switch to Design view and drag a few components onto
    the workspace and run the application.
    -->
    <mx:Button x="123" y="75" label="Button"/>
    <mx:CheckBox x="283" y="131" label="Checkbox"/>
    <mx:DateChooser x="45" y="116"/>
    <mx:NumericStepper x="283" y="230"/>
    <mx:RadioButton x="237" y="56" label="Radio"/>

</mx:WindowedApplication>
```

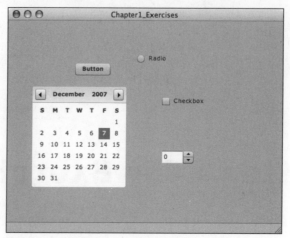

Figure B-1: Chapter 1 Exercise result.

Chapter 7 Exercise

By utilizing the classes created by the Import Web Services (WSDL) wizard, I was able to replicate the functionality demonstrated by Listing 7-13. Take a look at Listing B-2, and you will see that within the init() function, an instance of the StockQuote class is created and an event listener is added to handle the results of this service. There is also a getQuote() function, which when called simply passes the stock ticker symbol into the getQuote() function of the StockQuote class. Finally, the result handler function simply displays the results within an Alert window. The XML result can be seen in Figure B-2.

Listing B-2: The solution for the Chapter 7 Exercise

```
<?xml version="1.0" encoding="utf-8"?>
<mx:WindowedApplication xmlns:mx="http://www.adobe.com/2006/mxml"
    creationComplete="init()">
    <!--
    Use the project created in the Import Web Service section of this
    chapter to duplicate the functionality that was demonstrated
    in Listing 7-13 and Figure 7-10 of this chapter. Instead of
    calling the WSDL directly as demonstrated in Listing 7-13,
    utilize the ActionScript classes created by the WSDL import wizard.
    -->
    <mx:Script>
        <![CDATA[
        import net.webservicex.GetQuoteResultEvent;
        import net.webservicex.StockQuote;
        private var quote:StockQuote;

        private function init():void{
            quote = new StockQuote();
            quote.addgetQuoteEventListener(quoteResult);
```

```
        }

    private function getQuote():void{
        quote.getQuote(symbol.text)
    }

    private function quoteResult(event:GetQuoteResultEvent):void{
        mx.controls.Alert.show(event.result);
    }
    ]]>
</mx:Script>
<mx:TextInput text="" id="symbol" enter="getQuote()"/>
<mx:Button label="Get Quote" click="getQuote()" x="168"/>
</mx:WindowedApplication>
```

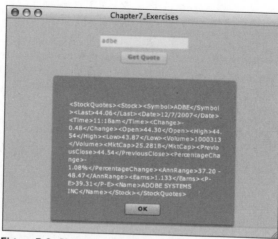

Figure B-2: Chapter 7 Exercise result.

Chapter 8 Exercise

This exercise asked you to create a new file and set its contents to a specific string. To do this, you will need to use both the `File` class for creating the file and the `FileStream` class to write out the contents of the file. If you look at Listing B-3, you will see that there is a single function named `createFile()`. This function first uses the `File` class to create a file named *Today.txt* on the desktop. It then creates the string in a variable named `s`, which was requested per the instructions by using the `Date` class to capture today's date. Finally, using the `FileStream` class, the new file is opened in Write mode, and the contents of the `s` variable are written to the file. The results can be seen in Figures B-3 and B-4.

Listing B-3: The solution for the Chapter 8 Exercise

```
<?xml version="1.0" encoding="utf-8"?>
<mx:WindowedApplication xmlns:mx="http://www.adobe.com/2006/mxml">
```

(Continued)

Listing B-3: The solution for the Chapter 8 Exercise *(continued)*

```
<!--
Create a new file on the desktop named Today.txt and set its contents to
be "Today is (insert the date using the Date class) and I have
created my first file from AIR."
-->
<mx:Script>
    <![CDATA[
    import mx.controls.Alert;
    private function createFile():void{
        var newFile:File = File.desktopDirectory.resolvePath("Today.txt");
        var d:Date = new Date();
        var s:String = "Today is " + d + "" +
                        " and I have created my first file from AIR.";
        var fileStream:FileStream = new FileStream();
        fileStream.open(newFile, FileMode.WRITE);
        fileStream.writeUTFBytes(s);
        fileStream.close();
        mx.controls.Alert.show("File created successfully","Notice");
    }

    ]]>
</mx:Script>
<mx:Button label="Create File" click="createFile()"
            horizontalCenter="0" verticalCenter="0"/>
</mx:WindowedApplication>
```

Figure B-3: Chapter 8 Exercise file after the file has been created.

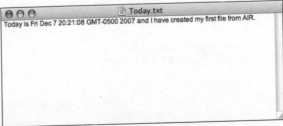

Figure B-4: The file created by the Chapter 8 Exercise.

Chapter 9 Exercise

The exercise in Chapter 9 asked you to create an application that spawns two windows. The windows need to communicate with each other. This will be demonstrated by having a TextInput component in Window 1 and a Label component in Window 2, which will show the text as it is keyed into Window 1. The solution is demonstrated in Listings B-4, B-5, and B-6.

If we examine Listing B-4, you will notice that there are two variables at the top of the Script block, which define the two Windows components that will be used in this application. They are defined as class variables, so that we will have a reference to them that will be used to set the text in the LabelWindow. Next, there is a function named createWindows(), which creates and opens the two windows. Now, looking at Listing B-5, you will see there is a myParent variable that was set to be a reference of the main application file within the createWindows() function within Listing B-4. You will also notice that when the TextInput contents change, there is a call to myParent.setLabelText() where the text property of the TextInput component is passed along. This setLabelText() function, which is on the main application file, then sets the text property of the Label component within the LabelWindow. The results can be seen in Figure B-5.

Listing B-4: The main solution file for the Chapter 9 Exercise

```
<?xml version="1.0" encoding="utf-8"?>
<mx:WindowedApplication xmlns:mx="http://www.adobe.com/2006/mxml"
    layout="absolute" width="400" height="200">
    <!--
    Create an application that creates two windows. The first window
    should have a TextInput component and the second should have a
    Label component that shows the current contents of the TextInput
    in the first window. Hint: Be sure to create the windows as
    instances of the main class and pass a reference of the main
    application into each window. Then you can reference them by
    instance name.
    -->
    <mx:Script>
        <![CDATA[
        private var textWindow:TextWindow;
        private var labelWindow:LabelWindow;

        private function createWindows():void{
            textWindow = new TextWindow();
            textWindow.myParent = this;
            textWindow.open();
            labelWindow = new LabelWindow();
            labelWindow.open();
        }

        public function setLabelText(s:String):void{
            labelWindow.l.text = s;
        }
        ]]>
    </mx:Script>
    <mx:Button label="Open Windows" click="createWindows()"
            horizontalCenter="0" verticalCenter="0"/>

</mx:WindowedApplication>
```

Listing B-5: The TextWindow component

```
<?xml version="1.0" encoding="utf-8"?>
<mx:Window xmlns:mx="http://www.adobe.com/2006/mxml" width="300" height="150"
    layout="absolute" title="Text Window">
    <mx:Script>
        <![CDATA[
        public var myParent:Object;
        ]]>
    </mx:Script>
    <mx:TextInput id="ti" horizontalCenter="0" verticalCenter="0"
                change="myParent.setLabelText(ti.text)"/>

</mx:Window>
```

Listing B-6: The LabelWindow component

```
<?xml version="1.0" encoding="utf-8"?>
<mx:Window xmlns:mx="http://www.adobe.com/2006/mxml" width="300" height="150"
            layout="absolute" title="Label Window">
    <mx:Label id="l" horizontalCenter="0" verticalCenter="0"/>
</mx:Window>
```

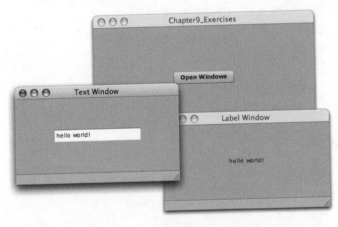

Figure B-5: The results of the Chapter 9 Exercise.

Chapter 10 Exercise

The goal of this exercise is to assign a different dock or system tray icon when each of four windows is in focus. Listing B-7 contains the mail file for the Chapter 10 exercise. This file declares the four windows that will be used within the application and then includes four Button components to create each window.

Listing B-8 shows an example of one of the four windows. The only difference in the other three that is not included in this section is the source for the icon that will be used. Looking further at Listing B-8, you will see that upon `creationComplete` of the window, an event listener is added, which will fire whenever the window is being interacted with. The `init()` function also calls the `addIcon()` function to set when the window is first opened. The event listener previously mentioned will handle the call to `addIcon()` when the window is interacted with after it is already open. Figures B-6 and B-7 show the icons for Window 2 and Window 4 being displayed in the Mac OS X dock.

Listing B-7: The main solution file for the Chapter 10 Exercise

```xml
<?xml version="1.0" encoding="utf-8"?>
<mx:WindowedApplication xmlns:mx="http://www.adobe.com/2006/mxml"
    layout="absolute">
    <!--
    Create an application that assigns a different icon
    (either dock or system tray) when each window is in focus.
    -->
    <mx:Script>
        <![CDATA[
        import mx.core.Window;
        private var win1:Win1 = new Win1();
        private var win2:Win2 = new Win2();
        private var win3:Win3 = new Win3();
        private var win4:Win4 = new Win4();

        private function openWin(w:Window):void{
            w.open();
        }

        ]]>
    </mx:Script>
    <mx:Button click="openWin(win1)" label="Open Window 1"
            horizontalCenter="0" y="33"/>
    <mx:Button click="openWin(win2)" label="Open Window 2"
            horizontalCenter="0" y="63"/>
    <mx:Button click="openWin(win3)" label="Open Window 3"
            horizontalCenter="0" y="93"/>
    <mx:Button click="openWin(win4)" label="Open Window 4"
            horizontalCenter="0" y="123"/>
</mx:WindowedApplication>
```

Listing B-8: An example of one of the four Window components used in this exercise

```xml
<?xml version="1.0" encoding="utf-8"?>
<mx:Window xmlns:mx="http://www.adobe.com/2006/mxml"
            layout="absolute" width="400" height="300"
            creationComplete="init()">
```

(Continued)

Listing B-8: An example of one of the four Window components used in this exercise
(continued)

```
<mx:Script>
    <![CDATA[
    [Embed(source="win-1.tif")]
    private var Icon:Class;

    private function init():void{
        this.nativeWindow.addEventListener(Event.ACTIVATE,nowActive);
        addIcon();
    }
    private function nowActive(event:Event):void{
        addIcon();
    }
    private function addIcon():void{
        var bitmap:Bitmap = new Icon();
        NativeApplication.nativeApplication.icon.bitmaps = [bitmap.bitmapData];
    }
    ]]>
</mx:Script>

<mx:Label text="Window 1" horizontalCenter="0"
        verticalCenter="0" fontSize="20"/>
</mx:Window>
```

Figure B-6: The icon for Window 2.

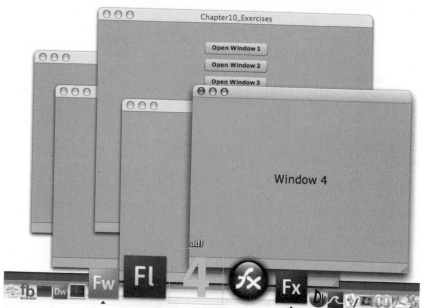

Figure B-7: The icon for Window 4.

Chapter 11 Exercise

The task with this exercise was to take the XML from Listing B-9, parse it, and insert it into a new SQLite database. Thus you'll need to do two things to accomplish this task. First, you'll need to create the code needed to create a new database and table to hold the month data. Second, you'll need to load the XML, parse it, and insert it into the new database.

Take a look at the solution file in Listing B-10. You will see that the `init()` function that is called on `creationComplete` makes a call to the `openOrCreateDatabase()` function. This function will either open the database if it already exists or create the database file, which will then call the `createTable()` function. The `createTable()` function will create the Months table with five fields needed to hold a unique identifier, the `SortOrder`, and the `English`, `Spanish`, and `Italian` translations.

The Months.xml file will be loaded using an HTTPService. The button labeled "Save XML to database" will load in the Months.xml file by calling the `send()` method on the HTTPService when it is clicked. The `onLoad()` function is called after the Months.xml file is loaded. This function parses the XML, loops through the months, and calls the `insertMonth()` function on each iteration of the loop. The `insertMonth()` function accepts the XMLNode, parses out each property, and inserts them into the Months database table. The results can be seen in Figures B-8 and B-9.

Appendix B: Solutions for Exercises

Listing B-9: The Months.xml file

```xml
<?xml version="1.0" encoding="utf-8"?>
<months>
    <month sortOrder="1" english="January" spanish="enero" italian="gennaio"/>
    <month sortOrder="2" english="February" spanish="febrero" italian="febbraio"/>
    <month sortOrder="3" english="March" spanish="marzo" italian="marzo"/>
    <month sortOrder="4" english="April" spanish="abril" italian="aprile"/>
    <month sortOrder="5" english="May" spanish="mayo" italian="maggio"/>
    <month sortOrder="6" english="June" spanish="junio" italian="giugno"/>
    <month sortOrder="7" english="July" spanish="julio" italian="luglio"/>
    <month sortOrder="8" english="August" spanish="agosto" italian="agosto"/>
    <month sortOrder="9" english="September" spanish="septiembre"
italian="settembre"/>
    <month sortOrder="10" english="October" spanish="octubre" italian="ottobre"/>
    <month sortOrder="11" english="November" spanish="noviembre"
italian="novembre"/>
    <month sortOrder="12" english="December" spanish="diciembre"
italian="dicembre"/>
</months>
```

Listing B-10: The solution file for the Chapter 11 Exercise

```xml
<?xml version="1.0" encoding="utf-8"?>
<mx:WindowedApplication xmlns:mx="http://www.adobe.com/2006/mxml"
    layout="absolute"
    creationComplete="init()">
<!--
Read in the Months.xml file and write it to a SQLite database
-->
<mx:Script>
    <![CDATA[
    import mx.rpc.events.ResultEvent;

    private var conn:SQLConnection;
    private var createTableStatement:SQLStatement;
    private var insertStatement:SQLStatement;
    private var dbFile:File;

    private function init():void{
        openOrCreateDatabase();
    }

    // open or create database
    private function openOrCreateDatabase():void{
        conn = new SQLConnection();
        dbFile =
    File.applicationStorageDirectory.resolvePath("Chapter11_Exercises.db");
        if(dbFile.exists) {
            conn.addEventListener(SQLEvent.OPEN, openHandler);
```

```
        } else {
            conn.addEventListener(SQLEvent.OPEN, createHandler);
        }
        conn.openAsync(dbFile);
    }


    // if called, call createTable()
    private function createHandler(event:SQLEvent):void {
        createTable();
    }


    private function openHandler(event:SQLEvent):void {
        log.text += "Database opened successfully \n";
    }


    private function errorHandler(event:SQLErrorEvent):void {
        var err:String = "Error id:" + event.error.errorID + "\nDetails:" +
                         event.error.message;
        log.text += err + "\n";
    }


    // create the table to hold months data
    private function createTable():void{
        var sqlText:String = "CREATE TABLE Months(ID INTEGER PRIMARY KEY, " +
                             "SortOrder INTEGER, English TEXT," +
                             "Spanish TEXT, Italian TEXT)";
        createTableStatement = new SQLStatement();
        createTableStatement.sqlConnection = conn;
        createTableStatement.addEventListener(SQLEvent.RESULT,
                                        createTableResult);
        createTableStatement.text = sqlText;
        createTableStatement.execute();
    }


    private function createTableResult(event:SQLEvent):void {
        log.text += "the table was created successfully \n";
    }


    private function onLoad(event:ResultEvent):void{
        var xml:XMLDocument = new XMLDocument();
        xml.ignoreWhite = true;
        xml.parseXML(event.result as XML);
        for each(var item:XMLNode in xml.firstChild.childNodes) {
            insertMonth(item);
        }
    }


    // insert month data
    private function insertMonth(node:XMLNode):void {
        var sqlText:String = "INSERT INTO Months(SortOrder, English, " +
                             "Spanish, Italian)" +
                             "VALUES(:sortOrder, :english, " +
                             ":spanish, :italian)";
```

(Continued)

Listing B-10: The solution file for the Chapter 11 Exercise *(continued)*

```
            insertStatement = new SQLStatement();
            insertStatement.sqlConnection = conn;
            insertStatement.addEventListener(SQLEvent.RESULT, insertResult);
            insertStatement.addEventListener(SQLErrorEvent.ERROR, errorHandler);
            insertStatement.text = sqlText;
            insertStatement.parameters[":sortOrder"] = node.attributes.sortOrder;
            insertStatement.parameters[":english"] = node.attributes.english;
            insertStatement.parameters[":spanish"] = node.attributes.spanish;
            insertStatement.parameters[":italian"] = node.attributes.italian;
            insertStatement.execute();
        }

        private function insertResult(event:SQLEvent):void {
            log.text += "new record was inserted successfully with id " +
            event.target.getResult().lastInsertRowID + "\n";
        }
        ]]>
    </mx:Script>

    <mx:HTTPService
        id="httpService"
        url="months.xml"
        resultFormat="e4x"
        result="onLoad(event)"/>

    <mx:Button click="httpService.send();"
        label="Save XML to Database" x="158" y="10"/>

    <mx:TextArea id="log"  x="10" y="50" width="449" height="232"/>
</mx:WindowedApplication>
```

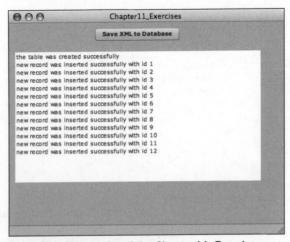

Figure B-8: The results of the Chapter11_Exercises application.

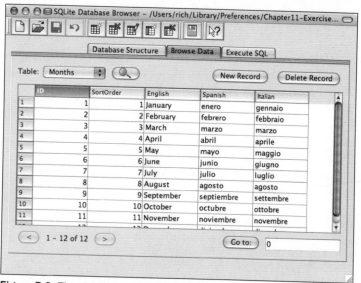

Figure B-9: The data after being added within the SQLite Browser.

Chapter 12 Exercise

This exercise asked for you to integrate keyboard events to trigger the paste functionality of the Chapter12_Paste sample. To do this, you'll need to use the KeyboardEvent class to listen for keystrokes. Take a look at Listing B-11, and you'll notice that the init() function is called on applicationComplete of the WindowedApplication tag. The init() function adds an event listener to the nativeApplication property of the application. This event listens for the KeyDown event and also has the third parameter set to True, which will intercept the key capture. If you leave out this property or set it to False, you will notice that the NativeMenu (on Mac) will be triggered by the KeyDown events. So if you do have a NativeMenu in your application with keyboard shortcuts attached, you will need to code for them, since the application will no longer handle them automatically. The event listener will trigger the onKeyDown() function whenever the keyboard is used when the AIR application is in use. Within the onKeyDown() function, there is some logic to evaluate the keys that have been pressed. If the key combination includes the controlKey and keyCode number 86 (the "V" key) on Windows or the commandKey and keyCode number 86 on Mac, the paste() function is called. From this point on, the application is exactly the same as the Chapter12_Paste example.

Listing B-11: The solution file for the Chapter 12 Exercise

```
<?xml version="1.0" encoding="utf-8"?>
<mx:WindowedApplication xmlns:mx="http://www.adobe.com/2006/mxml"
   layout="vertical"
     applicationComplete="init()">
```

(Continued)

Listing B-11: The solution file for the Chapter 12 Exercise *(continued)*

```
<!--
Using the Flex 3 KeyboardEvent class add support to the Chapter12_Paste example
for ctrl-v keyboard shortcut for pasting an image into the application.
-->
<mx:Script>
    <![CDATA[
    import mx.controls.Alert;
    import mx.controls.Image;
    import flash.filesystem.File;

    private function init():void{
        this.nativeApplication.addEventListener(KeyboardEvent.KEY_DOWN,
                                             onKeyDown,true);
    }

    private function onKeyDown(event:KeyboardEvent):void {
        if(event.controlKey && event.keyCode == 86 ||
           event.commandKey && event.keyCode == 86){
           paste();
        }
    }

    private function paste():void{
        var clipboardfiles:Array = Clipboard.generalClipboard.getData(
                    ClipboardFormats.FILE_LIST_FORMAT) as Array;
        for each (var file:File in clipboardfiles){
            switch (file.extension.toLowerCase()){
                case "png" :
                    addImage(file.nativePath);
                    break;
                case "jpg" :
                    addImage(file.nativePath);
                    break;
                case "jpeg" :
                    addImage(file.nativePath);
                    break;
                case "gif" :
                    addImage(file.nativePath);
                    break;
                default:
                    Alert.show("Unmapped Extension");
            }
        }
    }

    private function addImage(nativePath:String):void{
        var i:Image = new Image();
        if(Capabilities.os.search("Mac") >= 0){
            i.source = "file://" + nativePath;
        } else {
            i.source = nativePath;
        }
        this.addChild(i);
    }

    ]]>
```

```
    </mx:Script>
    <mx:Label text="Try ctrl-v to paste an image" fontWeight="bold"/>
    <mx:Button click="paste()" label="Paste an image"/>
</mx:WindowedApplication>
```

Chapter 13 Exercise

This exercise asked you to create a simple application and then integrate both the ConnectionManager and UpdateManager classes that I have provided within the AIR Central section of http://blog .everythingflex.com.

Listing B-12 shows the ConnectionManager class. The constructor of the ConnectionManager class accepts three optional arguments. The first is a Boolean, which, when true, will show the Alert message; when a connection failure occurs, it defaults to True. The second is the URL that the ConnectionManager will attempt to connect to. It defaults to www.google.com. The last is a string that holds the Alert message. It defaults to "This application requires an Internet connection." The ConnectionManager has a public property named isConnected, which will hold the current status of the application. To use the ConnectionManager, you will simply need to create an instance of the ConnectionManager class and set any of the optional arguments. Once an instance is created, it will create an instance of the URLMonitor, which will announce any changes in status and set the isConnection property to True or False.

Listing B-13 shows the UpdateManager class. The UpdateManager examines the applicationDescriptor property of the NativeApplication.nativeApplication to determine the version of the installed application. This is then stored in the currentVersion property. The constructor accepts one required argument and one optional argument. The first required argument is the URL that holds the version.xml file to test. To see an example of the version.xml file, please refer to Listing B-14. The second is a Boolean telling the UpdateManager whether to check automatically for an update or wait until the user triggers the check. It defaults to True. If true, it will load this XML file, parse it, and compare the version property of the XML file with the version that was parsed from the applicationDescriptor. If there is a difference and the forceUpdate property of the version.xml file is True, the application is automatically updated. If there is a difference and forceUpdate is False, the user is alerted of the available update, given a description of the update, and given the option to update his or her application. The UpdateManager will then perform the update using the File and FileStream classes to download and write the new AIR file to disk, and then the Updater class to complete the update.

The UpdateManager also contains a checkForUpdate() method that will allow your application to provide a way for its user to manually trigger a check for an update. To use the UpdateManager, you will simply need to create an instance of the UpdateManager and pass in the URL of the version.xml file. You may also pass in the optional second argument.

The solution file, which incorporates these two classes, is in Listing B-15. As you can see, the usage is pretty simple. A variable named cm with the type ConnectionManager is created as a class variable. Remember that, upon creation, this class will automatically start monitoring the connection status. Notice that this variable was set as Bindable. Next, an instance of the UpdateManager is created with a version .xml URL passed in as well as the auto-check set to False. There is a Label component, which simply states "Hello World!" and a Button component, which will check for the update. If you look at the Button component, you will notice that the enabled property is bound to the isConnected property of the Connection Manager. This will only allow this button to be enabled when the isConnected property is True. Once clicked, the UpdateManager's checkForUpdate() method is called. The results can be seen in Figures B-10 and B-11.

Listing B-12: The ConnectionManager **class**

```
package com.everythingflex.air.managers
{
    import air.net.URLMonitor;
    import flash.events.StatusEvent;
    import flash.net.URLRequest;
    import mx.controls.Alert;

    public class ConnectionManager
    {
        private var eventObj:StatusEvent;
        private var urlMonitor:URLMonitor;
        // if true, show the Alert window
        private var showMessage:Boolean;
        // message to display when connection fails and showMessage is true
        private var message:String;
        // URL to test for a connection
        [Bindable]
        public var connectionURL:String;
        [Bindable]
        public var isConnected:Boolean = false;

        public function ConnectionManager(showMessage:Boolean=true,
          connectionURL:String="http://www.google.com",
          message:String="This application requires\nan Internet connection"):void{

            this.showMessage = showMessage;
            this.connectionURL = connectionURL;
            this.message = message;
            startMonitor();
        }

        // start the URLMonitor and test against the connectionURL
        public function startMonitor():void{
          var urlRequest:URLRequest = new URLRequest(connectionURL)
          urlRequest.method = "HEAD";
          urlMonitor = new URLMonitor(urlRequest);
          urlMonitor.addEventListener(StatusEvent.STATUS, statusChanged);
          urlMonitor.start();
        }

        // handle changes in the connection status and dispatches StatusEvent
        public function statusChanged(event:StatusEvent):void{
          this.isConnected =  urlMonitor.available;
          if(!this.isConnected && this.showMessage){
              Alert.show(this.message, "Connection Failure");
          }
          eventObj = new StatusEvent(StatusEvent.STATUS);
         dispatchEvent(eventObj);
        }
    }
}
```

Listing B-13: The UpdateManager class

```
package com.everythingflex.air.managers
{
    import flash.desktop.NativeApplication;
    import flash.desktop.Updater;
    import flash.events.Event;
    import flash.filesystem.File;
    import flash.filesystem.FileMode;
    import flash.filesystem.FileStream;
    import flash.net.URLRequest;
    import flash.net.URLStream;
    import flash.utils.ByteArray;

    import mx.controls.Alert;
    import mx.events.CloseEvent;
    import mx.rpc.events.FaultEvent;
    import mx.rpc.events.ResultEvent;
    import mx.rpc.http.HTTPService;

    public class UpdateManager
    {
        // URL of the remote version.xml file
        private var versionURL:String;
        // load in the applicationDescriptor
        private var appXML:XML =
NativeApplication.nativeApplication.applicationDescriptor;
        private var ns : Namespace = appXML.namespace();
        // set the currentVersion information
        private var currentVersion:String = appXML.ns::version;
        // holder for remote version.xml XML data
        private var version:XML;
        private var urlStream:URLStream = new URLStream();
        private var fileData:ByteArray = new ByteArray();

        // the constructor requires the versionURL
        public function UpdateManager(versionURL:String,
                                    autoCheck:Boolean=true):void{
            this.versionURL = versionURL;
            if(autoCheck)loadRemoteFile();
        }

        // load the remote version.xml file
        private function loadRemoteFile():void{
            var http:HTTPService = new HTTPService();
            http.url = this.versionURL;
            http.useProxy=false;
            http.method = "GET";
            http.resultFormat="xml";
            http.send();
            http.addEventListener(ResultEvent.RESULT,testVersion);
            http.addEventListener(FaultEvent.FAULT,versionLoadFailure);
        }
```

(Continued)

Listing B-13: The `UpdateManager` **class** *(continued)*

```
/*
test the currentVersion against the remote version file and
either alert      the user of
an update available or force the update, if no update available,
alert user
*/
public function checkForUpdate():Boolean{
    if(version  ==  null){
        this.loadRemoteFile();
        return true;
    }
    if((currentVersion != version.@version)&&version.@forceUpdate == true){
        getUpdate();
    }else if(currentVersion != version.@version){
        Alert.show("There is an update available,\nwould you like to " +
                   "get it now? \n\nDetails:\n" + version.@message,
                "Choose Yes or No", 3, null, alertClickHandler);
    }else{
        Alert.show("There are no new updates available", "NOTICE");
    }
    return true;
}


/*
test the currentVersion against the remote version file and
either alert the user of
an update available or force the update
*/
private function testVersion(event:ResultEvent):void{
    version = XML(event.result);
    if((currentVersion != version.@version)&&version.@forceUpdate == true){
        getUpdate();
    }else if(currentVersion != version.@version){
        Alert.show("There is an update available,\nwould you like to " +
                   "get it now? \n\nDetails:\n" + version.@message,
                "Choose Yes or No", 3, null, alertClickHandler);

    }
}


/*
Load of the version.xml file failed
*/
private function versionLoadFailure(event:FaultEvent):void{
    Alert.show("Failed to load version.xml file from "+
    this.versionURL,"ERROR");
}

// handle the Alert window decission
private function alertClickHandler(event:CloseEvent):void {
```

```
        if (event.detail==Alert.YES){
            getUpdate();
        }
    }

    // get the new version from the remote server
    private function getUpdate():void{
        var urlReq:URLRequest = new URLRequest(version.@downloadLocation);
        urlStream.addEventListener(Event.COMPLETE, loaded);
        urlStream.load(urlReq);
    }

    // read in the new AIR package
    private function loaded(event:Event):void {
        urlStream.readBytes(fileData, 0, urlStream.bytesAvailable);
        writeAirFile();
    }

    /*
    write the newly downloaded AIR package to the
    application storage directory
    */
    private function writeAirFile():void {
        var file:File =
File.applicationStorageDirectory.resolvePath("Update.air");
        var fileStream:FileStream = new FileStream();
        fileStream.addEventListener(Event.CLOSE, fileClosed);
        fileStream.openAsync(file, FileMode.WRITE);
        fileStream.writeBytes(fileData, 0, fileData.length);
        fileStream.close();
    }

    // after the write is complete, call the update method on the Updater class
    private function fileClosed(event:Event):void {
        var updater:Updater = new Updater();
        var airFile:File =
File.applicationStorageDirectory.resolvePath("Update.air");
        updater.update(airFile,version.@version);
    }

    }
}
```

Listing B-14: Sample of a version.xml file

```
<?xml version="1.0" encoding="ISO-8859-1"?>
<currentVersion version="2"
            downloadLocation="http://www.yourdomain.com/appName/AppName.air"
            forceUpdate="false"
          message="Added new features"/>
```

Listing B-15: The main solution file for the Chapter 13 Exercise

```
<?xml version="1.0" encoding="utf-8"?>
<mx:WindowedApplication xmlns:mx="http://www.adobe.com/2006/mxml"
    layout="absolute">
    <!--
    Start out with a simple HelloWorld application and  add the
    functionality to test for an Internet connection.
    Next, add functionality to make your HelloWorld application
    a self-updating application.
    Note, you may use the ConnectionManager and UpdateManager
    classes that I have provided at http://blog.everythingflex.com
    -->

    <mx:Script>
        <![CDATA[
        import com.everythingflex.air.managers.UpdateManager;
        import com.everythingflex.air.managers.ConnectionManager;
        [Bindable]
        private var cm:ConnectionManager = new ConnectionManager();

        private var um:UpdateManager = new
UpdateManager("http://www.yourdomain.com/appName/version.xml");

        ]]>
    </mx:Script>

    <mx:Label text="Hello World!" fontSize="20"
        horizontalCenter="0" y="120"/>

    <mx:Button label="Check for Update"
        click="um.checkForUpdate()"
        enabled="{cm.isConnected}"
        horizontalCenter="0" y="160"/>

</mx:WindowedApplication>
```

Figure B-10: Screen showing a failure of an Internet connection.

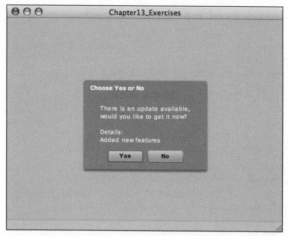

Figure B-11: An Alert notification of an available update.

Chapter 14 Exercise

This exercise asked you to create an application that reads the folder or file properties from the selected row of both the FileSystemDataGrid and FileSystemList components. The solution file is shown in Listing B-16. This file has two functions that operate in the same way. Each will cast the selectedItem from either the FileSystemDataGrid or FileSystemList as a File and then write name and size properties to one of the TextArea components. The results of this can be seen in Figure B-12.

Listing B-16: The solution file for the Chapter 14 Exercise

```
<?xml version="1.0" encoding="utf-8"?>
<mx:WindowedApplication xmlns:mx="http://www.adobe.com/2006/mxml"
    layout="absolute" width="650" height="525">
    <!--
    Create a sample application by reading the selected folder or file
    properties from the selected rows of a  FileSystemDataGrid
    and the FileSystemList component.
    -->
    <mx:Script>
        <![CDATA[
        import mx.controls.FileSystemEnumerationMode;
        import flash.filesystem.File;

        public function showFSDGDetails():void {
            var file:File = fsdg.selectedItem as File;
            log1.text += "name: " + file.name  + " size: " + file.size + "\n";
            log1.text += "          nativepath: " + file.nativePath + "\n";
        }
```

(Continued)

Listing B-16: The solution file for the Chapter 14 Exercise *(continued)*

```
        public function showFSLDetails():void {
            var file:File = fsl.selectedItem as File;
            log2.text += "name: " + file.name  + " size: " + file.size + "\n";
            log2.text += "            nativepath: " + file.nativePath + "\n";
        }


    ]]>
    </mx:Script>

    <mx:FileSystemDataGrid id="fsdg"
        horizontalCenter="0" y="10" width="600" height="250"
        enumerationMode="{FileSystemEnumerationMode.FILES_FIRST}"
        showExtensions="false" change="showFSDGDetails()"/>

    <mx:FileSystemList id="fsl" x="243" y="268" extensions="['.jpg','.gif']"
        change="showFSLDetails()" height="225"/>

    <mx:TextArea id="log1" x="24" y="268" width="204" height="225"/>
    <mx:TextArea id="log2" x="420" y="268" width="204" height="225"/>

</mx:WindowedApplication>
```

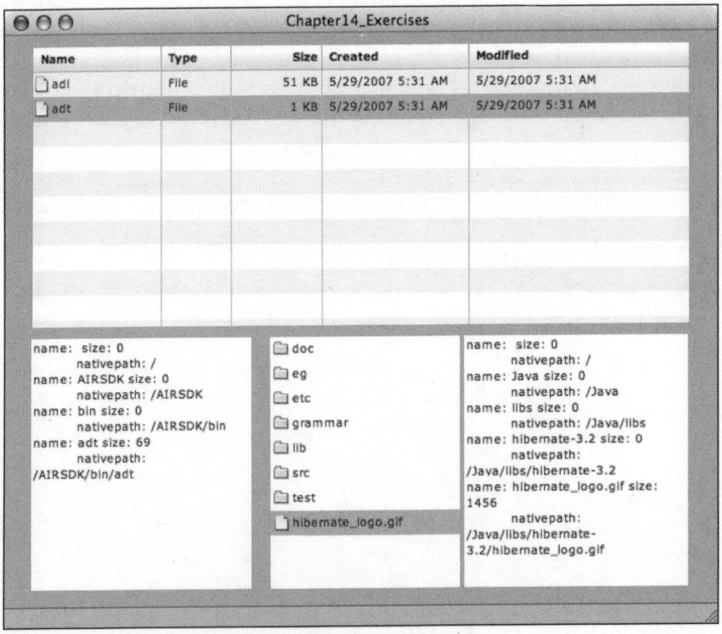

Figure B-12: The results of Chapter14_Exercises.

Chapter 15 Exercise

This exercise asked you to create an application that uses an HTML component to load in a web page, then upon request create a new window that displays all the images that were part of the HTML content within the HTML component. Take a look at Listing B-17, and you will see that there is an HTML component with an ID of HTML that will display `http://images.google.com`. There is a second component of type Button that will call the `showImages()` function when clicked. The `showImages()` function is the heart of this application. It first searches for images within the HTML component by calling getElementsByTagName ("img") on `html.htmlLoader.window.document.documentElement`. These images are stored as an object. A new Window component is created, the images object is looped through, and a new Image component is created on each iteration; the image source is set to the source of the image from the images object. The new Image component is then added to the window as a child. The results can be seen in Figure B-13.

Listing B-17: The solution file for the Chapter 15 Exercise

```
    <?xml version="1.0" encoding="utf-8"?>
<mx:WindowedApplication xmlns:mx="http://www.adobe.com/2006/mxml"
    layout="absolute" width="850" height="575">
    <!--
    Create an application that shows all of the images that a
    Web page contains in a separate window.
    Hint, you will need to parse out the images using
    getElementsByTagName(). Also, see Chapter 9 for
    information on the Windowing API.
    -->
    <mx:Script>
        <![CDATA[
        import mx.core.Window;
        import mx.controls.Image;

        private function showImages():void{
            var images:Object =
html.htmlLoader.window.document.documentElement.getElementsByTagName("img");
            if(images != null){
                var win:Window = new Window();
                win.layout = "horizontal";
                win.width=600;
                win.height=200;
                win.open();
                for(var i:Number=0; i < images.length; i++) {
                    var img:Image = new Image();
                    img.source = images[i].src;
                    win.addChild(img);
                }
            }
        }
        ]]>
    </mx:Script>
```

(Continued)

Listing B-17: The solution file for the Chapter 15 Exercise *(continued)*

```
<mx:HTML id="html" location="http://images.google.com" width="800" height="509"
    horizontalCenter="0" y="40"/>
<mx:Button click="showImages()" x="375.5" label="Show Image" y="10"/>
</mx:WindowedApplication>
```

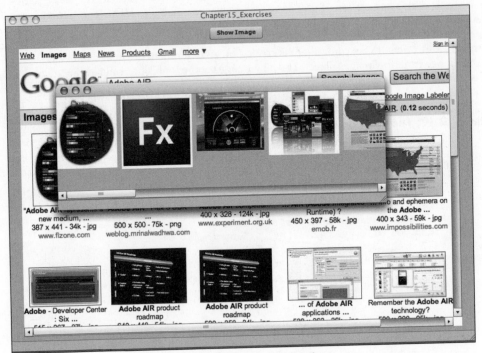

Figure B-13: The results of the Chapter15_Exercises application.

Index

Index

C

Category property-view, Flex Builder 3, 40

C/C++, development of, 19

changeFonts function, 255

changeImage function, 254

checkForUpdate function, 224–225, 229, 276

click handler, 237

clipboard
  clipboardFiles array, 205
  ClipboardFormats property, 205, 208
  copy and paste, 205–209
  copyToClipboard, 208–209

Code view, Dreamweaver CS3, 49

ColdFusion
  AIR application, updating, 92–95
  arrays, returning, 94
  backend files, creating, 89–90
  new AIR project, creating, 90–91
  server, downloading, 89
  value object, 91–92

common section, Flex Builder 3, 38–39

Components panel, Flex Builder 3, 36

Components window, Flash CS3, 46

configuration file. See AIR configuration file

ConnectionManager, 261–262

connectionStatusChanged function, 276

connection variable, SQLite database, 170

Console view, Flex debugger, 42

<content> tag, 71

context menus, 163–167
  assigning to objects, 164
  creating, 164–167
  Flex/AIR application, adding menu, 272
  functions of, 163
  functions required for, 165
  images used for, 165–166
  on root of application, 165

copy, 207–210
  copyToClipboard, 208–209
  Image components, 208
  import statements, 208

copy and paste. See copy; paste

copying
  directories, 116, 119
  files, 124, 126

<copyright> tag, 68

copyToAsync, 127

create directories, 114–115, 118

create files, 121–122, 125

createHandler, SQLite database, 170–171

createImageMenu, 164–165

createMainMenu function, 163–164

createMenu function, 155–156, 161

createTable, SQLite database, 172–174

createTransferableData function, drag-and-drop, 202–203

CSS (Cascading Style Sheets)
  development of, 28
  elements of, 28–30
  files example of, 29–30
  within HTML file, example of, 29
  withing MXML file, example of, 29–30

<customUpdateUI> tag, 74

D

database. See SQLite database

data exchange
  ActionScript Message Format (AMF), 89
  ColdFusion, 89–95
  database. See SQLite database
  JSON (JavaScript Object Notation), 96–97
  MashUp, 104–107
  REST (Representational State Transfer), 96
  SOAP (Simple Object Access Protocol), 100
  web services, 99–104
  WSDL (Web Services Description Language), 100–104
  XML (Extensible Markup Language), 98–99

DataManager, SQLite database integration, 265–267, 276–277